Library Management

Introduction to Public Services for Library Technicians. 2nd ed. By Marty Bloomberg.

Introduction to Technical Services for Library Technicians. 4th ed. By Marty Bloomberg and G. Edward Evans.

Immroth's Guide to the Library of Congress Classification. 3rd ed. By Lois Mai Chan.

Science and Engineering Literature: A Guide to Reference Sources. 3rd ed. By H. Robert Malinowsky and Jeanne M. Richardson.

The Vertical File and Its Satellites: A Handbook of Acquisition, Processing, and Organization. 2nd ed. By Shirley Miller.

Introduction to United States Public Documents. 2nd ed. By Joe Morehead.

The School Library Media Center. 2nd ed. By Emanuel T. Prostano and Joyce S. Prostano.

The Humanities: A Selective Guide to Information Sources. 2nd ed. By A. Robert Rogers.

The School Library and Educational Change. By Martin Rossoff (o.p.).

Introduction to Library Science: Basic Elements of Library Service. By Jesse H. Shera.

The School Librarian as Educator. By Lillian Biermann Wehmeyer.

Introduction to Cataloging and Classification. 6th ed. By Bohdan S. Wynar, with the assistance of Arlene Taylor Dowell and Jeanne Osborn.

Library Management. 2nd ed. By Robert D. Stueart and John Taylor Eastlick.

An Introduction to Classification and Number Building in Dewey. By Marty Bloomberg and Hans Weber.

Map Librarianship: An Introduction. By Mary Larsgaard.

Micrographics. By William Saffady.

Developing Library Collections. By G. Edward Evans.

Library Management

Second Edition

**Robert D. Stueart
John Taylor Eastlick**

1981
Libraries Unlimited, Inc.
Littleton, Colorado

LIBRARIES UNLIMITED, INC.
P.O. Box 263
Littleton, Colorado 80160

Library of Congress Cataloging in Publication Data

Stueart, Robert D
 Library management.

 (Library science text series)
 Biblography: p. 29
 Includes index.
 1. Library administration.   I. Eastlick, John T.,
joint author.   II. Title.
Z678.S799 1980   025.1'068   80-22895
ISBN 0-87287-241-6
ISBN 0-87287-243-2 (pbk.)

Libraries Unlimited books are bound with Type II nonwoven material that meets and exceeds National Association of State Textbook Administrators' Type II nonwoven material specifications Class A through E.

For
CHRISTIAN, SABINE, and VIRGINIA

PREFACE TO THE REVISED EDITION

This revised and enlarged edition comes with the encouragement of students, colleagues who are teaching library management, and library management practitioners who have been enthusiastic and constructive in their comments about the first edition and about the usefulness of a management text. The authors have incorporated many of their thoughtful suggestions into this current volume. One often repeated request was for more examples, and this has been accomplished by providing more in the text itself and by including appendices, for each chapter, which are policies, forms, plans, etc. from different types of libraries and which further illustrate the principles being presented in the chapters.

The purpose of this edition, as with the previous one, is to present the principles of management for libraries and information centers in a conceptual framework. Thus, this volume can serve the needs of practitioners and students, both as a text for formal classroom situations and as a guide for self-instructed or group-related continuing education. The genesis of this volume was in the almost total void in the area of writings on library management. Some important articles and some texts have appeared concerning special types of libraries (school, media centers, community college, college, university, public, and special), but there has been little in them of a comprehensive approach to the management of libraries. The intent of this volume, then, is to examine the dynamics of the library as an organization—the behavior of individuals and groups within the library, the policies and programs of the library, and the relationship of the library to its staff and its clientele. The present volume should prove just as valuable to the manager of a small library, who has had relatively little administrative experience as to the student who has had no experience at all.

The challenge of management in libraries has increased tremendously in recent years, influenced to a great degree by the rapid advance of technology and the expanding scope of library and information center activities, which has made many libraries into large, complex organizations. A separate chapter in this revised edition addresses the impact of change and its challenge for library managers.

Although most would agree that the principles of management are applicable to all types and sizes of enterprises, this volume presents those principles and theories in the context of libraries and information centers. It is assumed that techniques such as case studies, in-basket exercises, action mazes, and other simulated techniques will be used to supplement and magnify the principles that are important to management and that are developed here. For this reason, a particularly useful companion volume of case studies, written by Dr. A. J. Anderson who has written other case books, is to be published by Libraries Unlimited. Dr. Anderson's work is a most valuable tool and can be easily used with this volume. In fact, its arrangement coincides with the separate chapters of this volume on Planning, Organizing, Staffing, Directing, and Controlling.

In preparing for the management "jungle," one should keep in mind that anyone who is supervising another—whether another professional, a paraprofessional, a clerical worker, or a student assistant—is involved in the management process. Analysis of the workings of organizations shows that management must use the theories and techniques of many disciplines. For example, planning cannot be done without forecasting, and this requires some knowledge of economics.

Despite the documented advantages of combining theory with practice in operating an organization, many discount the importance of theory in a practical situation. There are practitioners who refuse to acknowledge that principles of management exist, but these same people must, in reality, apply the principles every day in their work situations. Decisions, if they are rational, are always based on some theory, whether or not one is aware of the theoretical basis. Even a "hunch" has a theoretical base. The manager must also be concerned with the human aspect and must be familiar with the conceptual framework of managing.

We have used the "traditional" headings that relate to planning, organizing, staffing, directing, and controlling simply to categorize discussion. This volume is arranged according to those five basic principles. Other writers would perhaps break down the functions in a different way, but this arrangement combines some principles and makes for what the authors feel is a better organization of the text. The actual operation of a library or information center follows no such precise linear pattern, for almost all elements are progressing simultaneously and they usually do not occur in a hierarchical relationship. It is recognized that by stating management in terms of "principles" some might tend to feel that management is being looked on as a rigid system. That is not the case. Although these principles may not be best in all situations, and different approaches may be appropriate under different conditions, it cannot be ignored that these basic principles generally apply to libraries as to all other organizations. Taken as a whole, the readings and/or footnotes at the end of each chapter represent a classified bibliography since they address particular topics for students who wish to pursue a subject in greater depth. Each idea, each concept discussed is related to or builds upon others, and each concept also relates to all levels of management and supervision in library organizations.

Contemporary management theory would define the library organization as a "system" in which each part of the organization interrelates with other parts to form a whole. The library itself, as an open system, interacts with its larger environment by drawing from that environment and exporting to that environment. Therefore, each concept mentioned, each principle discussed, each example used in this volume, rather than being narrowly defined and considered in isolation, must be set into the larger context of the library, its immediate environment, and, to an extent, its extended environment.

In writing this volume the authors have drawn freely upon research and writings in the fields of business management, public administration, and related fields of the social sciences. The text also reflects the authors' experience, at all management levels, in both public and academic libraries. Their experience in teaching management to graduate students in universities and colleges and their participation — often as leaders — in workshops, institutes, and seminars on many aspects of management, have also been helpful in organizing the concepts and examples used in this volume. These experiences, readings, writings, and teachings have blended together to form the basis for this volume.

The authors express their sincere appreciation to the following libraries for permission to reproduce documents emanating from the several institutions: University of California, Los Angeles; Cornell University Libraries; Dallas Public Library, City of Dallas; Duke University; Houston Public Library;

Massachusetts Institute of Technology Libraries; University of Michigan; Minneapolis Public Library and Information Center; New York State Library; Watertown (MA) Public Library; and Washington State Library.

The authors also wish to acknowledge the encouragement and patience given us by the publishers, Libraries Unlimited, and the willing help of Rudy Witthus and Fran Berger.

Robert D. Stueart   John Taylor Eastlick
Simmons College   Denver, Colorado
Boston, Massachusetts

1

MANAGEMENT DEVELOPMENT:
A Historical Overview

Management has been of some concern to organized society throughout civilized history, although its systematic study as a separate branch of human knowledge is fairly recent. The epoch of management inquiry and research has largely developed during this century, and many schools of thought have tried to formulate the underlying principles of management.

As early as 3000 B.C., the Sumerians kept records on clay tablets; many of those records applied to the management practices of the priests in Ur. Early Babylonia implemented a system of very strict control of business enterprises with its Codes of Akkadian and Hammurabi. Nebuchadnezzar, for instance, used color codes to control production on the Hanging Gardens, and these checks were performed every week and cumulated yearly. Reward was for piecework, which established norms for performance. The Hebrews' understanding of hierarchy and the importance of delegation is reflected in the *Old Testament*, particularly in "Exodus," chapter 18, which indicates that Moses "chose able men out of all Israel and made them heads over the people, rulers of thousands, rulers of hundreds, rulers of fifties and rulers of tens. And they judged the people at all seasons; the hard causes they brought unto Moses, but every small matter they judged themselves."

Construction of the pyramids, around 5000 B.C., was accomplished by about 100,000 men working for 20 years on only one of the larger ones. Around 2000 B.C. the principle of decentralized control was illustrated by the fact that control was vested in the individual states of Egypt (only later did the Pharaoh establish central control over all).[1] The Egyptians also employed long-range planning and staff advisers. Interpretations of early Egyptian papyri, extending as far back as 1300 B.C., indicate that the bureaucratic states of antiquity recognized the importance of organization and administration. Similar records exist for ancient China. Confucius' parables include practical suggestions for proper public administration. Claude George points out that one could find, in the China of 3000 years ago, "concepts that have a contemporary managerial ring: organization, functions, cooperation, procedures to bring efficiency, and various control techniques."[2] The staff principle, later perfected by the military organizations, was also used very effectively by the Chinese dynasty as far back as 2250 B.C.

Although the records of early Greece do not give much insight to the principles of management, the very existence of the Athenian commonwealth, with its councils, popular courts, administrative officials, and board of generals, indicates an appreciation of the managerial function. Socrates' definition of management as a skill separate from technical knowledge and experience is remarkably close to current understanding of the function. The Greek influence on scientific management is also revealed in their writings — Cicero wrote about the practice of motion study in 400 B.C., Plato wrote about specialization.

It is known that in ancient Rome the complexity of the administrative job evoked considerable development of management techniques. It is thought that the Roman Empire's secret of success lay in the ability of the Romans to organize.

Even Hannibal's crossing of the Alps in 218 B.C., with his Carthaginian troops and equipment, was a remarkable organizational feat.

Many of the techniques that we employ today in modern organizations can be traced to ancient origins. For instance, the first record of motion studies even predates Cicero; it appeared in the time of Cyrus, the Persian King, about 600 B.C. These records indicate that flute and pipe governed the motions, with songs for each task. They introduced rhythm, standard motion, and work tempo.

The most efficient formal organization in the history of Western civilization has been the Catholic Church. This is due not only to the appeal of its objectives but also to the effectiveness of its organization and management techniques. The scalar chain of command was introduced early in the organization of the Church, as was the concept of specialization.

The Arsenal of Venice, probably the largest industrial plant in the world of the sixteenth century, was an outstanding example of organizational efficiency. It appeared in the time of Machiavelli, whose writings emphasized the principle that authority developed from the consent of the masses. His ideas, particularly as set forth in *The Prince*, have application to our current study of leadership and communications.

Some of the most important principles and practices of modern business management can be traced to military organizations. The principles of unity of command, staff advisers, and division of work all evolved from early military order, probably as early as Cyrus and certainly refined by Alexander the Great. Although such organizations were fairly simple until recent times, they have gradually improved their techniques of direction. Among the most important of these has been the staff principle. The "general staff," for example, organized under a chief of staff, furnished specialized advice and information and supplied auxiliary services that have come to be essential features of military and business enterprise. The line of command concept also had its origin in the armies of antiquity and medieval ages, and the scalar principle is still a very important part of military organizations today.

The development of technology during the Industrial Revolution produced a factory system that brought workers into a central location and into contact with other workers. It was during the development of effective and efficient management control of those newly founded organizations that many management concepts began to emerge. Adam Smith in his writings, and particularly in *The Wealth of Nations*, described the "division of work" and "time and motion studies" as they should be employed in organizations. Other writers of that period, including Robert Owen, Charles Babbage, and Charles Dupin, wrote on the problems of management in factories.[3] Many of the principles that were later reemphasized and further refined in both the scientific management school and the human relations school were actually first developed by those writers during the eighteenth and nineteenth centuries. For instance, Babbage in his writing encouraged managers to use time study techniques, to centralize production, to inaugurate research and development, etc.[4] He contributed much thought to the scientific management approach and was a pioneer in developing the first digital computer.

Various methods have been used in the study of administration in this century. The first systematic approach was legalistic, being devoted to a study of the organization, powers, and activities and limitations of the public authorities. Later, a more scientific approach was used, concerned chiefly with administrative organization as the instrument of management. An attempt was made to determine, on the basis of empirical evidence, rules for efficient and effective administrative organization and operation. More recently the behaviorists have been using the methods of psychology, sociology, and anthropology in an effort to secure a better understanding of group behavior, leadership, and decision-making. This is now a major movement. These "schools" are referred to differently in different texts, but the content of each school is more or less defined so that it can be recognized.

No student can afford not to be familiar with the ideas of some pioneer thinkers in the field. This is not to say that their ideas should be accepted without question; however, the ideas of those thinkers are the basis for the development of management as we know it today, and these "schools" provide insight into the essence of management. As Harold Koontz puts it:

> There are the behaviorists ... who see management as a complex of interpersonal relationships and the basis of management theory the tentative tenets of the new and undeveloped science of psychology. There are also those who see management theory as simply a manifestation of the institutional and cultural aspects of sociology. Still others, observing that the central core of management is decision-making, branch in all directions from this core to encompass everything in organization life. Then, there are mathematicians, who think of management primarily as an exercise in logical relationships expressed in symbols and the omnipresent and ever revered model. But the entanglement of growth reaches its ultimate when the study of management is regarded as one of a number of systems and sub-systems, with an understandable tendency for the researcher to be dissatisfied until he has encompassed the entire physical and cultural universe as a management system.[5]

It is apparent, from studying the schools of management thought which have developed in this century, that they reflect the problems of the times in which they were popular. A few of them have survived and are influencing management thought today. For purposes of discussion, these can be grouped into the Scientific, Human Relations, and Decision Theory Schools.

SCIENTIFIC SCHOOLS

Scientific Management School

The term "scientific management" was coined in 1910 by Louis Brandeis in his appearance before the Interstate Commerce Commission. The basic assumption of this school is the philosophy that workers are economically motivated and that they will respond with their best efforts if material rewards are closely related to work efforts. The emphasis is on maximum output with minimum effort by eliminating waste and inefficiency at the operative level. In the United States, the work of Frederick Winslow Taylor dominates the thinking in this field of management. Taylor's views followed closely those of the protestant work ethic.

His attitude toward work was that man and machine were one, as he stated, "it is no single element, but rather this whole combination, that constitutes scientific management, which may be summarized as: Science, not rule of thumb; Harmony, not discord; Cooperation, not individualism; Maximum output, in place of restricted output; The Development of each man to his greatest efficiency and prosperity."[6] Taylor expounded several basic principles:

1) To gather all traditional knowledge and classify, tabulate, and reduce it to rules, laws, and formulas so as to help workers in their daily work.
2) To develop a science for each element of man's work to replace the rule-of-thumb method.
3) To scientifically select and then train, teach, and develop the worker.
4) To cooperate with workers to ensure that work is done according to developed scientific principles.
5) To effect an almost equal division of work and responsibility between workers and managers; that is, managers are to be given work for which they are best fitted, as are employees.[7]

Efficiency was the central theme of Taylor's writings. A steel works manager in Philadelphia, he was interested in knowing how to get more work out of workers, who are "naturally lazy and engage in systematic soldiering." This attitude was contributed to by poor management. He observed "when a naturally energetic man works for a few days beside a lazy one, the logic of the situation is unanswerable. 'Why should I work hard when the lazy fellow gets the same pay that I do and does only half as much work?' "[8] He proposed using scientific research methods to discover the best way. He felt that faster work could be assured only through 1) enforced standardization of methods; 2) enforced adaptation of best instruments and working conditions; and 3) enforced cooperation. He performed several experiments:

1) **Work study.** One experiment detailed movements of workers in a shop and suggested short cuts or more efficient ways of performing certain operations. Within three years the output of the shop had doubled.
2) **Standardized tools for shops.** In another area he found that the coal shovels being used weighed from 16 to 38 pounds. After experimenting, it was found that 21-22 pounds was the best weight. Again after three years 140 men were doing what had previously been done by between 400 and 600 men.
3) **Selection and training of workers.** Taylor insisted that each worker be assigned to do what he was best suited for and that those who exceeded the defined work be paid "bonuses." Production, as might be expected, rose ʓo an all-time high.

Taylor, therefore, advocated assignment of supervisors by "function"—i.e., one for training, one for discipline, etc. This functional approach is evident today in many organizations, including libraries.

Taylor's efforts were resented by workers and managers alike. Managers at first resisted Taylor's scientific method because it replaced their own intuition and discretion. At the same time it was challenged by unions because it questioned their roles. He was fired from his original job in Philadelphia. He then went to

Bethlehem Steel, where he was again fired after three years. The unions, indignant by this time, obtained investigation of his methods by a special congressional committee and were successful in forbidding "stop watches" or "bonuses" in Army arsenals until World War II. However, Eastern shipping concerns adopted his techniques and their popularity grew. The concepts spread to Europe and Britain and received impetus in Russia after the Revolution. Many maintain that this school represents techniques only and "hinders" a philosophy.

Taylor was the most important advocate of the scientific method approach, but there were others who worked in the same area. Frank and Lillian Gilbreth were contemporaries of Taylor. Frank, an engineer, and Lillian, a Ph.D. in psychology, expanded the concepts of motion study and fatigue. Their merit systems eventually evolved into performance appraisals. They devised the "one best way," which involved the fewest motions performed in the most comfortable position. They identified 17 basic elements in on-the-job motions (such as "grasp," "hold," "position," "search," etc.). These motions were called THERBLIGS, Gilbreth spelled backward, with one transposition.[9]

Taylor's work and the Gilbreths' work were complementary—Taylor stressed time study and the Gilbreths, motion study. Out of these two systems emerged the industrial engineering discipline.

Henry L. Gantt, of the Gantt Chart fame, writing and experimenting at the same time, developed the task-and-bonus system, which was similar to Taylor's awards incentive. His system set rates; if those rates were exceeded bonuses were paid, and in some cases production did double. Along the horizontal axis, the Gantt Chart shows time, work schedule, and work completed, and along the vertical axis it shows the individuals and machines assigned to those schedules. This early development of scientific management had little concern with the external environment of the organization, but rather was more concerned with the internal operations. Taylor took many of his concepts from the bureaucratic model developed by Weber, particularly in regard to rules and procedures for the conduct of work in organizations. The concept of bureaucracy developed at the same time as scientific management and thoughts on specialization of work, levels of authority, and control all emerged from Weber's writings.

Max Weber characterized a bureaucratic organization as:

1) An organization of functions bound by rules [in which]:
2) Area of competence or division of labor provides specialization and contributes to standardization.
3) The principles of hierarchy exists.
4) Promotion into management ranks is only by demonstrated technical competence.
5) Rules are to be recorded in writing.[10]

Weber further stated that "experience tends universally to show that the purely bureaucratic type of administrative organization ... is, from a pure theoretical point of view, capable of attaining the highest degree of efficiency and is in this sense formally the most rational known means of carrying out imperative control over human beings.[11] Ironically, Weber later changed his attitude and stated that "a passion for bureaucracy is enough to drive one to despair."

Classical School

Another "school," which began to develop in France at about the same time as Taylor's experiment in the United States, purports to analyze the management process, establish a conceptual framework for it, identify principles, and build a theory of management from them. It regards management as a universal process. This school, most often called the classical school, is sometimes referred to as the "traditional" or "universalist" school. Koontz and O'Donnel cite the value of universal principles: "When management principles can be developed, proved, and used, managerial efficiency will inevitably improve. Then the conscientious manager can become more effective by using established guidelines or help solve his problems, without engaging in original laborious research or the risky practice of trial and error."[12] Just as Taylor is considered the father of the Scientific Management School, the father of the classical school is a Frenchman, Henri Fayol. In his works, Fayol took the scientific approach, but he looked at administration from the top down. He emphasized the need to teach administration at all levels. Briefly, his stated principles were:

1) **Division of work.** As the enterprise grows, there should be an early division of duties, and the activities concerning management should be separated out and become distinct. Specialization naturally develops with division of work.

2) **Authority.** The authority that individuals possess in an organization should be equal to their given responsibility. If one is responsible for the results of a task, that person should be given the authority to take actions necessary to ensure its success.

3) **Discipline.** There should be complete obedience, energy, and behavior in the best interest of the organization.

4) **Unity of command.** An employee should receive orders from only one superior. This unity of command was in direct opposition to Taylor's idea of having workers take instructions from several "foremen."

5) **Unity of direction.** A body with two heads is a monster and has difficulty in surviving. There should be one head and one plan to ensure a coordinated effort.

6) **Subordination of individual interest to general interest.** Primary concern should be the growth of the organization.

7) **Remuneration of personnel.** Wages should be fair.

8) **Centralization.** Everything that goes to increase the importance of the subordinate's role is decentralization, everything that goes to reduce it is centralization. Centralization is the desirable arrangement within an organization.

9) **Scalar chain.** Gangplanks should be used to prevent the scalar chain from bogging down. The gangplank (illustrated by the dotted line in Figure 1-1) can be thrown across without weakening the chain of command, as long as this relationship is advisory and not policy making.

Figure 1-1
Gangplank Principle

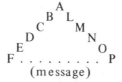

(message)

10) **Order.** There is a right place for everything and everyone in the organization. That place or job must be identified.

11) **Equity.** Equality of treatment must be taken into account in dealing with employees. Justice should be tempered with kindness.

12) **Stability of tenure of personnel.** It is important to keep people on the job.

13) **Initiative.** Incentive rewards may be provided to stimulate production.

14) **Esprit de corps.** Communication is the key to a satisfied working group.[13]

Fayol considered qualities required by managers as physical (health, vigor); mental (ability to understand and learn, judgment, and adaptability); moral (energy, firmness, willingness to accept responsibility, initiative, loyalty, tact, dignity); educational (general acquaintance with matters not belonging exclusively to the function performed); technical (peculiar to the function); and related to experience (arising from the work proper).

Fayol saw workers as people who: 1) are naturally lazy; 2) resist work more effectively when working in groups; 3) must be subjected to sharp discipline; 4) can best be motivated by the incentive of higher wages; 5) can do much better when properly instructed; and 6) differ markedly in native ability and capacity. However, he was more concerned than was Taylor with human relations and with defining the activities of managers and thus the division of labor. He and Luther Gulick, among others, advised managers to break down complicated jobs into more specialized activities. This was achieved through a "pyramid of control." Gulick and Urwick followed Fayol's lead by popularizing several principles:

1) Fit people to the administrative structure.
2) Recognize one top executive as the source of authority.
3) Adhere to unity of command.
4) Use special and general staff.
5) Departmentalize by purpose, process, person, and place.
6) Delegate and utilize the exception principle.
7) Make responsibility commensurate with authority.
8) Consider appropriate spans of control.[14]

Taylor and Fayol, then, may be considered the founders of the theory of administration or management. There is little doubt that many organizations, including libraries, still depend heavily on these classical theories for the bases of their formal organizations. The greatest criticisms of these schools have been that they place undue emphasis on the formal aspects of organization and neglected entirely the effects of individual personality, informal groups, intra-organizational conflicts, and the decision-making process on the formal structure.

System School

World War I gave great impetus to the study of efficiency, and by 1930 the idea of applying theory to organization and system was emphasized in the organization and system school. This theory distinguished between administration—representing the ownership point of view—and scientific management—an approach to work at the operative level—as they related to organization and system. This school expanded the work of Fayol and at the same time began to explore the behavioral aspects of management. For example, Max Weber and his disciples, studying bureaucracy, considered administrators as the key to governmental control in any modern state. As a structuralist, Weber, a German sociologist, emphasized specialization within an organization and gave a great deal of importance to the hierarchy of the decision-making process. Weber, writing about the same time as Taylor and Fayol, analyzed the authority and responsibility of the "office" rather than the individual. The theory that he developed about authority structures in a complex organization is monumental.[15]

Other significant writers of this movement who were mentioned above were Lyndell Urwick, an Englishman, and Luther Gulick, an American, who edited a landmark work on scientific administration.[16] Gulick, in a paper to President Roosevelt in 1937, summed up an executive's functions in the acronym POSDCORB:

1) **P**lanning. That is, working out in broad outline the things that need to be done and the methods for doing them in order to accomplish the enterprise's set purpose.

2) **O**rganizing. That is, the establishment of the formal structure of authority through which work subdivisions are arranged, defined, and coordinated for the defined objectives.

3) **S**taffing. That is, the whole personnel function of bringing in and training the staff and maintaining favorable conditions for work.

4) **D**irecting. That is, the continuous task of making decisions and embodying them in specific and general orders and instructions and serving as the leader of the enterprise.

5) **CO**ordinating. That is, the all-important duty of interrelating the various parts of the work.

6) **R**eporting. That is, keeping those to whom the executive is responsible informed through records, research, and inspection.

7) **B**udgeting. This encompasses all that goes with budgeting in the form of fiscal planning, accounting, and control.

HUMAN RELATIONS SCHOOLS

Developing during the 1930s, the human relations schools compensated for some of the deficiencies of the classical theories. The thesis of the human relations schools is that, since managing involves getting things done through people, management study should center on interpersonal relations. The main emphasis of those schools, then, is on the individual and the informal group in the formal organization; it is concerned with integrating people into a work environment. The phrase "personnel administration" came into prominence at this time, and increasing efforts toward democratization and staff participation became evident.

This "school" is primarily concerned with the study of people as human beings rather than as work units. A primary concern is the recognition of basic human needs, with the idea that once those needs are recognized and a willing ear is given to the suggestions and complaints, then morale will increase, as will production. Sociologists and psychologists have contributed to the development of this school.

Human Behavior School

Research emanating from this school of thought has focused on behavior of the individual, the group, and the organization. The major assumption is that if management can make employees happy, maximum performance will result. Mary Follett, a political philosopher, was concerned with the human aspect and called for intensive research within the organization. She emphasized the psychological and sociological aspects of management, viewing it as a social process and felt that coordination was the most important principle: coordination by direct contact with the people concerned; coordination that was a continuous process; coordination found in the initial steps of every endeavor; and coordination as a reciprocal arrangement of all aspects of a situation. She was mainly concerned with the workers in the organization and their involvement in deciding their destiny within the organization. Early efforts in this type of research were the experiments of Elton Mayo and a group of industrial psychologists at the Western Electric Hawthorne Plant, in Chicago. These researchers began to study physical working conditions and their influence on worker productivity. Their studies revealed the importance of social interaction and psychological factors in determining productivity and satisfaction. Since that time, of course, behavioral scientists have refined the research tools used to evaluate human responses to their work environment. Several principles were demonstrated in their studies: 1) that workers are more motivated by social rewards and sanctions than by economic incentives; 2) that workers in their acts are influenced by the group; and 3) that whenever formal organizations exist, both formal and informal norms exist. They found that when the work group associated itself with management, productivity rose. When the group felt itself to be in opposition to management, productivity stayed close to the minimum accepted level. In general, the human behavior school maintains that if the organization makes employees happy, it will gain their full cooperation and effort, and reach optimum efficiency. Two other disciples of this school are Rensis Likert and Frederick Herzberg.

It can be seen that Mayo's conclusions were quite different from those of Taylor. Taylor said that man at work is an entirely economic man; Mayo maintained that workers are motivated by "togetherness" and crave individual recognition within the group.

Social System School

This school is closely related to the human relations school and is often confused or intertwined with it. It encourages management to let employees develop social groups on the job, to move toward employee participation in management, and to allow democracy in the organization. The spiritual father of this school is perhaps Chester Barnard, who in his writings dwells on the contribution-satisfaction equilibrium and identifies four specific inducements: 1) material inducements, such as money and other physical securities; 2) personal non-material opportunities for distinction, prestige, and personal power; 3) desirable physical conditions of work; and 4) ideal benefactions, such as pride of workmanship, sense of adequacy, loyalty to the organization, etc.[17] Barnard emphasized communications as the "first function" of managers. Some prominent disciples of this school are Herbert Simon, Chris Argyris, Ralph Stogdill, Peter Drucker, Douglas McGregor, and Abraham Maslow.

Several new theories and concepts regarding the individual have emerged from the works of these authors. For instance, "Management by Objectives," a concept introduced in the 1950s by Peter Drucker, has been supported by Douglas McGregor in his "Theory Y." The idea is that information sharing is desirable and that management and workers should share planning and analysis of the operations. Abraham Maslow's "Need Theory" further builds on this concept by arguing that man has a hierarchy of needs starting with the basic physical ones of food, shelter, and clothing, and working through five steps to the intangible needs of self-actualization and fulfillment. These concepts will be further discussed in other chapters.

More recently, attention has been paid to the matter of individuals and group behavior in the work situation and to their relationship in a larger social, cultural, and political system. A topic of current exploration is both the behavior of individuals and groups within organizations and the behavior of organizations as social systems interacting with the environment.

DECISION THEORY SCHOOLS

In the 1950s, 1960s, 1970s, and into the 1980s contributions have been made to management through disciplines such as mathematics, statistics, and economics: by use of mathematical models for decision making and prediction; through control techniques such as cost benefit analyses; through game theory and strategies in creative planning; and through psychology and sociology, with theories of leadership and organization, human motivation and behavior, organizational relationships, and nature of authority. These schools draw on the common element in all those previously discussed — the decision-making aspect. The advent of technology has greatly aided researchers in the development of information systems.

The decision theory school is primarily concerned with the study of rational decision procedures and of the way managers actually reach decisions. The implications are that mathematical models and quantitative processes could serve as the basis for all management. Many of the researchers have concentrated on *describing*[18] the decision-making process, drawing on psychology and economics, or on *prescribing*[19] how decisions should be made. The mathematical school, a branch of the decision theory school, is concerned with what to measure and why, with the thought of indicating how best to improve a system or solve a problem.

These management scientists share common characteristics, namely: 1) the application of scientific analysis to managerial problems; 2) the goal of improving the manager's decision-making ability; 3) a high regard for economic effectiveness criteria; 4) a reliance on mathematical models; and 5) the utilization of electronic computers.[20] This school, as might be suspected, uses techniques such as game theory, simulation, and linear programming in presenting alternatives to the decision maker.

GENERAL SYSTEMS THEORY

Undoubtedly the most accepted theoretical base for modern management is a movement that is currently emerging called General Systems Theory (GST). This movement is integrating the knowledge that has been gleaned from the biological, physical and behavioral sciences into one system. Its disciples call themselves "revisionists" and are working to combine the thoughts of the behavioral scientists with those of systems theorists, mathematicians, statisticians, and computer scientists by merging the theories of the scientific management movement with those of the human relations movement. Some of the authors, previously mentioned, are now part of this movement. Those researchers include Herbert Simon, Chris Argyris and Rensis Likert, to mention only a few. The movement is described by some as not really a theory but rather "a direction in the contemporary philosophy of science."[21]

Ludwig von Bertlanffy is credited with being the founder of GST by being the first to talk about the "systems theory of the organism."[22] He defines a system as "a set of elements standing in interrelation among themselves and with the environment."[23] (These elements for libraries would include personnel, materials, and money). The really important aspect is the interaction among the elements to create a whole, dynamic system. This system, if it is an open one, interacts with its environment. It draws from the environment and feeds back into the environment. It is influenced by the environment and in return influences other parts of the environment. If the system is dissected it becomes evident that the organization is made up of a number of subsystems; likewise the organization is but one subsystem of a larger environment.

Kast points out that there is a "rather loose, conglomeration of interests and approaches" in this developing field and that the key concepts that permeate the field are:

1. Emphasis upon scientific method;
2. Systematic approach to problem solving;
3. Mathematical model building;
4. Quantification and utilization of mathematical and statistical procedures;
5. Concern with economic-technical rather than psychosocial aspects;
6. Utilization of electronic computers as tools;

7. Emphasis on total systems approach;
8. Seeking optimal decision under closed-system assumption;
9. Orientation to normative rather than descriptive methods.[24]

SUMMARY

Very briefly summarized, then, the scientific schools' approach to organization is to study the activities that need to be undertaken to achieve objectives; the human relations approach starts with a study of man's motives and behavior; and the decision theory approach concentrates on the decisions that need to be made to achieve objectives. All of these schools of management thought are interrelated. Simon states that "it is not clear that operations research embodies any philosophy different from that of scientific management.... No meaningful line can be drawn any more to demarcate operations research from scientific management or scientific management from management science."[25] All are concerned with the management process, but no one school can begin to provide a comprehensive view. All have strong points and weak points. Some of the best and some of the worst of each can be observed in library operations today.

NOTES

[1]J. H. Breasted, *Ancient Records of Egypt* (Chicago: University of Chicago Press, 1906), pp. 150-250.

[2]Claude S. George, Jr., *The History of Management Thought*, 2nd ed. (Englewood Cliffs, NJ: Prentice-Hall, 1972), p. 12.

[3]Larry N. Killough, "Management and the Industrial Revolution," *Advanced Management Journal* (July 1970): 67-70.

[4]Charles Babbage, *On the Economy of Machinery and Manufacturers* (London: Charles Knight, 1832).

[5]Harold Koontz, "The Management Theory Jungle," *Academy of Management Journal*, v. 4, no. 3 (Dec. 1961): 174-75.

[6]Frederick W. Taylor, *Scientific Management* (New York: Harper and Row, 1947), p. 10.

[7]Frederick Winslow Taylor, *Principles of Scientific Management* (New York: Harper and Brothers Publishers, 1941), pp. 36-37.

[8]"Shop Management," in Frederick Winslow Taylor, *Scientific Management* (New York: Harper and Row, 1947), p. 31.

[9]Edna Yost, *Frank and Lillian Gilbreth* (New Brunswick, NJ: Rutgers University Press, 1949), p. 262.

[10]Max Weber, *Theory of Social and Economic Organization*, tr. and ed. by A. M. Henderson and T. Parsons (Oxford: Oxford University Press, 1947).

[11]Gerald D. Bell, ed., *Organizations and Human Behavior* (Englewood Cliffs, NJ: Prentice-Hall, 1967), p. 88.

[12]Harold Koontz and Cyril O'Donnell, *Principles of Management*, 5th ed. (New York: McGraw-Hill, 1972), pp. 14-15.

[13]Henri Fayol, *General and Industrial Management*, tr. by Constance Storrs (London: Pitman & Sons, 1949), p. 22.

[14]Luther Gulick and Lyndall Urwick, eds., *Papers on the Science of Administration* (New York: Institute of Public Administration, Columbia University, 1937).

[15]Max Weber, *The Theory of Social and Economic Organizations* (New York: Free Press, 1947).

[16]Gulick and Urwick, eds., *Papers on the Science of Administration.*

[17]Chester I. Barnard, *The Functions of the Executive* (Cambridge, MA: Harvard University Press, 1950).

[18]James March and Herbert Simon, *Organizations* (New York: Wiley, 1958).

[19]Sheen Kassouf, *Normative Decision Making* (Englewood Cliffs, NJ: Prentice-Hall, 1970).

[20]Richard M. Hodgetts, *Management: Theory Process and Practice* (Philadelphia, PA: W. B. Saunders Company, 1975), p. 113.

[21]Anatol Rapoport, "General Systems Theory," in David Sells, ed., *International Encyclopedia of the Social Sciences*, v. 15 (New York: Macmillan, 1968), p. 452.

[22]Ludwig von Bertlanffy, "The History and Status of General Systems Theory," *Academy of Management Journal* 15 (Dec. 1972): 407.

[23]Bertlanffy, p. 417.

[24]Fremont E. Kast and Jonas E. Rosenzweig, *Organization and Management* (New York: McGraw-Hill, 1974), p. 89.

[25]Herbert A. Simon, *The Shape of Automation: For Men and Management* (New York: Harper and Row, 1965), p. 69.

READINGS

Barnard, C. I. *The Functions of the Executive.* Cambridge, MA: Harvard University Press, 1938.

Fayol, H. *General and Industrial Management.* New York: Pitman, 1949.

George, Claude S., Jr. *History of Management Thought.* 2nd ed. Englewood Cliffs, NJ: Prentice-Hall, 1972. paper.

Gulick, L., and L. Urwick, eds. *Papers on the Science of Administration.* New York: Columbia University Press, 1937.

Herzberg, Frederick, et al. *The Motivation at Work*. 2nd ed. New York: Wiley, 1959.

Howard, Paul. "The Functions of Library Management," *Library Quarterly* (July 1940): 315-40.

Koontz, H., and C. O'Donnell. *Principles of Management*. New York: McGraw-Hill, 1964.

Likert, Rensis. *The Human Organization*. New York: McGraw-Hill, 1967.

Maslow, Abraham H. *Motivation and Personality*. New York: Harper and Row, 1954.

Mayo, Elton. *The Human Problems of an Industrial Civilization*. 2nd ed. Cambridge, MA: Harvard University Press, 1946.

McGregor, Douglas. *The Human Side of Enterprise*. New York: McGraw-Hill, 1960.

Taylor, Frederick W. *Scientific Management*. New York: Harper and Row, 1947.

2

THE PLANNING PROCESS

LIBRARY PLANNING

One of the most easily avoided activities in libraries, as in many other organizations, is the planning process. This phenomenon exists despite the fact that planning is the most basic function — all other functions must reflect it. Changing environments make planning much more vital, more alive today, than it has ever been, and that is why it is so important. Although there are numerous reasons that libraries neglect planning, the main reason is that it is an extremely difficult, time-consuming process that is further complicated by economic uncertainty, shrinking federal, state, and local support and changing societal priorities. Added to this is the fact that many managers resist proper planning. Too many librarians still tend to emphasize current operations at the expense of planning. This resistance to systematic and comprehensive planning is often couched in such phrases as "Planning is just crystal-ball gazing in these days of technological change" or "There's no time to devote to planning because we are too busy with the present." Libraries are often being mandated by parent institutions to develop long-range plans in an attempt to anticipate the programs that will be desirable in some future period. These plans, which become the basis for budgeting, include expansion of programs, staffs, materials, and the physical plant. For instance, in September 1973, the University of Washington initiated implementation of a formal long-range planning process for the total university system.[1]

Since planning is an effort to anticipate the future and the inevitable changes that come with it, it can be accomplished only by choosing from among possible alternatives. Though planning is most often a line function, a specialized cadre of people has been developed in some libraries and information centers whose primary functions are those of planning. Those officers, rather than replacing line responsibilities, supplement their planning efforts. They, for example, might provide factual data and propose new services, but their primary role is to coordinate the entire planning program. Some libraries have instituted planning committees, and others (mainly large public and academic library systems such as Columbia University Libraries) have created planning offices within the staff structure of the library. These groups are responsible for developing or guiding the development of certain plans, particularly those that are long range in nature. Such groups, with responsibilities clearly defined, are able to perform more intensive investigations and to analyze and coordinate plans more thoroughly. Columbia University Library's Planning Office is administered by the Assistant University Librarian for Planning, with specific objectives to:

1) Provide a direction and framework for library and information service operations that will guide decision making and problem solving.

2) Improve library service, operations and fiscal control through the application of computer technology and management science to library procedures.

3) Ensure the rational and effective development of information services and resources in the context of university academic planning.

4) Permit the anticipation of future resource needs for information service by establishing plans based on present decisions.

5) Bring the skills and experience of university and libraries staff members into the planning process.[2]

In developing the planning process, several university libraries[3] have used the MRAP (Management Review and Analysis Program) technique as a self-study guide; this technique was developed by the Management Studies Office of the Association of Research Libraries.

Because of successful operations that resulted from an over-abundance of funds, librarians have often been led to attribute these successful programs to their own imagination and intuition. Lack of success, however, is often blamed on "circumstances beyond our control" instead of on the lack of planning. Planning for library service in these days of technological and economic uncertainty and change becomes much more important but even more difficult. Many plans may become obsolete before they are implemented. Considerations of what planning is and is not will be helpful in developing a planning attitude.

What Is Planning?

Planning is not just behavior but also a process; it is the process of getting an organization from where it is to where it wants to be in a given period of time by setting it on a predetermined course of action. It is deciding what to do, how to do it, when to do it, and who is to do it. Thus, planning consists of making decisions now regarding possible courses of action in light of established missions, goals, objectives, and other available information. Perhaps the most important reasons for planning are to offset uncertainty and change, to focus attention on clearly defined objectives, to gain economical operation, and to facilitate control. It is, of course, impossible and impractical to plan for every action the organization might want to take. To create a planning "attitude" the concept must begin at the top and be implemented through policies, procedures, projects, and programs of the library. A planning document becomes today's design for tomorrow's action, an outline of the steps to be taken starting now but continuing into some future period. The process leading to the written document should be discussed with the people most concerned. This is an idealistic attitude, of course, because it is not always feasible for everyone to participate in the varied stages of the planning process. The degree of involvement, perhaps, depends upon several factors: cost, time, the importance of the particular plan in question, the perceived knowledge of participants about the question as well as their own particular interest in the plan, etc. However, the whole organization should be, at the least, informed about the plans that are taking shape. When this involvement takes place the greatest commitment will be achieved. If the staff and the funding authorities are in agreement at this basic stage, then it is realistic to expect that the written plan will be used consistently as a guide by all members of the organization.

This planning process, then, forces action on the part of the institution as a whole. Members of the institution must evaluate and set goals and progress towards them. Planning should be used daily in the mainstream of the library; it is not a process that the manager uses at occasional intervals when he or she thinks there is time for it. Without daily planning, decisions become ad hoc choices, activities become random, and confusion and chaos often prevail.

Factors in Planning

The planning process can be arbitrarily divided into four elements:

Time

Time is the first element in the planning process. There are two categories of plans with respect to time: long-range and short-term. These categories refer to the span of time over which the plan is effective, starting with the time when the plan is initiated and ending with the time when the objectives of the plan are actually achieved. Long-range, strategic, or master planning necessitates looking at operations of the library in a most critical and comprehensive way, in order to develop a planning network that connects the sub-plans of individual units, departments, and divisions of the library into one master plan. Perhaps the most touted examples of long-range planning are those produced by communist governments in the form of five- to ten-year plans.

Master planning is a concept that is relatively new to libraries and information centers, whether one is considering total university planning, which would affect academic libraries; city planning, which would have bearing on public libraries; school systems planning, which affects media centers; or corporation planning, which might affect special libraries. Many large library and information centers are now involved in the long-range planning process. An example is the "Academic Plan for the Davis Campus 1970-1980" and the "University of California at San Diego's Long Range Plan to 1984."[4]

Impetus for master planning, a desirable approach for most complex organizations, came primarily after World War II, when "postwar planning" was important to companies in the United States; this was particularly true because technology was changing and becoming more expensive and companies had to be sure of the need. According to Drucker, strategic planning is,

> the continuous process of making present entrepreneurial (*risk-taking*) *decisions* systematically and with the greatest knowledge of their futurity; organizing systematically the *efforts* needed to carry out these decisions; and measuring the results of these decisions against the expectations through organized, systematic feedbacks.[5]

Another definition that proves helpful is the one supplied by Steiner, who states that strategic planning is "the process of determining the major objectives of an organization and the policies and strategies that will govern the acquisition, use, and disposition of resources to achieve those objectives."[6]

Most experts agree that long-range plans should reflect programs five or ten years from the present time. One of the most difficult aspects of long-range plans is that they force the librarian to make certain assumptions about the future, concerning such things as population trends for higher education or urban centers or on-going technological changes reflected through networks such as the Ohio

College Library Center's operations or through bibliographic data bases. Since there is no way of being absolutely certain about the future, the further ahead one plans the greater is the uncertainty. This makes it even more imperative that such written plans receive periodic review, so that certain aspects can be updated, deleted, or rethought as the library's priorities shift or change completely. As Fred Luthans points out, one weakness is that strategic planners seldom, if ever, plan for cutbacks or failures.[7]

Short-term plans, on the other hand, usually coincide with the accounting year. Examples of short-term plans are next year's budgets or staff work schedules. This type of planning, often called operational planning, reflects the day-to-day operational decisions that need to be made. These plans are much more detailed than the long-range ones and the objectives that are developed are much more specific. Long-range plans are used as general guides, while short-range plans bring the concept to an operational stage. Since they are more specific and immediate, they do not carry the uncertainty that long-range plans do.

Collecting and Analyzing Data

The second element in planning is collecting and analyzing data—the more pertinent the information available, the better the planning process will be. This step includes systematic collection of data concerning libraries and information centers, their activities, operations, staff, use, and users, at a given time and over a given period—in other words, a study of the whole organization and its operation. Techniques for collecting this data are discussed in the chapter on principles of control.

Levels of Planning

All supervisors, whether they are at the upper, middle, or lower levels in the organizational structure, should engage in planning and should be responsible for planning. Involvement of lower echelon personnel in planning has the advantage of getting the practical point of view of those closer to the scene of the operations. Long-range planning is usually carried out primarily by the upper echelon and is general in nature, while short-range planning is usually conducted by middle- and lower-level supervisors. In libraries where committees or planning offices have been created, this hierarchical approach has disappeared and input from all levels is encouraged. It is easy to see the consequence if the two types of plans are not coordinated.

Flexibility

Flexibility—that is, meeting the changing needs—is the essence of good planning. Any planning that is too rigid to accommodate change is an exercise in futility. This is why it is so important to review long-range plans periodically with a thought to revising priorities that may no longer be paramount. In this respect, it is important to be sure that the library's plans remain consistent with those of the larger organization of which the library is a part.

It should be evident from the previous comments that planning is an attitude, a state of mind, a way of thinking. The whole concept of planning is a network of mutually dependent components ranging from an overall plan to technical plans for specific operations.

Planning Techniques

There are many techniques that are important to the planning process but that are often mistaken for the process itself. Four of these are discussed here:

Standards or Guidelines

These have been established by different groups to present the authorities with standards and to act as guidelines for planning. For example, standards developed by the American Library Association are now in existence for most types of libraries and library service, and they are based on actual, or known, demands for library services. But these are not plans; they are simply a means of differentiating between acceptable and unacceptable service. What each library must do is to develop individual plans based on demands of that library's clientele, using the standards as guidelines. Both human and technical factors are necessary considerations in developing sound standards.

Forecasting

This is an attempt to find the most probable course of events or a range of possibilities. Forecasts are building blocks, the foundation on which managers can do their own planning, but forecasting is only one part of planning. The whole process of forecasting involves predicting future trends, influences, and developments that may be beyond the librarian's control. There are three basic strategies for forecasting:

    a.   The deterministic one assures that there is a close causal relation between the present and the future. There is great reliance on information gathered from past performance. The past is used to project the future.

    b.   The symptomatic one searches for signs which might be indicators of the future. "Leading Economic Indicators" in business is an example. This approach is based on the concept that the sequence of events in a cycle is consistent enough to use this approach.

    c.   The systematic strategy looks for underlying regularities. Econometrics is an example of this type of forecasting.[8]

Some techniques that have been used in industry are currently being adapted by libraries for use in forecasting. These include the survey approach, which is used in technological forecasting. Futurology has become a hot topic in today's world, particularly for managers. Many new techniques are currently being employed to predict the future. One popular technique employed by librarians is the Delphi technique. The steps, briefly outlined, for this technique are as follows:

1) A panel of experts on the subject, for instance library funding, is developed.

2) The panel predicts developments over a specified period of time. There is no group interaction; each member works alone.

3) Results of this list of "developments" are then used to draw up a survey that is sent to each panelist for further reaction — refinement, deletion, etc. This process is repeated until the investigator is convinced that no further alterations in predictions will be made.

This technique is sure to gain popularity as more libraries become involved in the long-range planning process.

Another technique that has been used to one degree or another in most libraries is that of "Trend Projection." This technique, in its formal approach, graphically plots future trends based on past experience. For instance, the number of volumes put on reserve and the number of times they have circulated during a semester, if plotted on a graph, can reveal significant trends. These are only two of the forecasting techniques that can be used by librarians.

Future Decisions

These are not plans. Plans deal not with future decisions but with the future of present decisions — not with what one should do tomorrow but with what one must do today to be prepared for the events of tomorrow. Often the library planning approach tends toward making plans for something one will decide to do in the future. Such planning makes for interesting reading, but its purposes are moot.

Bound Documents

Such documents are desirable, but planning is not simply a bound document that results from periodic planning sessions. Changes in environment require changes in plans, so there must be flexibility. Planning should be done when a change is needed or because of dissatisfaction with the current process. This change should be accomplished at that moment.

Environment for Planning

Planning is committing library resources — personnel and material — with the best possible knowledge of the future, systematically organizing the effort needed to utilize these resources, and measuring the results of planning decisions through systematic feedback so that needed changes can be effected. In order to establish a climate for planning within the library or information center at least two things are desirable: 1) the entire organization should know the direction, goals, and expectations of the library; and 2) the library and institutional administration should know of all decisions, commitments, and efforts of the organizational members. At this point the library can proceed with a systematic planning process.

Several forces work simultaneously to have an effect on library planning. Both the external and the internal environment influence library planning. For instance, general information on social trends, cultural changes, and political and economic forces is needed if there is to be effective planning of the operations of libraries and information centers. Awareness of national and regional library plans, including cooperative programs and networking, is an important professional factor.

The institutional environment also creates a competitive relationship with other departments in the broader organization, whether these are, for instance, other academic units of the college, university, or school; other departments, such as the Department of Parks and Recreation, in a city government; or other units of a business concern of which the special library is a part. Particularly in the light of revenue sharing from the federal government, public libraries must compete for federal support and local attention. This puts a much greater responsibility on the librarian for "selling" programs and being accountable for their outcome. Both the internal and external environments must be taken into consideration in the process. Factors such as economic conditions, political climate, legislation, demographics of population and technological developments are all important external trends. Likewise, personnel, organizational structure, likely financial future, etc. are internal factors that must be considered.

Future of Library Planning

The immediate problem for library administrators is gaining an understanding of how and why to plan. The first step in improving library services is to recognize all the factors that have been discussed above. The next step is individual planning, which each library must do, and in so doing, it must provide the services that represent the goals of that library. A number of libraries have now developed formal long-range plans that might serve as models. "Tomorrow's libraries will be the result of today's planning." Today's planning, then, must be based on clearly formulated objectives that will encourage all parts of the organization to work toward the same goal. It is a challenge and a responsibility for libraries to be able to integrate resources toward achieving common goals. Setting these goals and objectives is the basic step in developing long-range plans for the library.

OBJECTIVES FOR LIBRARIES

An objective, according to Webster's Unabridged, is that toward which effort is directed; an aim or end of action. Identification of the broad objectives, the service objectives, of a library or information center is the first step in the planning process. One of the difficulties of developing a set of goals and objectives is the confusion that exists in the terminology used; objectives are variously referred to as philosophy, mission, goals, guiding principles, targets, quotas, activities, deadlines, or purposes. There are probably shades of difference between those terms, but there does not seem to be consistency in this interpretation. For instance, the University of Tennessee, in its "Goals and Objectives Statement," defines goals as "statements which are subordinate to objectives and reflect specific measurable steps to be taken," while the University of Washington describes goals as "a long term mission or policy statement describing the direction in which the organization is moving."

Just as planning may be thought of in a hierarchy from strategic or long-range plans to the short-range or operational ones, so the objectives of the library can be indicated in such a hierarchy. The peak of the pyramid consists of the most general, all-encompassing ones, and the lower ones build from that. In the formulation of plans, mission should precede goal, which should precede objectives, if there is to be an integral relationship among them.

Figure 2-1
Objectives Hierarchy

Note: Each goal interacts with and influences every other goal, just as every objective does with every other objective, and every activity does with every other activity. Each level is derived from the level above. In other words, activities are derived from objectives, and objectives from goals.

Formulating Objectives

Clearly formulated objectives enable all parts of an organization to work toward common goals. Objectives provide a focus for policy making and for management decisions of all types. The first question that must be addressed in the process of setting objectives is "What is the purpose of this organization?" After this has been answered, other planning can be undertaken. Of course, libraries and information centers are typically born with service objectives. For public libraries the mission has traditionally been education, information, and recreation; the library emerged as the vehicle to accomplish this mission. One should take this mission one step further by defining the overlap between the needs of the user and the capabilities of the library or information center. This intersection is the basis of the library's goals. Failure to identify this common ground correctly leads to the selection of goals—and later objectives—that are non-related or unrealistic. Likewise, it must be remembered that objectives are dependent on time and that they are likely to change over a period of time.

All activities and policies should be directed to the achievement of these goals and objectives. Clear objectives also encourage a consistency in management planning and decision making over an extended period of time. Unfortunately, objectives often exist in the thinking of management without being made explicit, or at least they often remain unverbalized. Such an approach can lead to confusion and discouragement, and a great deal of energy can be expended on faulty assumptions. Objectives should set the pattern for the structure of the organization and be action oriented. It is difficult, if not impossible, to be accountable for performance if objectives are not stated and communicated. These objectives may change as the feedback mechanism begins to work. The objectives should not be viewed as passive but rather should provide not only direction but also an incentive to achieve.

Levels of Objectives

Four distinct levels of "objectives" can be identified in libaries and information centers:

Broad General Mission

These could be called the "creed" or statement of mission or purpose of the organization. As examples, Cornell University Library states that its mission is "to provide bibliographical, physical, and intellectual access to recorded knowledge and information consistent with the present and anticipated teaching and research responsibilities and social concerns of Cornell"; Duke University Libraries states its mission as that of providing "services and resources to meet the present and future scholarly and informational needs of the Duke University community and, insofar as possible, to share resources with those outside the University"; the Minneapolis Public Library states its function as being "a dynamic civic resource that provides information, materials, and services to stimulate ideas, advance knowledge, and enhance the quality of life for the community."[9] Likewise, Public Law 941, Section 371, states that the purpose of the National Library of Medicine is "to assist the advancement of medical and related sciences, and to aid the dissemination and exchange of scientific and other information important to the progress of medicine and to the public health." The official mission indicates the general purposes of the organization; the mission statement is most often set forth in the charter, annual report, or other authoritative pronouncement of the organization. It is the justification for the organization's existence.

Organization-Wide Goals

Often referred to as the long-range goals of the organization, these are broad aspirations that represent a philosophical basis for the operation of the library. Since goals provide not only the direction but also the incentive to achieve, it is almost impossible to be accountable for performance if goals are not stated and communicated.

Every organization is naturally a goal seeking.one, because goals provide a direction and produce effectiveness in the organization. They also provide a framework for planning and help motivate individuals toward achieving those goals. Goals must be flexible and are subject to constant modifications to reflect change. Goals are not operational because they are not specific enough;

therefore, objectives and activities are necessary to quantify goals statements. They serve as the basis for development and as measures against which the success or failure of the objectives can be determined. Goals are action oriented, in other words, they cannot simply be stated, there must follow action, in the form of objectives, which will accomplish them. Stated goals and real goals, although most often identical, are sometimes different. If they are "real goals they will have an impact on the organizations policies, structure, operations and, in general, on the behavior of people."[10] For example, the library may want to offer a high quality bookmobile service (stated goal), but if it does not adequately finance such an operation its real goal cannot be the offering of high quality bookmobile service.

The University of Illinois Library states the following as its goals:

a) Effective organization and administration
b) Adequate financial support
c) Continued rational development of the collections
d) Strong staffing and staff development
e) Quality and efficiency of operations
f) Effective services to users
g) Adequate physical facilities[11]

The University of California at San Diego Library states its goals as follows:[12]

1. To provide a collection of resource materials adequate to support the instructional and research programs.
2. To develop and maintain adequate library facilities.
3. To make the Library's collections and its reference and other public services accessible to faculty, students and staff of the university, and as far as possible, to individuals, public and private institutions, and industries in the San Diego region. In order to meet these goals it is the Library's objective to select, develop, and maintain the qualified staff necessary to provide the collection and services.

Specific Objectives

These can either be departmental objectives or short-range ones for the whole organization. Some objectives are tangible or measurable, while others are not — for instance, one objective may be to improve morale, but how can one measure morale? A real challenge also arises when it is determined that there are multiple service objectives. What, for example, is the major service objective of a university library? Is it to provide needed materials for students at the undergraduate level, or is it to provide materials that will allow faculty and graduate students to do research and therefore advance the state of knowledge? Or is it both? Specific objectives can be related to each goal; for instance, the goal may be to develop library collections using general guidelines set down. One specific objective, to use Oklahoma State University's plan as an example, might be stated in this way:

the annual budget for library materials (books, periodicals, binding and other media) should closely approximate the following for the years indicated:

By 1975 — $600,000
By 1980 — $800,000
By 1985 — $960,000[13]

Further examples of library goals and objectives are provided in Appendix 1 of this volume.

Activities

These more elemental tasks are directly related subsets of the objectives. They are usually short-term or repetitive and measurable.

All four elements of the hierarchy of objectives involve: 1) the clients — who they are and who they are not; 2) the services — what services are needed, which should be added, and which deleted; 3) the personnel resources — what professional and clerical skills are needed to provide services; 4) the financial resources — what and where they are and how to get them; 5) the community responsibilities — whether the library is a social institution.

Unlike business, where the first objective is often to make the highest profit possible, libraries have as one of their primary objectives "socialization" — to pay good wages, to make the organization a good place to work in, to provide a useful service, and to attract a competent staff. Libraries, however, are responsible to higher authorities, which to some extent dictate the social objectives. Therefore, objectives of libraries can be forced on them by the community through social obligations or by the employees through collective bargaining or other means. Just as profit and social objecives in business organizations often dictate opposite courses that force a compromise, so in libraries the individual's objectives and those of the organization as a whole can conflict and force compromise.

Setting Objectives

Objectives can be conservative or expansive, but should be such that they "stretch" the enterprise. There is a real danger of setting objectives that are in reality hopes and not attainable ends. In setting objectives many things must be taken into account: the strengths of the library, the limitations of the library and how much can be accomplished with the resources available, and the objectives of the larger institution of which the library is but one part. Questions that must be addressed in the objective setting exercise are:

Is the objective suitable?
Does it take the organization in the direction it wants to go?
Does it support the overall mission?
Is it compatible with other objectives?
Is it acceptable to the majority who will be charged with
    implementing it?

Can the organization afford it?
Is it achievable?
Is it ambitious enough to be challenging?

A balance must be reached between what is obtainable and what is challenging. The greatest problem in planning is bridging the gap between what is desirable (stated objectives) and what is possible (real objectives). The approach to management by objectives has forced organizations to provide an accurate picture of real, actual, operating objectives. Also, because most libraries have multiple goals, management by objectives, a technique to be discussed later, forces the organization to establish each objective in light of the others. They must fit and must be consistent and harmonious. It is also important to remember that many forces influence the process, and it must therefore be viewed from a number of perspectives. The three primary ones are:

1) the environmental level—that is, considering those constraints imposed on the organization by society in general
2) the organizational level—that is, consideration of the goals of the organization as a system
3) the individual level—the goals of the individuals working in the organization.

There must be a maximum degree of goal compatibility if the organization is to achieve its goals.[14] If an individual working in the organization does not see a relationship between his or her own well-being and success (personal goals) and those of the organization, then he or she is likely to have little motivation to serve the objectives of the organization.

Improper selection or faulty specifications of objectives will waste planning time and money, will result in frustration, and will make the entire planning activity futile. Every library should spell out its own objectives instead of relying totally on those of other organizations, because these objectives determine the policy, planning, and organizational structure of that library. This also represents the end toward which organizing, staffing, and controlling are aimed. The goal of every library is to survive. To do this, it cannot even stand still, let alone decline in vigor. It must produce services that are in demand; therefore, it must state its general objectives in terms that apply to all libraries of a given type, but also in specific terms aimed at service to that particular library's clientele. To say that the objectives of a library are to provide the right book to the right reader at the right time is not enough. It may be more accurate to state its objectives as being: 1) to provide all materials necessary to meet the needs of all patrons, and 2) to attract highly qualified staff.

Once a master plan to achieve goals has been developed and approved, the individual objectives are assigned to one or more subordinate units of the organization for execution, and these units in turn assign activities for individual sections of the unit. Ideally, each unit executes several plans simultaneously, making consistent progress toward several objectives but keeping in mind the priorities that have been established. In practice this may not work effectively. Every person seems to invest more time in fulfilling objectives related to his or her own particular interests, thus losing sight of the priorities established by that unit. For instance, the major objective of a catalog department may be to catalog all current, incoming materials. Other objectives (e.g., getting rid of a backlog that may have accrued or reclassifying the already classified collection) may take priority with some staff members—particularly those who are responsible for reclassifying or cataloging the backlog—so that the department falls behind in achieving its major objective. Then, too, unforeseen circumstances arise to unbalance the accomplishment of a group of objectives. The loss of a key person is a good example of something that can jeopardize the achievement of objectives or that can at least force major revisions or delays.

Unfortunately, most people carry out tasks; they do not achieve objectives. Most do not even know the objectives of an organization. Ask librarians what justifies their positions and they will nearly always answer, if the answer is serious, by listing the work they do, the tasks or machines they control or supervise. Each librarian is concerned with the means and methods, and may not be able to describe the objectives. Perhaps the main benefit of having aims and setting objectives is that this step provides a new way of looking at the old job; it concentrates thought and often gives a sense of purpose. Organizations with clear aims and objectives tend to have a higher staff morale. Understanding of objectives and their environment, plus participation, is the best assurance of loyalty to them. By setting written objectives and communicating them to the staff, the organization encourages individuals to think through the more logical courses of action and provides them with a yardstick for activities. Setting objectives is also an excellent way of measuring output for the organization.

Management by Objectives

The process of goal setting involves decision making, choosing from among alternatives, and translating those decisions into objectives that act as behavioral guides for individuals and groups within the organization. One technique that has been used to merge individual goals with those of the organization and that is being used regularly by management in libraries is "management by objectives," which combines individual and institutional goal setting with the decision-making process. Much has been written on management by objectives, a technique that has been in favor with industry and commerce for some time. Peter Drucker, in *Practices of Management*, first defined the technique:

> This approach involves the establishment and communication of organizational goals, the setting of individual objectives pursuant to the organizational goals, and the periodic and then final review of performance as it relates to the objectives.[15]

He cautions, however, that, although it means the ability to direct oneself and one's work on the one hand, it can also mean domination of one person by another:

> Objectives are the basis of "control" in the first sense; but they must never become the basis of "control" in the second, for this would defeat their purpose. Indeed, one of the major contributions of management by objectives is that it enables us to substitute management by self-control for management by domination.[16]

Description of the technique has been further refined by Odiorne, who defines it as,

> a process whereby the superior and subordinate managers of an organization jointly identify its common goals, define each individual's major areas of responsibility in terms of the results expected of him, and use these measures as guides for operating the unit and assessing the contribution of each of its members.[17]

In essence, management by objectives means establishing sets of objectives and approaching them as a team over a stated period of time. Objectives must be measurable, with time limits, and they must require specific and realistic action. Perhaps the two most important factors are the interactive goal setting and the performance appraisal. The interactive aspect identifies mutually agreed upon objectives for a person to pursue, making that person, then, accountable for results. True interactive sessions involve the supervisor and the employee both giving input to the situation and the follow-up or appraisal aspect. This follow-up requires open and free communication without fear of retaliation and without judgment but rather with trust and respect. Some feel that these sessions can be "self-defeating over the long run because they are based on a reward-punishment psychology that serves to intensify the pressure on the individual."[18] Indeed, the process is a very delicate one which can only improve with experience.

Management by objectives is perhaps the most evident example of participative management because it involves everyone, to an extent, in the management process. It can clarify responsibilities, strengthen planning and control, and establish better relationships between supervisors and other staff members. In this process, at the start of appraisal periods, supervisor and subordinates agree upon specific results to be obtained during this period; they establish what is to be done, how long it will take, and who is to do it. The whole process rests upon several premises:

1) **Clearly stated objectives.** If they are not clear, they should be clarified.
2) **A succession of specific objectives.** Bench marks must be established to measure progress.
3) **Delegation of specific objectives.** Certain people should be responsible for accomplishing specific objectives.
4) **Freedom to act.** Subordinates should be presented objectives and authority and then be charged with accomplishment of those specific objectives.
5) **Verifiable results.** To achieve objectives, it is best to quantify them. If they are non-quantifiable objectives, they may relate to quantifiable ones. For example, if one wants to reduce absenteeism by 50%, the reasons for absenteeism must be considered. If the reasons relate to morale, then morale must be improved, etc.
6) **Clear communication.** This exists only when objectives are specific, are agreed upon by all parties, are budgeted, and are known by all individuals who have a reason for knowing.
7) **Shared responsibilities.** Team effort is the key to management by objectives.

8) **Personal accountability.** Each person must be accountable for the achievement of his assigned objectives.
9) **Improving management ability.** Management is able to plan more objectively when these premises are accepted.

The approach to management by objectives is set in phases of operation: 1) finding the objectives; 2) setting the objectives; 3) validating the objectives; 4) implementing the objectives; and 5) controlling and reporting the status of the objectives. Research studies have confirmed that the process does, indeed, improve communications, increase mutual understanding, improve planning, create positive attitudes toward the evaluation system, utilize management abilities, and promote innovation within organizations which have used it.[19] Figure 2-2 illustrates the steps in a MBO process.

Figure 2-2
The Cycle of Management by Objectives
From *Management by Objectives*, by George S. Odiorne,
Copyright © 1965 by Fearon-Pitman Publishers, Inc.,
Belmont, California. Reprinted by permission.

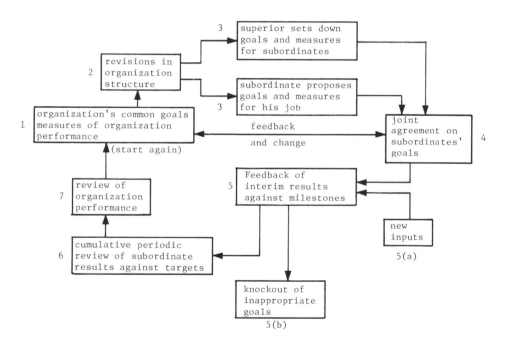

Simply stated by Odiorne, management by objectives helps solve management problems by:

a. Providing a means of measuring the true contribution of managerial and professional personnel.

b. Defining the common goals of people and organizations and measuring individual contributions to them; it enhances the possibility of obtaining coordinated effort and teamwork without eliminating personal risk taking.

c. Providing solutions to the key problem of defining the major areas of responsibility for each person in the organization, including joint or shared responsibilities.

d. Processes are geared to achieving the results desired, both for the organization as a whole and for the individual contributors.

e. Eliminating the need for people to change their personalities, as well as for appraising people on the basis of their personality traits.

f. Providing a means of determining each manager's span of control.

g. Offering an answer to the key question of salary administration—"How should we allocate pay increase from available funds, if we want to pay for results?"

h. Aiding in identifying potential for advancement and in finding promotable people.[20]

Libraries and information centers are beginning to explore this technique's potential for their operations. The things that must be guarded against are: making the individual's objectives too easy; making them too difficult; setting objectives that conflict with policy; or setting objectives that then hold an individual accountable for something beyond his or her control. Also, some concern has been expressed as to whether there is a deterioration of motivation over time. Such deterioration would be reflected, among other ways, in lack of participation by all members, the mountains of paper work which have accumulated, emphasis on quantitative aspects, and in increased administrative concerns.[21] This concept is expanded in other chapters of this volume.

Finally, objectives, as distinguished from policy, emphasize aims and are stated as expectations; policies emphasize rules and are stated in the form of directions.

POLICY MAKING

In many discourses "policy making" and "decision making" are synonomous terms. In actual practice, however, policy making is a part of decision making, in that policies emanate from these original decisions and become general statements or understandings that channel thinking in future decision making. Once policies have been established, they can become effective tools for transferring decision making to lower levels in the organization, because, given the broad policy outline, individuals at all levels can make operational decisions. Perhaps a working definition of policy might be "a verbal, written, or implied overall guide setting up boundaries that supply the general limits and direction in which managerial action will take place."[22]

Policies and objectives are both guides to thinking and action, but there are differences between them. Objectives, as already discussed, are end points of planning, while policies channel decisions along the way to these ends. Another difference is that a policy is usually effective or operational the day it is formulated and continues to be in effect until it is revised or deleted. A policy, then, leads to the achievement of objectives and aids in the decision-making process. As mentioned before, by adopting policies guidance can be given to all levels of the organization. For instance, by adopting the "Equal Opportunity Employer" policy an institution is ensuring that all qualified individuals are seriously considered, by all hiring units within the organization, for any position vacancy. The policy does not dictate the choice of a particular individual but does eliminate one factor — discrimination — as an element in the final decision.

Policy making is not reserved for top management; it is developed at all levels. These levels include, on the one hand, major policies involving all segments of the organization and, on the other, minor policies applicable to only a small segment of the organization. There are many policies in existence in libraries that cover basic directions toward the achievement of the library's stated goals. These include policies relating to materials, personnel, and money (more particularly, the acquisition of materials, personnel appointment and promotion, budgeting, etc.). Examples of library policies might be: 1) all new staff will be rotated through all departments during their first year on the staff (staff development policy); or 2) library materials should present all sides of controversial issues (book selection policy). The kinds of library policies are too numerous to expound here, but policy manuals for all types of libraries enumerate them. Such a policy manual is an important record that is invaluable as a decision-making tool and as a way of communicating within the organization. It is also a basic tool for indoctrinating new staff members.

All libraries have policies, whether they are written or unwritten, sound or unsound, followed or not followed, understood or not understood, complete or incomplete. It is almost impossible to delegate authority and clarify relationships without the existence of policy, since one cannot make decisions without some kind of guidelines. It is important to remember that policies can provide freedom as well as restrict it and that there are as many cases of frustration within organizations about the lack of rules, regulations, procedures, and policies as there are about arbitrarily established ones. In the absence of policy, each case is resolved on its own merit, so consistency is lacking. Lack of policy means that questions may be considered time after time, by a number of different individuals, with the result that energy is wasted, conflicting decisions are made, and confusion develops. Policy ensures some degree of consistency in the operation. Just as with objectives, policies may fall into a general area and be stated in the form of principles that guide the library (these being broad, comprehensive, and basic), while others are specific or operational and deal with day-to-day activities.

Sources of Policy

Sources of policy making are easily categorized:

1) **Originated policy.** Policies developed to guide in the general operations of the library. These flow mainly from the objectives and are the main source of policy making within the organization.

2) **Appealed policy.** Decisions needed by supervisors, in their assigned areas of responsibility, who take it through the chain-of-command where a common law is established. This type of policy can cause confusion because it is forced and often does not have the thorough consideration that is required. To draw an extreme example, it may be the "forced" policy of the catalog department — for administrative convenience only — to make no more than two subject headings for each monograph. One can imagine the effect this could have on the reference department's work with patrons.

3) **Implied policy.** Developed from actions that people see about them and believe to constitute policy. Repetitive actions, such as promotion from within, may be interpreted by subordinates as policy. This may or may not be the case, but particularly in these areas staff must be informed and briefed so that misunderstandings do not arise.

4) **Externally imposed policy.** Such policies, which come through several channels, are policies that dictate the working of an institution but that may be beyond its control. For example, laws have a direct bearing on the policies that libraries may formulate. These laws are both general, such as those relating to destruction of public property (Malicious Damage Act 1861), and specific, such as those relating to copyright (Copyright Act 1976). When policies are being formulated the laws must be remembered.

No matter what objectives are set for, say, public libraries, the objectives are also subject to the law. In the case of public libraries, the process of setting objectives must reflect the government's policy on public libraries at the local, state, and national levels. If, for instance, for local economic reasons, a local authority decides to spend all library funds on its children's services or, at the other extreme, to close the library down completely — such an action might be in conflict with its obligation, and thus illegal. Perhaps a better example might be if a library decides to re-plan its service points, with the result that a branch library is closed down. People living nearby may object and petition their representative, who may decide that such a policy is not securing an improvement and may prevent the authority from carrying out its policy no matter how well-intended it may be.

Another example of library laws relates to finance. An excellent example of this is the set of conditions under which British universities regulate the spending of funds. The Universities Grant Committee's document states very precisely the standards for capital investment, book stock, etc. It states, for example, that library space should be 25 square feet per reader and 60 square feet for each 1,000 books at a cost of 5.37½p. per square foot. Because this is an external control upon all university grant spending, it necessarily affects the planning and administration of the university library.

Levels of Policy

Policies fall into two groups: those that deal with the managerial functions of planning, organizing, staffing, directing, and controlling; and those that deal with the functions of the enterprise, such as selection and development of resources, finance, and personnel and public relations – all of these relating to the characteristic behavior of the library to gain its objectives.

Effective Policy Making

Several basic rules should be considered when policies are being formulated. Some of these may seem simplistic and even redundant, but it is surprising how many organizations ignore these basics when they are formulating policy. To be most effective, policies should be:

1) reflective of the objectives and plans of the organization. The three should dovetail so that each builds on the other instead of working against it. For this reason, any policy should have received detailed consideration before being proposed and certainly before implementation.

2) consistent, so that efficiency is maintained. Again, the existence of contradicting policies simply dissipates the desired effect.

3) flexible, so that they can be changed as new needs arise. Many organizations adhere to out-of-date policies. On the other hand, a laissez-faire approach to policy formulation and revision may lead to disillusionment on the part of those who are charged with carrying it out. Therefore, some degree of stability must be maintained. Policies should be controlled through regular and careful review. Although the application of policies requires an exercise of judgment, violation of the policy under the guise of "flexibility" should be avoided.

4) distinguished from rules and procedures. Rules and procedures are firm, while policies, as guides, allow for latitude in their use.

5) written, so that they are easily communicated to staff. A clear policy, well written, is an aid to information dissemination. Since policies most often affect individuals who have not been involved in their formulation, they should receive discussion and wide distribution through letters, announcements, policy manuals, etc.

Stated policies have several advantages: 1) they become available to all in the same form; 2) they can be referred to so that anyone who wishes can check the policy; 3) misunderstandings can be referred to a particular set of words; 4) they indicate a basic honesty and integrity of the organization's intentions; 5) they can more readily be disseminated to all who are affected; 6) they can be taught to new employees more easily; 7) the process of writing forces managers to think more sharply about the policy, thus helping achieve further clarity; and 8) they generate confidence of all persons in the organization in the leadership of top management and in the fact that everyone will be treated substantially the same under given conditions.[23]

Procedures, Rules, and Regulations

A number of techniques are available for carrying out policy. Each of these has some unique aspect.

Procedures are guides to action rather than guides to thinking, and they are subordinate to policies. They establish a method of handling repetitive tasks or problems and may be thought of as measures by which work is performed. Greater efficiency in routine jobs can be achieved through procedures that identify the best way of getting the job done. Procedures tend to be chronological in listing what is to be done. Examples of procedures are: 1) timetable for budget preparation; 2) sequence of steps to be followed in searching and ordering library materials; or 3) interlibrary loan procedures. Procedures are helpful in routine decisions because they break down the process into steps.

The relationship between procedures and policies can be indicated by an example: library policy may grant employees a month's annual vacation; procedures, established to implement this policy, will schedule holidays to avoid disruption of service, will maintain records to assure each employee a holiday, and will provide a means of applying for the holiday.

Rules and regulations, constituting the simplest type of plan, spell out a required course of action or conduct that must be followed. A rule prescribes a specific action for a given situation and creates uniformity of action. Rules may place positive limits (*should*), negative limits (*should not*) or value constraints (*good or bad*) on the behavior of individuals working in the institution or on individuals using the institution as a service. These rules ensure a stable, consistent, and uniform behavior by those individuals. Like procedures, rules and regulations guide action, but they specify no time sequence. Like decisions, rules are guides, but they allow no discretion or initiative in their application. Examples of rules might be the prohibition of smoking in the library or the fact that reference books do not circulate. Regulations also establish a course of action that is authoritative in nature; failure to adhere to regulations can elicit discipline.

DECISION MAKING

Actual selection from among alternatives is the core of planning. A decision must be made, with a course of action in mind, by choosing the alternative one "thinks" is best. This is not necessarily the alternative that *is* best, because that can be determined only later. Of course, such a choice implies an awareness of alternatives and of the important factors that need to be considered. It is a conscious choice and is a much slower process than one would imagine. The decision-making process involves a blend of thinking, deciding, and acting: "information" is the key to this process. The stereotype of finger-snapping and button-pushing fades with systematic research and analysis. Deliberation, evaluation, and thought must be brought into play before a final decision is made. In the generic sense, many decisions are mundane. However, others are of unmeasured consequence and could change the library's course of action. An example might be the decision to open a new branch library or the decision to purchase an exit control system for a small public library. The decision is probably made after a long period of review, analysis, and discussion, and the manager who has the ultimate say makes a decision that will affect a great many people, both staff and patrons. Concentration on the final act obscures the fact that a number of steps were necessary, and the announcement of the decision is only the final step. Although this discussion is primarily about the steps in a "major" decision process, it is important to remember that we all make decisions in our daily lives and that most of these decisions, to one degree or another, are reached by the same process discussed here. Some organizational decision making, which was originally thought of as in the power of the executive alone, is now being delegated to others in the organization. According to Drucker,

> decision making can no longer be confined to the very small group at the top. In one way or another almost every knowledge worker in an organization will either have to become a decision-maker himself or will at least have to be able to play an active, an intelligent, and an autonomous part in the decision-making process. What in the past has been a highly specialized function, discharged by a small and usually clearly defined organ — with the rest adapting within a mold of custom and usage — is rapidly becoming a normal if not an everyday task of every single unit in this new social institution, the large-scale knowledge organization. The ability to make effective decisions increasingly determines the ability of every knowledge worker, at least of those in responsible positions, to be effective altogether.[24]

Group Decision Making

The approach to decision making by groups is quite different from individual decision making, primarily because of group dynamics. However, group decision making should follow the same process, the same steps, if it is to be constructive. Although techniques of both decision making and participatory management will be discussed in other sections of this volume, it is pertinent to discuss very briefly here the group decision process. Again we are talking about the broad strategies, objectives, etc., that reflect organizational decisions in the library. Simon points out that, "almost no decision made in an organization is the task of a single individual."[25] Not everyone would agree. Max Weber, for instance, when he formulated the concept of bureaucracy with emphasis on the position rather than the person, detailed the delegation of responsibility, channels of communication for decision making, and the need for specialization for decision-making purposes. His theory, for all intents, rejects interaction among subordinates for decision-making purposes.

There are, nevertheless, several advantages to group decision making:

1) **Group judgment.** The old adage that "two heads are better than one" applies here. Group deliberation is important in identifying alternative solutions to a problem.

2) **Group authority.** There is a great fear of allowing one person to have too much authority. Group decisions avoid this problem to an extent. However, it must be remembered that one person must ultimately answer for decisions that have been made. Thus, the role of leadership in the organization is not diminished but changed.

3) **Communication.** It is much easier to inform and receive input from all parts of the organization through a group. Also, if various interest groups have been represented during the process of making major decisions, there is less resistance to the decisions. Also, communication permits a wider participation in decision making and therefore can have some influence on employee motivation.

There are also distinct disadvantages to the group approach. As Townsend cynically writes, a committee developed to make decisions is a group of "unfits appointed by the incompetent to do the unnecessary." More realistically, disadvantages might be:

1) **Cost.** Group decision requires a great deal of time, and therefore money.

2) **Compromise.** Group decisions can be diluted to the least common denominator. Pressures of uniformity force compliance. There are two ways of viewing this problem. The major drawback may be that "majority rules." The desirability of a consensus should not take precedence over critical evaluation in such a situation. On the other hand, a group can prevent an individual from "riding his own hobby horse" by forcing him into line with the thinking of the rest of the group.

3) **Indecision.** There are delays in reaching a final decision because of the lengthy deliberations required. Groups are often charged with engaging in too much irrelevant talk and not enough concrete action.

4) **Power.** One individual usually emerges as a leader. This person may be one who is already in a position of influence in the organization. The authoritarian personality of an administrator can be used as a tactical weapon, so that the group process simply becomes one way of minimizing opposition to an action that has already been decided on by that individual. The degree of cohesiveness of the group and the attitudes of one person toward another are important factors in this group process.

4) **Authority.** One great disadvantage is that groups are frequently used to make decisions that are beyond their authority. This can cause great delay and only enhances a feeling of frustration on the part of members. The responsibility and authority of the group should be clearly set down at the beginning.

This democratic approach of group decision making affects morale, stresses team approach, keeps individuals aware, and provides a forum for free discussion of ideas and thoughts. Librarians have traditionally not demanded a greater voice in decision-making affairs because they have had an "employee" rather than a "professional" orientation. The higher a person is on the administrative scale, the less aware he or she is of the inadequate opportunities given for staff participation. This is an area of great discussion and disagreement in all types of organizations.

Steps in Decision Making

If goals for the organization are clear, the first step in decision making is to develop alternatives. This step is possible for almost all situations. Effective planning involves a search for these alternatives. If there is only one solution, management is powerless to devise alternatives and no decision is required, although some adjustments may be necessary. In most cases, however, the process may lead to several alternatives, so judgment or opinions become a very necessary factor.

Final selection of a course of action is a matter of weighing expected results against enterprise objectives. What is best for one segment is not necessarily best for the whole. Making only two subject cards for the catalog, for instance, is easier for the cataloging department but harder for the reference department. Choosing a course of action commits the entire enterprise to the chosen position.

The scientific approach to decision making requires that one first identify the problem. Once that has been done, the decision maker must collect and analyze all data available on that particular problem. This includes intuition, opinion, and impression in addition to the concrete data that may have been collected or that should be collected before the final decision is made. It may involve techniques that will be discussed under operational research. After all alternatives have been developed, one must select what appears to be the most appropriate alternative. Often this alternative is then expressed as policy for the functioning of the organization. This selection process involves a great deal of risk as well as uncertainty because it is only after the decision has been implemented, that one can tell whether or not it was an appropriate decision. The final step of implementation, then, brings the decision into the "control" aspect of the organization.

Factors in Decision Making

Several factors influence decision making for libraries. For instance, such things as population trends, educational achievement, user and non-user needs, all point to the necessity of a community analysis before final decisions can be made on services to be offered by the library. Selection from among alternatives is made on the basis of:

1) **Experience** (relying on one's past experience). In this regard, mistakes as well as accomplishments should act as guides. If experience is carefully analyzed and not blindly followed, it can be extremely useful.

2) **Experimentation.** This approach toward deciding among alternatives is expensive where capital expenditure and personnel are concerned.

3) **Research and analysis.** Although this is the most general and effective technique used, it may be expensive, and its benefits must be considered by the individual library. However, the approach is probably more beneficial and cheaper in the long run for larger academic, public, and special libraries. Those advantages and disadvantages will be discussed in the section on operational research.

Evaluating the Decision's Importance

One important factor in the decision-making process, is the perceived level of importance of a particular decision. There are two basic types of decisions: a major one affecting the total organization, and a lesser one, which has less impact on the overall organization but is nonetheless important. These latter ones are of a more routine nature and probably compose as much as 90% of the total decisions made in an organization. Decisions of lesser importance do not require thorough analysis. However, politics are paramount in decision making, and this is an area that rests largely in the channels of communication. Consideration of the human factor in the decision-making process is very important; acceptance of change is essential to the success of a decision. Those who will be affected by the decision should be told early on—preferably, they should be involved in the decision from the beginning.

A final, practical list of suggestions may facilitate involvement in the decision-making process:

1) Distinguish big from little problems to avoid getting caught in a situation that is rapid-fire and not effective.

2) Rely on policy to settle routine problems, and reserve the big problems for thorough analysis.

3) Delegate as many decisions as possible to the level of authority most qualified and most interested in handling the problem.

4) Avoid crisis decisions by planning ahead.

5) Don't expect to be right all the time; no one ever is.

Decision making is at the heart of any organization. The approach that the librarian takes to decision making and to the involvement of others will determine the directions the library will take in the future.

NOTES

[1]University of Washington, "The Libraries Planning Guide Adapted from the University of Washington Planning Guide for Fiscal Years 1974-1981" (Nov. 1973) (mimeo).

[2]Columbia University, "Detailed Organization Description of the Columbia University Libraries (June 1973)," p. II.3.1. (April 12, 1973) (mimeo).

[3]"The Management Review and Analysis Program: A Symposium," ed. by Michael K. Buckland, *Journal of Academic Librarianship* 1, no. 6 (Jan. 1976), p. 14.

[4]University of California, San Diego, "Academic Plan for the Davis Campus 1970-1980" (mimeo); and "UCSD Library—Long Range Plan to 1984" (mimeo).

[5]Peter F. Drucker, *Management* (New York: Harper and Row, 1974), p. 25.

[6]George Steiner, *Top Management Planning* (New York: Macmillan, 1969), p. 34.

[7]Fred Luthans, *Introduction to Management: A Contingency Approach* (New York: McGraw-Hill, 1976), p. 95.

[8]*Leonard S. Silk and M. Louise Curley, A Primer on Business Forecasting* (New York: Random House, 1970), pp. 3-4.

[9]Cornell University, "Statement of Mission," Cornell University Libraries (Dec. 19, 1972) (mimeo); Duke University, "Statement of Mission," Duke University Libraries, p. 11 (mimeo); and Minneapolis Public Library and Information Center, "Goals and Objectives Statement," 1979 (mimeo).

[10]Amitai Etzioni, "The Organization Goal: Master or Servant," in *Modern Organization* (Englewood Cliffs, NJ: Prentice-Hall, 1964), p. 7.

[11]University of Illinois, "Statement of Goals and Objectives of the Library of the University of Illinois at Urbana-Champaign" (Oct. 25, 1972) (mimeo).

[12]University of California, San Diego, "UCSD Library—Long Range Plan to 1984," p. 2 (mimeo).

[13]Oklahoma State University, "OSU Library Mission Statement and Goals" (Feb. 8, 1972), p. 2 (mimeo).

[14]Fremont E. Kast and James E. Rosenzweig, *Organization and Management: A Systems Approach* (New York: McGraw-Hill, 1974), pp. 158-59.

[15]Stephen J. Carrol, Jr. and Henry L. Tosi, Jr., *Management by Objectives* (New York: Macmillan, 1973), p. 3.

[16]Peter F. Drucker, *The Practice of Management* (New York: Harper and Row, 1954), p. 131.

[17]George S. Odiorne, *Management by Objectives* (Belmont, CA: Fearon-Pitman, 1965), pp. 55-56.

[18]Harry Levinson, "Management by Whose Objectives?" *Harvard Business Review* 48 (July-Aug. 1970): 134.

[19]Stephen J. Carroll, Jr., and Henry L. Tosi, "Goal Characteristics and Personality Factors in a Management-by-Objectives Program," *Administrative Science Quarterly* 15 (Sept. 1970): 295-305.

[20]George S. Odiorne, *Management by Objectives* (Belmont, CA: Fearon-Pitman, 1965), p. 55.

[21]John M. Ivancevich, "A Longitudinal Assessment of Management by Objectives," *Administrative Science Quarterly* 17 (March 1972): 127.

[22]M. Valliant Higginson, "Putting Policies in Context," in *Business Policy*, ed. by Alfred and Walter Gross (New York: Ronald Press, 1967), p. 207.

[23]Dalton E. McFarland, "Policy Administration," in *Business Policy*, ed. by Alfred and Walter Gross (New York: Ronald Press, 1967), p. 230.

[24]Peter F. Drucker, *The Effective Executive* (New York: Harper and Row, 1966), p. 162.

[25]Herbert Simon, *Administrative Behavior* (New York: Macmillan, 1957), p. 133.

3
ORGANIZING

Upon the completion of the planning process described in chapter 2, clearly defined goals and objectives for an organization will have been established and the programs necessary to achieve the goals and objectives will have been determined. Only after this planning process is complete is the process of organizing undertaken. That planning comes before organizing cannot be emphasized too much. To reverse the process is to encourage the development of an organization that will not permit the accomplishment of planned goals and objectives.

WHAT IS AN ORGANIZATION?

An organization is a structure (man-created) that provides a system through which people can perform assigned activities contributing to the goals, objectives, and programs of the organization. Any activities that do not contribute to the accomplishment of the organization's goals and objectives have no place in the organization.

Since this structure is man-created, it should in no way be considered permanent, fixed, or sacred. Many managers are reluctant to alter an organizational structure once it has been established. This may be due to fear of change or to a failure to recognize that new activities bring new or modified organizational structures. It has been said that most of the organizations existing today were created to meet goals and objectives that no longer exist for those organizations. To impose new goals and objectives on our old organizational structure can only result in inefficiency, duplication of endeavor, and confusion.

An organizational structure that provides for the efficient achievement of the planned goals and objectives is not an easy structure to develop. In an organization consisting of one person, there is no need to develop an elaborate structure. The one person does everything. But as the organization grows from two to more individuals a structure must be established. Even with two people in one organization, a differentiation of activities occurs and a structure emerges.

As the organizational structure gets larger and more people are involved, more complex problems are encountered. Except for the one-person organization, the planned organizational structure must provide an activity-authority environment in which people can work. The organizational process must provide for the identification and grouping of similar or related activities necessary for achieving the organization's goals and objectives; it must permit the assignment of these activities to appropriate units of the emerging organization. It must provide for the coordination of activities under a manager and the delegation of authority and responsibility necessary for the manager to carry out the assigned activities.

Peter Drucker identifies three ways to determine the kind of structure needed for a specific organization: activities analysis, decision analysis, and relations analysis.[1] He emphasizes that only by detailed and thorough analysis of activities can managers determine what work has to be performed, what activities belong together, and where the activities are placed in the organizational structure. Drucker's decision analysis identifies the kinds of decisions that are needed, where in the structure of the organization they should be made, and the degree of involvement of each manager in the decision-making process. In relations analysis, Drucker emphasizes the relationship of the units of the organizational structure and the responsibilities of each manager to the other units as well as the responsibilities of other units to him.

Koontz and O'Donnell summarize the process of organizing as "a process by which the manager brings order out of chaos, removes conflicts between people over work or responsibility, and establishes an environment suitable for teamwork."[2] Implicit also is recognition of the human factor—that jobs must be structured for people, with all their strengths and weaknesses, and that people must be motivated.

The modern organizational structure will provide an environment that encourages easy communication between organizational units so that everyone understands the function and purpose of all units within the structure, and so that any obstacle to performance—be it organizational or personal—can be removed. The modern-day organizational structure will provide a decision-making communications network that will permit the accomplishment of the goals and objectives of the organization.

DEPARTMENTATION

An organization is structured by identifying and grouping similar or related required activities or tasks into departments. To identify similar or related tasks sounds like a simple process. But it becomes more complex when the tasks are examined to determine how they contribute to the organization's goals and objectives. Such grouping of tasks creates blocks of activity-oriented tasks or people-oriented tasks. How the blocks are placed in relation to one another will indicate the true goals and objectives of the organization—which may be different from those originally stated.

Blocks of activity tasks are those that put primary emphasis on process, procedure, or technique. These tasks can vary from the most routine, which require little skill, to very complex tasks requiring extensive ability and knowledge but also conformity with a process, procedure, or technique. People-oriented tasks, which place primary emphasis on human relationships, require the ability to communicate, to guide or direct, and to motivate other individuals.

Most of the older forms of organization put primary emphasis on the activity-oriented tasks. Since World War II, however, it has been recognized that the people-oriented tasks fulfill very important roles in any organization. An example of routine activity-oriented tasks in a library is the task of shelving books or preparing catalog cards; complex activity-oriented tasks might include the selection of books in accordance with a book selection policy or the development of a computer-based program. People-oriented tasks might include the relationship of the reference librarian to the library user, the attitude of the supervisor to subordinates, or the ability of the chief library manager to work with officials in government or academic institutions.

Having identified blocks of tasks, the job of the organizer is to place them together in a logical order. The question "What blocks should be put together or kept apart?" must be answered. Unrelated tasks will be separated. Likewise, the question "What is the proper relationship of the blocks?" must be resolved. Some task blocks will be primary in importance and some secondary. Some will be subservient to larger or primary blocks.

Drucker[3] suggests that it is not as important to identify all tasks that are required in an organization as it is to identify the key tasks. He proposes that any organization design start with the following questions:

> In what area is excellence required to obtain the company's objectives?

> In what areas would lack of performance endanger the results, if not the survival, of the enterprise?

These are questions that libraries have not traditionally asked themselves. Perhaps the answers will change library organization. At best, these questions are a real challenge to library administrators.

METHODS OF DEPARTMENTATION

Business and industry have generally used six methods to establish departments: 1) numbers, 2) function, 3) territory, 4) product, 5) customer, 6) process or equipment.[4] Libraries have used some of the same methods, but in many cases they have interpreted them differently from industry. Libraries use the following methods for departmentation:

Numbers

This concept comes mainly from the military, where a designated number of troops make a squad, a platoon, a regiment, etc. Only in a few situations do libraries use this as a basis for organization—for example, in a situation such as the moving of a library, where no special skills except a strong back are required. A designated number of individuals are assigned to the moving process according to the method of moving, the distance the items are to be moved, and the timetable for completing the move. This is usually a temporary organizational structure for libraries that is soon eliminated.

Function

In business, organization by function has been widely accepted, and in libraries, too, this method has been extensively used. The functions of circulation, reference, acquisition, readers' advisor, shelving, to name but a few, have historically been the basis of library organization. The grouping of necessary library activities has identified these specific functions. In some of the organizational patterns that have emerged in the last 40 years, some of these functions have been combined to create one department with sub-departments performing related functions.

In the 1930s it was not unusual to have many functional departments working autonomously. In recent years, many of these have been combined into larger units because the assigned activities were related. A good example is the emergence in recent years of the major functional department of Technical Services, which includes many units that used to be autonomous functional departments. Order or acquisitions departments, catalog departments, serials departments, binding departments, and book processing departments, previously autonomous, are now usually combined because their activities are related to the organization's end goal of acquiring and organizing library resources.

Territory

In industry it has been a principle that all activities in a designated territory or area should be grouped together and placed under the direction of a manager. This has permitted industry to adapt to local situations as far as the local labor market, local needs and problems, and local production problems are concerned. Libraries have also used this principle of territory or area in their organizational structure. Public libraries and school media centers are much concerned about the location of their central facility; public libraries are concerned about the area to be served by their branch libraries, bookmobiles, and storefront libraries. Academic libraries that have branch libraries — such as a science library, architecture library, or education library — are concerned that these facilities be in the area where the appropriate clientele will be located.

Product

Large industries have used this method for organization because it allows for specialization. Organization by product is particularly prevalent in diversified industries. Libraries basically do not use this standard, though perhaps the product of a print shop (a printed bibliography, brochure, or a catalog card) might be interpreted as a product.

Customer

Industry has used this method of departmentation to appeal to the needs and desires of clearly defined customer groups; so, too, have libraries. Since the late 1800s, special children's rooms have been provided in public libraries. Also, public libraries have aimed their service at teenagers, blind persons, and physically handicapped persons, special groups in the community, and, since the late 1960s, economically or culturally disadvantaged persons. This has caused special organizational departmentation in the public library. The academic library has used this method when undergraduate libraries were established and when rare book libraries and special collections were developed for the researcher.

Process or Equipment

Industry has used this standard when large installations have been required — a smelting plant, a steel mill, etc. Libraries have used it, too, but on a much smaller scale. Those libraries that operate a book bindery centralize all the special, heavy binding equipment in one place. But generally this method has been used as a basis for centralizing such smaller equipment as printing equipment, microform readers, phonodisc players, cassettes, and films. There is a trend in school media centers and some public libraries to distribute this type of equipment throughout the library and to disregard this method of organization.

Libraries have developed two other methods on which the organizational structure is based:

Subject

Large public and academic libraries use this method extensively today. It provides for more in-depth reference service and reader guidance, and it requires a high degree of subject knowledge on the part of the staff. There is no set pattern that determines the subjects to be included in a subject department. In academic libraries subject departments are usually broad in scope and include all related subjects in such areas as humanities, social sciences, science, etc. In large public libraries more popular names are used for subject departments. Also, the number of subject departments created in a library varies. There was a period during the late 1930s and early 1940s when major libraries created as many as twelve subject departments in one organization. But, because of the financial problem of staffing so many departments, the present tendency is to create four to six subject departments in one public library.

Forms of Resources

Libraries have frequently used the form in which the resources have been issued as a basis for organization. It is not unusual to find a map department, a film library, a periodicals department, and a documents department as part of the library organizational structure. Large academic and public libraries tend to separate by form, whereas smaller libraries try to incorporate the various forms into broader departmental units.

Only in the most specialized library would a single one of these organizational methods be used; a library usually uses several of the methods. A large public library, for example, generally has a circulation department (function), subject departments (combining several functions), branch libraries (territory), children's services (clientele) and perhaps service to business (customer), a print shop (equipment), documents collection (form), etc. Academic libraries also use various methods in setting their organizational structure. Figure 3-1 shows how even the smallest one-room library uses various methods in its organization.

Much emphasis has been placed on the identification and grouping of tasks to create departments and sub-departments. But one more element is essential in the creation of an effective departmentation for an organization. To each department or sub-department a manager is assigned to whom adequate authority is delegated to permit him or her to carry out assigned tasks. If a manager in an organization is assigned the responsibility for the accomplishment of designated tasks and the supervision of employees, he or she must have the authority to guarantee efficient performance.

Figure 3-1
One-Room Library

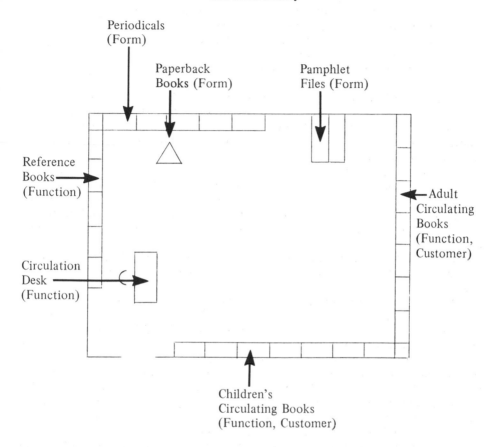

Periodicals
(Form)

Paperback
Books (Form)

Pamphlet
Files (Form)

Reference
Books
(Function)

Adult
Circulating
Books
(Function,
Customer)

Circulation
Desk
(Function)

Children's
Circulating Books
(Function, Customer)

THE SCALAR PRINCIPLE AND THE HIERARCHY

As departments and sub-departments are assigned various tasks, primary and secondary units of the organization emerge. Primary organizational departments are those that have numerous tasks and broad responsibilities; secondary or sub-departments are those that have more specific tasks and more limited responsibility. A sub-department is usually attached to a primary department because its tasks contribute to the fulfillment of the responsibilities of the primary department. The manager of the primary department supervises the manager of the sub-department to assure compliance with the needs of the primary department. Authority, therefore, flows from the primary to the secondary supervisor.

The scalar principle requires that there be a final, ultimate authority in every organization, and that lines of authority extend downward through the organization to every subordinate position. The clearer the line of authority, the more effective will be organizational performances and communication. Henri Fayol described the scalar principle as, the chain of supervisors ranging from the ultimate authority to the lowest ranks. The line of authority is the route followed—via every link in the chain—by all communications which start from or go to the ultimate authority. This path is dictated both by the need for some transmission and by the principle of unity of command, but it is not always the swiftest. It is even at times disastrously lengthy in large concerns, notably in governmental ones.[5]

A clear understanding by each subordinate in the line of authority or, in military terms, in the line of command, is necessary for effective organizational functioning. The subordinate knows to whom he or she is responsible and for what; further, the parameters of his or her authority in relation to other employees are clear.

As a result of the ranking of organizational units, a hierarchy develops. A hierarchy is defined as "any system of persons or things ranked one above the other."[6] The concept of the hierarchy has existed for centuries. While much of the development of this concept can be attributed to the military, it is the Roman Catholic Church that developed the concept as an efficient organizational device.[7]

A hierarchy is usually illustrated as a triangle with the ultimate authority at the apex of the triangle and authority flowing downward to all other parts of the triangle.

In an effective organization, the position holding ultimate authority will delegate authority to subordinate managers. The delegation of authority to subordinates does not mean that the final authority relinquishes that authority. A major supervisor is responsible for the actions of subordinates even if authority has been delegated. What actually has happened in many libraries is that the responsibility to perform designated activities has been assigned to a subordinate, but the authority to accomplish those designated activities has been withheld. Many administrators are afraid to delegate authority; they clutch it tenaciously. But a subordinate given responsibility without authority is in a difficult position and probably will not be able to function efficiently.

Thus, while the historical concept of the hierarchy centralized all authority in the primary administrator (king, queen, commander, or Pope), the current concept is that the primary administrator must delegate sufficient authority to a subordinate to enable that subordinate to accomplish assigned activities and responsibilities. Authority should be delegated downward to that place in the organization where decisions need to be made. This results in a decentralization of authority in place of the traditional centralization of command.

LINE AND STAFF

Line positions, those having authority and command in an organization, are the decision makers of the organization. In many organizations staff positions are advisory positions without authority. The concept of staff also developed from the military. It is said that Alexander perfected the staff concept during his conquest of Macedonia. The Catholic Church organization utilizes staff services in its central administration through the Sacred College and the Roman Curia.[8] Both institutions are regarded as advisory to the Pope, who delegates no authority to them and is not obligated to accept their advice.

Sometimes a staff unit is defined as one that deals with "ideas." But it is broader than that. In today's organizations, a staff unit may be a research unit, a personnel office, a public relations office, or a systems analyst. The important concept is that the unit has no authority; it functions in an advisory capacity only. The manager of a staff unit is supervised by a superior and in turn may supervise subordinates within the staff unit. But nowhere does the staff manager have authority over the organization.

A library personnel office, for example, may have the responsibility of receiving applications, interviewing applicants, maintaining personnel files, recommending promotion, transfer, etc. But it does not have the authority to cause any of these actions to take place. Only the line position – the authority position – can take action.

But staff positions in an organization are extremely important. They provide the facts, the information needed by the decision makers. They are the individuals skilled in specific functions and they apply their skills as a basis for action.

UNITY OF COMMAND

Organizations often have too many bosses. The organizational structure should guarantee that each employee is supervised by only one supervisor. Only one supervisor should make assignments and assess the success of the employee in achieving those assignments. Too often, however, in business and in libraries, employees have several supervisors. In libraries, this is particularly true of the clerical staff and shelvers. When more than one supervisor supervises an employee, the employee is placed in the awkward position of determining whose work to do first, the style in which the work is wanted, and which instruction to follow. The principle of unity of command protects the employee from undesirable situations that result from dual or multiple supervision.

SPAN OF CONTROL

The phrase "span of control" is well entrenched in management thought. And it is an important part of management. But the word "control" may be misleading. This phrase really raises the question of how many individuals one supervisor can supervise well. "Control" might better be replaced by "management," for the concept concerns the number of supervisors one manager can manage efficiently.

There are no established criteria to resolve this problem, and in actual practice the number of supervisors assigned to one manager varies extensively – usually from five to nine. But there are situations where many more than nine supervisors are assigned to one manager.

One of the criteria used to determine the number of people one manager can adequately manage concerns the kind of assignment given the various supervisors. If the activities of the various units assigned to one supervisor are similar, then perhaps the number can be increased; if the activities vary extensively and require a thorough knowledge of a great variety of activities, the number should be decreased. One must consider the knowledge the manager must have to do an adequate job of managing. The broader and more detailed the required knowledge, the fewer the number of assigned units there should be.

Another criterion concerns the amount of time involved in communication. Time is becoming a critical element in many enterprises. A good manager who has a number of supervisors to supervise will try to reduce the time necessary for the supervising. It will be necessary to spend more time in the initial training of a new supervisor, to give assignments in broad terms of goals or objectives to be achieved, and to delegate authority so that the supervisors may supervise their personnel. If the span of control is large and the manager fails to function as described, time will be consumed by frequent conferences, daily meetings, and repetitive instruction. Time will not be used efficiently.

When one manager has many organizational units reporting to him or her, a flat or horizontal organization is created and an extensive span of control obtains. There are few levels of operation in a flat organization.

Figure 3-2 shows only two levels of operation—the director and the supervisor of each unit to which specific activities have been assigned. But the scope of knowledge required of the director is extensive, indeed. While time would be saved because of the absence of many levels, the amount of supervision given each unit would probably be minimal.

Figure 3-2
Flat Organization

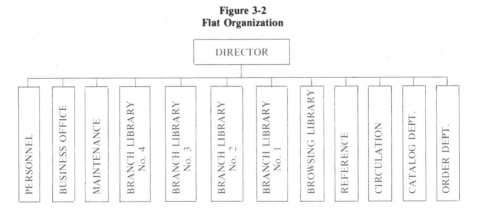

As related units are put together under one supervisor, a vertical organization is created and the span of control is reduced. Figure 3-7 (page 70) shows a vertical organization with four levels of operation. Each supervisor's span of control is small, except for the director, who has six people to supervise—a great reduction from the twelve people shown in Figure 3-2.

The principle of span of control is that there is a limit in each managerial position to the number of persons an individual can efficiently manage. But that number must be determined by the variety of activities assigned and the amount of time a manager can give to each subordinate supervisor.

FUNCTIONAL AUTHORITY

Functional authority is that supervisory power exercised on the unit by a position outside the organizational unit. Seldom is functional authority assigned by a major manager; rather, as the outside position assumes greater authority in the total organizational unit, it influences the authority and operation of the smaller organizational unit. While the outside power may be another line supervisor, more frequently a staff position is involved. It is dangerous for an administrator to permit the development of functional authority, since it violates the principle of unity of command.

When line supervisors need assistance that requires special knowledge, it is easy for the specialist, the staff position, to receive permission from the administrator to assist the line supervisor. Gradually this "permission" translates itself into authority. Such action erodes the authority of the major supervisor. While such authority is usually limited to "how" (and occasionally "when") action is to occur, it generally does not influence the "where, what, and who" aspects of personnel assignments.

The main supervisor may ask the library personnel officer to explain grievance procedures to a line supervisor. That request gradually changes to authority over the line supervisor in matters relating to grievances; functional authority develops as the line supervisor accepts the direction of the staff officer in place of the primary supervisor's direction.

In libraries, functional authority frequently develops in the area of the specialists who work with children, young adults, and adults. Frequently these specialists are called "coordinators." Regardless of their title, they are expected to work with employees who perform their type of specialty. Thus, the coordinator of work with children will be expected to train the children's librarian in public branch libraries. At the same time, the head of the branch library expects to do the same thing. So the coordinator is exercising functional authority and the branch librarian is exercising line authority—to the detriment of the children's librarian, who is caught in the middle.

In order to avoid internal conflicts, the role of the individual exercising functional authority needs to be clearly defined. All parties must understand the parameters within which the individual exercising functional authority operates.

ORGANIZATIONAL POLICIES

In order to maintain consistency and continuity, written organizational policies should be prepared as the organizational structure is established. Of course, any changes in the structure will require changes in the policy statements. The establishment of organizational policies helps to meet the requirements of the *principle of functional definition*. This principle establishes the concept that the more a position, a department, or any unit of an organization understands and has a clear definition of its authority and responsibility, of the results expected, and of its relationship to other organizational units, the better will the individuals concerned respond and the better will be their performance.

A policy may be defined as a statement that guides present and future action. It is a general statement that guides the action of employees in the decision-making process. It is true that policy has a restrictive effect on the decisions employees may make. But such policies assure compliance with the organizational structure, which has been created to achieve goals and objectives.

A policy is a public statement. It is available to all employees and is discussed with them to assure understanding. Employees should not have to try to identify organizational policy from the action or occasional statements of the manager.

Organizational policies should include the following:

1) Statements identifying the laws that authorize the establishment of the library. Libraries may operate under state law, county or municipal ordinances, or charters. All types of libraries (except special libraries operated by private industry or incorporated bodies) have a legal base for their operation.

2) Statements describing the departmentation that has been established as the organizational structure. The tasks and responsibilities of each unit — the large organizational unit as well as each sub-unit — must be defined. The relationship of one unit to another is established by describing the chain of command (line of authority). Statements describing activities and responsibilities naturally limit the scope of activities of the various organizational units.

3) Statements describing the resources of the organizational unit. In libraries it is possible to list the classification numbers for which a department is responsible or to identify the types of resources to be housed in that unit. For example, a fine arts department may be responsible for all books in the Dewey Classification 700. That department is responsible for the selection of all titles and for the replacement, duplication, and weeding of these resources. In addition, the department is assigned responsibility for maintaining a picture file, a phonodisc collection of classical and popular recordings, and a collection of large art prints. Because librarians tend to develop special indexes, it is wise to identify the authorized indexes that will be maintained by the department.

The purpose of such organizational policy statements is not to limit the creativity of the staff but rather to assure consistency in the operation of the organizational structure. Such policy statements also provide an excellent method of communicating to the employees the responsibility of each organizational unit other than the one to which they are assigned.

ORGANIZATION CHARTS

An organization chart is a graphic presentation of the organizational structure. Although it includes staff units, primarily it shows how departments are tied together by lines of authority. Lines of authority are solid lines; lines that show staff organizational units are broken lines. Formal communication follows the lines of staff and authority. Informal lines of communication are generally not shown on the traditional organization chart.

On an organization chart, authority flows down and out. It does not return to the original line of authority. For example, in Figure 3-3, the main line of authority flows from the director down to the assistant director and from that position down and out to the three functional departments.

In Figure 3-3, the business office is supervised by the director only. Authority flows from the director down and out to the business office and stops there. The business office has no authority over the assistant director or over other organizational structures shown in the figure. An understanding of the principle that authority flows out and stops is very important in interpreting organization charts.

Figure 3-3
Organization Chart Showing Authority Lines

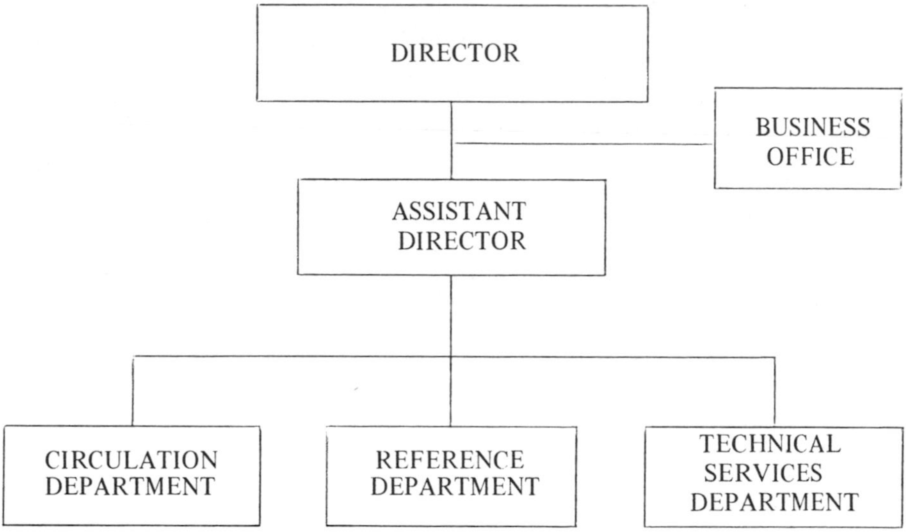

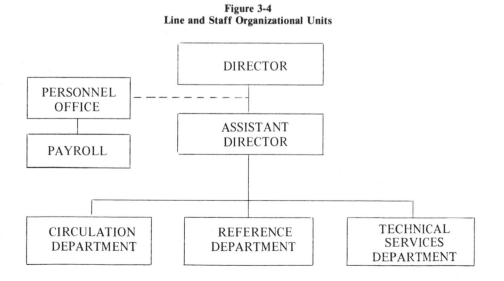

Figure 3-4 illustrates an organization that has both line and staff organizational units.

Figure 3-4
Line and Staff Organizational Units

In the library represented by Figure 3-4 the director has authority over the personnel officer. This authority goes down and out the broken line. The personnel office serves in an advisory capacity to the director and to all other units of the organization, without authority over any unit. However, the personnel office, in its own internal operation, has line authority in that it supervises the payroll functions.

Some of the blocks in Figures 3-3 and 3-4 seem to represent individuals (e.g., director and assistant director), while others represent functions (e.g., circulation, reference, and technical services). The blocks representing functions include all assigned activities and a manager. The blocks that seem to represent individuals actually represent all the activities assigned to that organizational unit. For the director, activities would include the direct supervision of the business office in Figure 3-3 and the personnel office in Figure 3-4. But, in addition, it is also expected (in both charts) that the director will perform such activities as planning, working with outside groups, organizations, and individuals (such as the public library board or the vice-president for academic affairs in a university library), and evaluating library services. The assistant director in both charts would be responsible for day-to-day supervision of the three operating units, but other activities would also be assigned to this organizational unit. Although it may appear that a unit of the organizational structure is designated by an individual's title, one must recognize that the organizational block includes all the activities of that position.

Not all organizations are as simple as those represented by Figures 3-3 and 3-4. Some become very complex. As a result, various means have been developed to show the authority relationship of one unit to another. If the function assigned to reference in Figure 3-3 were expanded, that expansion might be shown as in Figure 3-5.

Figure 3-5
Organization Chart Showing Two Sub-Units of a Department

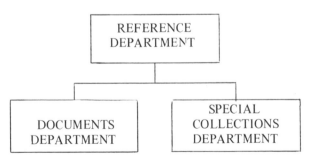

The added organizational units (both by type of material) are equal in status in that they are both immediately supervised by the manager of reference. This same relationship might be charted as follows:

Figure 3-6
Alternative Method of Showing Equal Sub-Units

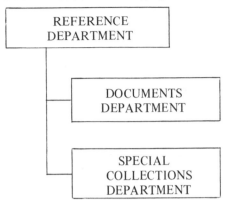

In Figure 3-6, authority flows down from the manager of reference, out to the documents department, and then stops. It continues to flow down and out to special collections and stops. Thus, Figure 3-6 presents a vertical method of showing equal units, while Figure 3-5 uses a horizontal method.

Sometimes the status of an organizational unit is misunderstood because of its location on the organization chart. The belief is frequently held that the higher on the chart the unit is represented, the greater is its status and authority. This is not true. The importance of an organizational unit is determined by the line of authority and the number of managers that authority passes through before reaching the final authority.

Following the line of authority in Figure 3-7 (page 70) reveals that the assistant director provides immediate supervision to circulation, reference, and technical services. It is also apparent that these organizational units are important because they are placed rather high on the organization chart. But what of extension—the unit that provides service outside the central building? It is shown low on the chart. But analyzing the authority line reveals that extension is equal in status, rank, and importance to the other three units. Extension reports to the same position—the assistant director—as do circulation, reference, and technical services.

The organization charts presented above are the traditional type. They are all based on the hierarchical concept and are designed to show the relationship of one organizational unit to another through lines of authority. The development of an organization chart will help the manager identify problems or inconsistencies in the organization. One common inconsistency readily identified is the assignment of unrelated or dissimilar activities to a unit. Also, through the analysis of an organization chart the span of control of each supervisor can be determined, and any problems of dual supervision can be readily detected.

Every library, regardless of size, should have an organization chart. It should be available to all staff so that they will understand relationships within the library. But it must be recognized that organization charts are limited in what they can do. While an organization chart can show formal relationships, informal relationships and communication lines between units are not shown. An organization chart shows lines of authority, but at no place does it show the degree of assigned authority. That will have to be described in organizational policies.

Figure 3-7
Vertical Organization Chart Showing Placement on a Chart
(Figures in parentheses indicate level according to authority lines)

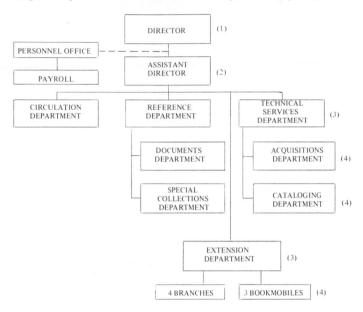

Occasionally, the creation of an organization chart may tend to freeze an organization. This can happen particularly under poor leadership. But if leadership is strong and if the organization is dynamic, the organization chart and organization will change. Four factors can cause the organization to change:

1) Change in property—the development of new buildings and facilities
2) Change in program—a change in goals and objectives and programs to achieve objectives
3) Change in techniques—the introduction of mechanization or automation
4) Change in financial support—the sudden increase or reduction of income

Appendix 2 includes organization charts of Dallas Public Library, Cornell University Libraries, University of Michigan Libraries, and New York State Library. An analysis of the charts indicates that in actual practice the principles of preparing an organization chart are sometimes seemingly violated. On some of the charts, it would appear that some positions have two or three supervisors. The span of control of any one supervisor is larger on some of the charts than is usually recommended. An organization chart will reflect local situations that may be historical in nature or that reflect the desire and intent of the administrator in spite of the general principles of organization chart development. It is also interesting to note that one organization chart is used as a "manning table." This term evolves from the military and designates the number and general level of staff assigned to each organizational unit. The organization chart of the state library shows in general terms the functions and responsibilities assigned to different organizational units. This is helpful in interpreting the organization chart to a large constituency. The organization chart of the University of Michigan Libraries is a very thoroughly prepared document. Issued as a small booklet, this organization chart first includes an overall diagram of the structure of this organization. For each of the various organizational components, individual organization charts are presented, showing the name of the organizational unit, basic functions or tasks assigned, and the number and level of staff assigned. Only one of these detailed charts, supplementing the main organization chart of the University of Michigan Libraries, is presented in Appendix 2.

CURRENT TRENDS IN ORGANIZATION AND ORGANIZATION CHARTS

The organizational process described above represents the historical and traditional method of organizing. However, different companies, industries, and libraries are testing new or modified methods of organization. These new forms basically retain the concept of the hierarchical triangle with the major authority at the top, though some patterns of organization have replaced the individual at the top with an "executive committee," which has final authority.

Odiorne identifies several of these modifications in organization processes. These modifications are based on the assumption that most employees in an organization can perform as they see fit as long as such action is not specifically prohibited by policy and as long as such action contributes to the organization's goals and objectives. He defines the following new management processes:[9]

Bottom-up Management

This process is achieved by delegating authority and the power of decision-making to the lowest possible point in the organization. This delegation of authority supposedly increases employee initiative and requires that employees in the lower echelons of the organization accept more responsibility for their actions.

Collegial Management

This concept, which affects only the top decision maker, has already been mentioned. Instead of a single final authority position, a group of individuals participate in the making of those decisions that affect the total organization. This structure not only brings more expertise into the decision-making process, but also gives more individuals a feeling of responsibility.

Project Management

The chart for this concept of organization (sometimes called a task force) may look like many small organizational units attached to one another by lines of authority. Odiorne compares it to a bunch of grapes.[10] Each unit has a specific temporary task to perform and, when the task is completed, the group working on a specific project returns to their primary jobs. This structure is widely used; the term "task force" is frequently used to identify the temporary organizational unit assembled to do a specific temporary project, but the terminology does not change the basic concept of organization.

The Doughnut

This method of illustrating an organizational pattern consists of a series of concentric circles, each of which shows a different level of operation. Top administrators are shown in the center and the levels of organization are represented by the successive circles. This is not a change in organizational structure but rather a different way of showing the organization. (*See* Figure 3-8).

Figure 3-8
Organization Chart Presented as a "Doughnut"

The Matrix

Some libraries are developing packages of information for specific community groups. In order to have representative resources and services from all organizational units of the library, it is necessary to create a matrix, a lateral slice across autonomous units. For example, the matrix might consist of the organizational unit responsible for services to the disadvantaged. The creation of a matrix structure might be temporary, but it is very important that the administrators of the autonomous units affected understand what is happening and cooperate with the endeavor. Without this understanding and cooperation, it is possible that the organizational principle of unity of command might be violated.

Regardless of new methods of illustrating organizational structure and new patterns of organization, the basic concept of the hierarchical structure is expected to remain. Managers will still be assigned responsibility and the authority to fulfill that responsibility. Possibly new criteria for structuring the organization will emerge. Drucker suggests four criteria for organizational structure:

> 1) Result-producing activities—activities which can be related ... to the results and performance of the entire enterprise,
>
> 2) Support activities—[activities]—which while ... essential do not produce direct results,
>
> 3) Hygiene and housekeeping activities—activities which are truly ancillary,
>
> 4) Top-management activities— ... activities that are the conscience of an organization. The conscience function of giving vision, of setting standards, and of auditing performance against these standards is basically a top-management function.[11]

New trends, such as "management by objectives" and "participative management" are not changes in the basic concept of organization. Rather, they represent the "humanistic school's" approach to management.

EVALUATION OF AN ORGANIZATIONAL STRUCTURE

Even though the process of organization has emerged over the years and some principles have been evolved, no one would claim that they are infallible laws. Rather, these principles are "truths of general application"[12] by which any organization can be evaluated.

In 1952, the American Management Association found through a survey that most companies used 9 criteria to evaluate their organizational structure.[13] Since that time additional criteria have been identified; at the present time, 15 criteria—stated as principles—can be applied to an evaluation of an organization:[14]

Principle of Unity of Objective. The structure of an organization is effective if all and every unit of the organization contributes to the accomplishment of the organization's goals and objectives.

Principle of Efficiency. The structure of an organization must not only be effective but must also be efficient. To be efficient the organizational structure must make it possible for every organizational unit to contribute its maximum endeavor toward the accomplishment of goals and objectives, without any unsought consequences or costs.

Principle of Span of Control. Each managerial position can manage a limited number of persons, but the number will vary according to the diversity of activities assigned and their impact on the time required for effective management.

The Scalar Principle. When the line of authority from the ultimate authority to each subordinate position is absolutely clear, effective decision making and organizational communication will result.

Principle of Delegation. The amount of authority delegated managers should be sufficient for them to achieve assigned responsibilities.

Principle of Responsibility. The subordinate is totally responsible to the superior for authority delegated, and the superior cannot escape responsibility for the activities of the subordinate.

Principle of Parity of Authority and Responsibility. The responsibility for actions taken under delegated authority cannot be greater than the authority delegated.

Principle of Unity of Command. An individual should report to only one superior.

The Authority Level Principle. An individual manager is required to make decisions according to the authority delegated to him or her and such decisions will be referred upward in the organizational structure.

Principle of Division of Work. An organizational structure assigned a group of activities that are necessary to achieve goals and objectives identifies and groups similar or related tasks into departments, thereby creating a series of inter-related roles that fit the capabilities and motivations of people. The principle of division of work, which permits broad grouping of tasks, should not be confused with occupational specialization, which allows for specialized and limited tasks only.

Principle of Functional Definition. If a position or a department has a clear understanding of expected results, activities assigned, amount of authority delegated, and informational relationships with other positions, individuals can contribute more adequately to the accomplishment of goals and objectives.

Principle of Separation. If an organizational unit is designed to be a check on the activities of another organizational unit, the individual in charge of the checking unit cannot perform his or her responsibility if he or she reports to the unit whose activity is to be evaluated.

Principle of Balance. A balance must be maintained in the application of organizational principles so that an effective structure evolves that permits the accomplishment of goals and objectives. In complex situations, not all principles will have the same priority, nor will they all pull in the same direction. Often, varying situations will require one principle to be emphasized more than another until the environment or situation changes.

Principle of Flexibility. Because of changing environments, the more provision made for building in organizational flexibility the more adequately can the organization fulfill its purposes. In a culture that is shifting rapidly, it is essential that an organization be able to adapt to change not only rapidly but efficiently.

Principle of Leadership Facilitation. The organizational structure and authority delegation within it should provide an environment for efficient leadership performance.

ORGANIZATIONAL RENEWAL

Both in industry and in libraries, organizations develop into structures that deter the achievement of desired goals and objectives. Recent industrial history shows that some larger organizations that expanded to meet the needs of World War II production were not able to adjust to changes required by the post-war era. The same structure, procedures, and rules appropriate for a large organization were retained even though the company had to reduce its size and the scope of its activities. Libraries have faced similar problems of adjustment. Having grown fat on federal grants, some libraries have not been able to adjust to the recent lean years of reduced or withdrawn federal funds.

All organizations need a high degree of stability. It is important that in spite of current trends and socio-economic movements, organizations keep sight of their primary goals, and that they have the stability to adapt to change without losing their basic thrust. Libraries usually have a high degree of stability even in times of economic stress. But some libraries are not able to adapt programs or eliminate tasks that in the long view are detrimental to their basic goals.

Stability is not rigidity. A library that has stability is able to adapt to new situations. A library that is rigid in its organizational structure is brittle and may break when change is required. Rigidity develops partly because of the attitudes of the managers and employees toward change. The existing structure is familiar and comfortable and the work habits and processes are personally satisfying and secure.

But other factors also encourage organizational rigidity. Large bodies of policies, procedures, and rules have been developed that prohibit the employees from exercising any initiative or judgment. Every action is dictated by recorded directions. The employee becomes literally frozen by the existence of those guidelines that were originally designed to be a positive force for the organization. It is not uncommon for chief managers to pull back any authority they might have delegated. An authority-centered organization prevents any decisions from being made except by the chief manager. Actual situations have been observed where large libraries operated under a strong authority-centered librarian. These libraries were so rigid in their compliance with written directions and the inability to make decisions where and when they needed to be made that the libraries literally ground to a halt. The organization was inoperable.

When a library becomes rigid in its organizational and operational structure, the general trend of the employee is either to accept the situation passively, to revolt and leave, or to unionize. Particularly in libraries, the attitude of the employee is to become arrogant toward the user. More concern for compliance with rules is demonstrated than concern for service. In reality, the organization is functioning more to meet its own needs than it is to fulfill its valid goals and objectives.

An organization operating in this manner is a bureaucratic organization serving itself. But an organization need not remain ineffectual, frozen, and rigid. An organization can be brought back to productive life and can return to the dynamic role its founders envisioned. John W. Gardner, when he was president of the Carnegie Corporation, said "Most ailing organizations have developed a functional blindness to their own defects. They are not suffering because they can't *solve* their problems but because they won't *see* their problems."[15] He proposed nine steps for organizational renewal:[16]

1)   There must be an effective program for the recruitment and development of talent. The organization must not only bring in highly talented and motivated people but it must also have a constructive career development program for its present employees.

2)   There must be a hospitable work environment for the employee permitting him to feel a part of the organization rather than just a cog in its operation.

3)   There must be built-in provisions for self-criticism. Most executives cannot trust themselves to be adequately self-critical. An atmosphere must be created wherein anyone with critical comments will not be afraid to speak up.

4)   There must be flexibility in the organizational structure. While specialization and division of labor are at the heart of modern organization, the complex modern organization must constantly be examining its structure.

5)   There must be an adequate system of internal communication. Ideas, the product of the human brain, must be examined, evaluated, and judged through a good communication system.

6)   There must be a way of combatting the process by which employees become the prisoner of their procedures. Evaluate and eliminate unnecessary rules, procedures, and policies.

7)   There must be a method of combatting the vested interests which develop in every organization. At every level there are vested interests and any change threatens someone's special interests, privileges, authority, or status. Everyone's overriding special interest is the continuing vitality of the organization, regardless of vested interests.

8)   The concern of the organization must be what it is going to become, not what it has been. It is the future strength and vitality of the organization which is of concern and not past successes.

9) Organizations are successful because of the motivation, conviction, and morale of their employees. Employees must care whether they do well or badly. They must believe that their efforts not only contribute to but will be recognized by the total organization.

Organizations are like individuals in that they cannot remain at a status quo. There is no permanent plateau. There is either improvement or decline. The managers of organizations and the total body of employees need to recognize this and to judge their organization's movement.

NOTES

[1] Peter F. Drucker, *The Practice of Management* (New York: Harper and Row, 1954), chapters 10-18.

[2] Harold Koontz and Cyril O'Donnell, *Principles of Management: An Analysis of Managerial Functions*, 4th ed. (New York: McGraw Hill, 1968), p. 239.

[3] Peter F. Drucker, *Management, Tasks, Responsibilities, Practices* (New York: Harper and Row, 1973), p. 530.

[4] Koontz and O'Donnell, *Principles of Management*, pp. 259-74.

[5] Henri Fayol, *General and Industrial Administration* (New York: Putnam, 1949), p. 14.

[6] *Random House Dictionary of the English Language* (New York: Random House, 1966).

[7] J. P. Mooney, *The Principles of Organization*, rev. ed. (New York: Harper and Row, 1939), chapters 3-5, 16-18.

[8] Mooney, *Principles.*

[9] George S. Odiorne, "Up the Pyramid ... or ... Doughnut ... or ... Beehive," *Nation's Business* 60, no. 1 (Jan. 1972): 62-64.

[10] Odiorne, "Up the Pyramid," p. 63.

[11] Drucker, *Management*, pp. 532-35.

[12] Koontz and O'Donnell, *Principles*, p. 423.

[13] Ernest Dale, *Planning and Developing the Company Organization Structure*, Research Report No. 20 (New York: American Management Association, 1952), pp. 138-44.

[14] Koontz and O'Donnell, *Principles*, pp. 424-28.

[15] John W. Gardner, "How to Prevent Organizational Dry Rot," *Harper's Magazine* 231, no. 1385 (Oct. 1965): 21.

[16] Ibid. Paraphrased from Gardner, "How to Prevent Organizational Dry Rot," p. 21.

4

STAFFING

Three components compose all libraries: 1) a physical facility or a group of facilities to house the activities of the library, 2) a collection of resources, and 3) personnel to collect and organize the resources and to retrieve information needed by users. Of the three components only the last — personnel — can bring a library to life and make it a dynamic, vital force for the community it serves. Most of these people — the personnel — are well educated. They are dedicated to a philosophy of service. They believe that education will improve the quality of life. And they recognize that in this age of change, a process of continuing education is essential if an individual is to be a self-sufficient, participating member of society.

LIBRARY EDUCATION

The aim here is to give no more than a historical overview of library education. However, it is important to note that the first School of Library Economy was started at Columbia College by Melvil Dewey in 1884. In 1889, the school was moved to Albany, New York, as part of the New York State Library.[1] One library school, however, was inadequate for a developing profession. In the early 1900s, many public libraries established training classes as the means of training staff. These training classes, which required a high school diploma for admission and which lasted for approximately nine months, were basically work-study programs. Students attended formal classes in the mornings and worked in the afternoons and evenings. Such subjects as cataloging, circulation, and reference were studied. Academic libraries developed in-service training programs for their potential staff.

In the 1920s and 1930s, library leaders recognized that this was an inadequate education for library professional personnel. It was recognized that the basis for library education was a broad education in the liberal arts. Strong training classes were moved from public libraries to academic institutions and the entrance requirements were raised so that a bachelor's degree was required. Basically, then, library education became a fifth year of study beyond secondary school for which a second bachelor's degree, BSLS or BALS, was awarded. There were, of course, some library education programs offered as undergraduate majors or minors as there are today. But the standard for the professional librarian until 1947 was a year of professional study beyond the baccalaureate degree, culminating in the awarding of a bachelor's degree in library science.

In 1947, the University of Denver's Graduate School of Librarianship changed the degree offered for the fifth year of study from a BSLS to a Master of Arts. Soon other schools across the nation followed this pattern, offering various degrees (e.g., Master of Arts in Librarianship, Master of Science in Librarianship, etc.) for the fifth year of study. The present standard is that a professional librarian is an individual who holds a fifth-year master's degree from a library school accredited by the American Library Association.

The American Library Association is authorized by the Council on Postsecondary Accreditation to accredit programs leading to the first professional degree in librarianship. At the present time, over 60 programs are accredited. The *Standards of Accreditation*, 1972, as adopted by the Council of the ALA in June 1972 but effective January 1, 1973, set forth the criteria for accreditation. Accreditation serves two primary purposes:

> 1) it should identify for the public, including prospective students and employers, educational institutions and programs of study which meet established standards of educational quality, and 2) it should stimulate improvement both in standards and in educational institutions and programs.[2]

Not all accredited programs are the same; they vary according to the goals and objectives of the individual library school. Some programs are rather prescriptive, in that they require a large group of core courses and do not permit much individualization of course selection. Others have a small core of required courses and permit students to specialize in such fields as administration, technical services, information science, and school media centers. Theoretically, at least, however, all accredited library schools should offer programs that present "the principles and procedures common to all types of libraries and library service."[3]

Employers of new graduates do not always evaluate the education that the prospective employee has received. It is assumed by employers that all accredited programs are the same. Employers should be sure that the education received by the new graduate meets the needs of the job for which the candidate is being considered.

Of course, not all personnel working in a library are required to have a master's degree and to be classified as professional librarians. Many other levels of education can be effectively utilized in libraries, ranging from a high school diploma, a baccalaureate degree, or a master's degree in subject fields or specialties, such as Master of Personnel Administration, to the Ed.D or Ph.D.

In June 1970, the Council of the American Library Association adopted a statement of policy on *Library Education and Manpower*, which was reworked in the spring of 1976 and reissued under the title, *Library Education and Personnel Utilization*. This policy statement is given in full below because it is basic to the problem of staffing a library.

LIBRARY EDUCATION
AND PERSONNEL UTILIZATION*

A Statement of Policy Adopted by the Council of
the American Library Association, June 30, 1970**

1 The purpose of the policy statement is to recommend categories of library personnel, and levels of training and education appropriate to the preparation of personnel for these categories, which will support the highest standards of library service for all kinds of libraries and the most effective use of the variety of skills and qualifications needed to provide it.

2 Library service as here understood is concerned with knowledge and information in their several forms—their identification, selection, acquisition, preservation, organization, communication and interpretation, and with assistance in their use.

3 To meet the goals of library service, both professional and supportive staff are needed in libraries. Thus the library occupation is much broader than that segment of it which is the library profession, but the library profession has responsibility for defining the training and education required for the preparation of personnel who work in libraries at any level, supportive or professional.

4 Skills other than those of librarianship may also have an important contribution to make to the achievement of superior library service. There should be equal recognition in both the professional and supportive ranks for those individuals whose expertise contributes to the effective performance of the library.

5 A constant effort must be made to promote the most effective utilization of personnel at all levels, both professional and supportive. The tables on page [81] (Figure 1) suggest a set of categories which illustrate a means for achieving this end.

*The policy statement adopted by ALA with the title "Library Education and Manpower." In the spring of 1976, the Office for Library Personnel Resources Advisory Committee edited this statement to remove sexist terminology.

**Throughout this statement, wherever the term "librarianship" is used, it is meant to be read in its broadest sense as encompassing the relevant concepts of information science and documentation; wherever the term "libraries" is used, the current models of media centers, learning centers, educational resources centers, information, documentation, and referral centers are also assumed. To avoid the necessity of repeating the entire gamut of variations and expansions, the traditional library terminology is employed in its most inclusive meaning.

Figure 1

CATEGORIES OF LIBRARY PERSONNEL—PROFESSIONAL

TITLE For positions requiring:		BASIC REQUIREMENTS	NATURE OF RESPONSIBILITY
library-related qualifications	nonlibrary-related qualifications		
Senior Librarian	Senior Specialist	In addition to relevant experience, education beyond the M.A. [i.e., a master's degree in any of its variant designations: M.A., M.L.S., M.S.L.S., M.Ed., etc.] as: post-master's degree; Ph.D.; relevant continuing education in many forms	Top-level responsibilities, including but not limited to administration; superior knowledge of some aspect of librarianship, or of other subject fields of value to the library
Librarian	Specialist	Master's degree	Professional responsibilities including those of management, which require independent judgment, interpretation of rules and procedures, analysis of library problems, and formulation of original and creative solutions for them (normally utilizing knowledge of the subject field represented by the academic degree)

CATEGORIES OF LIBRARY PERSONNEL—SUPPORTIVE

TITLE		BASIC REQUIREMENTS	NATURE OF RESPONSIBILITY
Library Associate	Associate Specialist	Bachelor's degree (with or without course work in library science); OR bachelor's degree, plus additional academic work short of the master's degree (in librarianship for the Library Associate; in other relevant subject fields for the Associate Specialist)	Supportive responsibilities at a high level, normally working within the established procedures and techniques, and with some supervision by a professional, but requiring judgment, and subject knowledge such as is represented by a full, four-year college education culminating in the bachelor's degree
Library Technical Assistant	Technical Assistant	At least two years of college-level study; OR A.A. degree, with or without Library Technical Assistant training; OR postsecondary school training in relevant skills	Tasks performed as supportive staff to Associates and higher ranks, following established rules and procedures, and including, at the top level, supervision of such tasks
Clerk		Business school or commercial courses, supplemented by in-service training or on-the-job experience	Clerical assignments as required by the individual library

6 The titles recommended here represent categories or broad classifications, within which it is assumed that there will be several levels of promotional steps. Specific job titles may be used within any category: for example, catalogers, reference librarians, children's librarians would be included in either the "Librarian" or (depending upon the level of their responsibilities and qualifications) "Senior Librarian" categories; department heads, the director of the library, and certain specialists would presumably have the additional qualifications and responsibilities which place them in the "Senior Librarian" category.

7 Where specific job titles dictated by local usage and tradition do not make clear the level of the staff member's qualification and responsibility, it is recommended that reference to the ALA category title be used parenthetically to provide the clarification desirable for communication and reciprocity. For example:

REFERENCE ASSISTANT (Librarian)   HEAD CATALOGER (Senior Librarian)

LIBRARY AIDE (Library Technical Assistant)

8 The title "Librarian" carries with it the connotation of "professional" in the sense that professional tasks are those which require a special background and education on the basis of which library needs are identified, problems are analyzed, goals are set, and original and creative solutions are formulated for them, integrating theory into practice, and planning, organizing, communicating, and administering successful programs of service to users of the library's materials and services. In defining services to users, the professional person recognizes potential users as well as current ones, and designs services which will reach all who could benefit from them.

9 The title "Librarian" therefore should be used only to designate positions in libraries which utilize the qualifications and impose the responsibilities suggested above. Positions which are primarily devoted to the routine application of established rules and techniques, however useful and essential to the effective operation of a library's ongoing services, should not carry the word "Librarian" in the job title.

10 It is recognized that every type and size of library may not need staff appointments in each of these categories. It is urged, however, that this basic scheme be introduced wherever possible to permit where needed·the necessary flexibility in staffing.

11 The salaries for each category should offer a range of promotional steps sufficient to permit a career-in-rank. The top salary in any category should overlap the beginning salary in.the next higher category, in order to give recognition to the value of experience and knowledge gained on the job.

12 Inadequately supported libraries or libraries too small to be able to afford professional staff should nevertheless have access to the services and supervision of a librarian. To obtain the professional guidance that they themselves cannot supply, such libraries should promote cooperative arrangements or join larger systems of cooperating libraries through which supervisory personnel can be supported. Smaller libraries which are part of such a system can often maintain the local service with building staff at the Associate level.

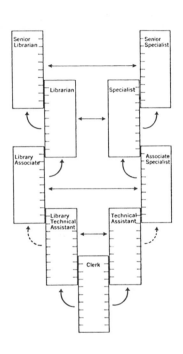

Figure 2

If one thinks of Career *Lattices* rather than Career *Ladders*, the flexibility intended by the Policy Statement may be better visualized. The movement among staff responsibilities, for example, is not necessarily directly up, but often may be lateral to increased responsibilities of equal importance. Each category embodies a number of promotional steps within it, as indicated by the gradation markings on each bar. The top of any category overlaps in responsibility and salary the next higher category.

Comments on the Categories

13 The *Clerk* classifications do not require formal academic training in library subjects. The assignments in these categories are based upon general clerical and secretarial proficiencies. Familiarity with basic library terminology and routines necessary to adapt clerical skills to the library's needs is best learned on the job.

14 The *Technical Assistant* categories assume certain kinds of specific "technical" skills; they are not meant simply to accommodate advanced clerks. While clerical skills might well be part of a Technical Assistant's equipment, the emphasis in an assignment should be on the special technical skill. For example, someone who is skilled in handling audiovisual equipment, or at

introductory data processing, or in making posters and other displays might well be hired in the Technical Assistant category for these skills, related to librarianship only to the extent that they are employed in a library. A *Library Technical Assistant* is a person with certain specifically library-related skills—in preliminary bibliographic searching for example, or utilization of certain mechanical equipment—the performance of whose duties seldom requires a background in general education.

15 The *Associate* categories assume a need for an educational background like that represented by a bachelor's degree from a good four-year institution of higher education in the United States. Assignments may be such that library knowledge is less important than general education, and whether the title is *Library* Associate or Associate *Specialist* depends upon the nature of the tasks and responsibilities assigned. Persons holding the B.A. degree, with or without a library science minor or practical experience in libraries, are eligible for employment in this category. Titles within the Associate category that are assigned to individuals will depend upon the relevance of their training and background to their specific assignments.

16 The Associate category also provides the opportunity for persons of promise and exceptional talent to begin library employment below the level of professional (as defined in this statement) and thus to combine employment in a library with course work at the graduate level. Where this kind of work/study arrangement is made, the combination of work and formal study should provide 1) increasing responsibility within the Associate ranks as the individual moves through the academic program, and 2) eligibility for promotion, upon completion of the master's degree, to positions of professional responsibility and attendant reclassification to the professional category.

17 The first professional category—*Librarian*, or *Specialist*—assumes responsibilities that are professional in the sense described in paragraph #8 above. A good liberal education plus graduate-level study in the field of specialization (either in librarianship or in a relevant field) are seen as the minimum preparation for the kinds of assignments implied. The title, however, is given for a position entailing professional responsibilities and not automatically upon achievement of the academic degree.

18 The *Senior* categories assume relevant professional experience as well as qualifications beyond those required for admission to the first professional ranks. Normally it is assumed that such advanced qualifications shall be held in some specialty, either in a particular aspect of librarianship or some relevant subject field. Subject specializations are as applicable in the *Senior Librarian* category as they are in the *Senior Specialist* category.

19 Administrative responsibilities entail advanced knowledge and skills comparable to those represented by any other high-level specialty, and appointment to positions in top administration should normally require the qualifications of a *Senior Librarian* with a specialization in administration.

This category, however, is not limited to administrators, whose specialty is only one of several specializations of value to the library service. There are many areas of special knowledge within librarianship which are equally important and to which equal recognition in prestige and salary should be given. Highly qualified persons with specialist responsibilities in some aspects of librarianship—archives, bibliography, reference, for example—should be eligible for advanced status and financial rewards without being forced to abandon for administrative responsibilities their areas of major competence.

Implications for Formal Education

20 Until examinations are identified that are valid and reliable tests of equivalent qualifications, the academic degree (or evidence of years of academic work completed) is recommended as the single best means for determining that an applicant has the background recommended for each category.

21 In the selection of applicants for positions at any level, and for admission to library schools, attention should be paid to personal aptitudes and qualifications in addition to academic ones. The nature of the position or specialty, and particularly the degree to which it entails working with others, with the public, or with special audiences or materials should be taken into account in the evaluation of a prospective student or employee.

22 As library services change and expand, as new audiences are reached, as new media take on greater importance in the communication process, and as new approaches to the handling of materials are introduced, the kinds of preparation required of those who will be employed in libraries will become more varied. Degrees in fields other than librarianship will be needed in the Specialist categories. For many Senior Librarian positions, an advanced degree in another subject field rather than an additional degree in librarianship, may be desirable. Previous experience need not always have been in libraries to have pertinence for appointment in a library.

23 Because the principles of librarianship are applied to the materials of information and knowledge broader than any single field, and because they are related to subject matter outside of librarianship itself, responsible education in these principles should be built upon a broad rather than a narrowly specialized background education. To the extent that courses in library science are introduced in the four-year, undergraduate program, they should be concentrated in the last two years and should not constitute a major inroad into course work in the basic disciplines: the humanities, the sciences, and the social sciences.

24 Training courses for Library Technical Assistants at the junior or community college level should be recognized as essentially terminal in intent (or as service courses rather than a formal program of education), designed for the preparation of supportive rather than professional staff. Students interested in librarianship as a career should be counselled to take the general four-year college course rather than the specific two-year program, with its inevitable loss of time and transferable content. Graduates of the two-year programs are not prohibited from taking the additional work leading to the bachelor's and master's degrees, provided they demonstrate the necessary qualifications for admission to the senior college program, but it is an indirect and less desirable way to prepare for a professional career, and the student should be so informed.

25 Emphasis in the two-year Technical Assistant programs should be more on skills training than on general library concepts and procedures. In many cases it would be better from the standpoint of the student to pursue more broadly-based vocational courses which will teach technical skills applicable in a variety of job situations rather than those limited solely to the library setting.

26 Undergraduate instruction in library science other than training courses for Library Technical Assistants should be primarily a contribution to liberal education rather than an opportunity to provide technological and methodological training. This does not preclude the inclusion of course work related to the basic skills of library practice, but it does affect teaching method and approach, and implies an emphasis on the principles that underlie practice rather than how-to-do-it, vocational training.

27 Certain practical skills and procedures at all levels are best learned on the job rather than in the academic classroom. These relate typically to details of operation which may vary from institution to institution, or to routines which require repetition and practice for their mastery. The responsibility for such in-service parts of the total preparation of both librarians and supportive staff rests with libraries and library systems rather than with the library schools.

28 The objective of the master's programs in librarianship should be to prepare librarians capable of anticipating and engineering the change and improvement required to move the profession constantly forward. The curriculum and teaching methods should be designed to serve this kind of education for the future rather than to train for the practice of the present.

29 Certain interdisciplinary concepts (information science is an example) are so intimately related to the basic concepts underlying library service that they properly become a part of the library school curriculum rather than simply an outside specialty. Where such content is introduced into the library school it should be incorporated into the entire curriculum, enriching every course where it is pertinent. The stop-gap addition of individual courses in such a specialty, not integrated into the program as a whole, is an inadequate assimilation of the intellectual contribution of the new concept to library education and thinking.

30 In recognition of the many areas of related subject matter of importance to library service, library schools should make knowledge in other fields readily available to students, either through the appointment of staff members from other disciplines or through permitting students to cross departmental, divisional, and institutional lines in reasoned programs in related fields. Intensive specializations at the graduate level, building upon strengths in the parent institution or the community, are a logical development in professional library education.

31 Library schools should be encouraged to experiment with new teaching methods, new learning devices, different patterns of scheduling and sequence, and other means, both traditional and nontraditional, that may increase the effectiveness of the students' educational experience.

32 Research has an important role to play in the educational process as a source of new knowledge both for the field of librarianship in general and for library education in particular. In its planning, budgeting, and organizational design, the library school should recognize research, both theoretical and applied, as an imperative responsibility.

Continuing Education

33 Continuing Education is essential for all library personnel, professional and supportive, whether they remain within a position category or are preparing to move into a higher one. Continuing education opportunities include both formal and informal learning situations, and need not be limited to library subjects or the offerings of library schools.

34 The "continuing education" which leads to eligibility for Senior Librarian or Specialist positions may take any of the forms suggested directly above so long as the additional education and experience are relevant to the responsibilities of the assignment.

35 Library administrators must accept responsibility for providing support and opportunities (in the form of leaves, sabbaticals, and released time) for the continuing education of their staffs.

Additional copies available from

Office for Library Personnel Resources
American Library Association
50 E. Huron St., Chicago, Ill., 60611

Many important concepts are presented in this policy statement. Attention is called particularly to paragraphs 8 and 9, which define the role of the professional librarian. Paragraph 11 describes the basis for salary scale development, which will be discussed in detail later. Paragraphs 13 through 19 categorize the various levels of employees needed in libraries. These paragraphs amplify Figure 1 of the statement. Special attention should be given to Figure 2, which proposes two lattices (or ladders) for career movement in libraries. This concept of the professional librarian advancing up the left lattice and the specialist advancing up the right lattice is a new concept in library personnel administration. But at the present time, when the role and function of libraries are rapidly changing, it is important to utilize many people with various skills, knowledge, and abilities. The dual lattice provides for such capability.

Up to the present few libraries have implemented the concept of the two career lattices. In most libraries, the traditional pattern of one lattice still exists. The line of authority in most libraries passes down the lattice of the professional librarian. Therefore, advancement in a professional career is possible only when the employee assumes greater supervisory responsibility. There is, however, a great need for administrators to recognize the important role the specialist plays in library service and administration, and to develop organizational patterns that permit the specialist to advance in the library hierarchy because of the value of that specialty, and not simply because greater authority and responsibility are assumed.

Libraries today are identified by the U.S. Internal Revenue Service as educational institutions. The U.S. Congress, when it established the National Commission on Libraries and Information Science, approved the following policy statement (P.L. 91-345, Section 2), which enforces the federal government's recognition of the importance of libraries in a rapidly growing technological society:

> The Congress hereby affirms that library and information science services adequate to meet the needs of the people of the United States are essential to achieve national goals and to utilize most effectively the Nation's educational resources and that the Federal Government will cooperate with State and local governments and public and private agencies in assuring optimum provision of such services.

The level of education achieved by members of the library staff, therefore, becomes one of the primary criteria for establishing library staffing patterns.

During the 1930s and early 1940s it was not uncommon to find libraries in which approximately 50% of the total staff positions were classified as professional. Following World War II and the development (at least in public institutions) of more structured personnel programs, the number of professional positions declined to approximately 30% of the total staff. It is anticipated that as the educational programs for professional librarians expand, the number of professional positions required in libraries may decline even more. This will occur as the professional librarian assumes more responsibility for decision-making, supervision, and training. Library Associates and other personnel as defined by the *Library Education and Personnel Utilization* policy will assume the more routine day-to-day activities.

WHAT IS A JOB?

It will be recalled that in chapter 3, departmentation was defined as the process of identifying similar or related activities and grouping these activities into departments according to such principles as territory, function, clientele, subject, etc. The development of a job follows a similar pattern. Of the related or similar activities assigned to a department, similar or related tasks must be identified and grouped together to create a job.

Jobs should not be allowed just to emerge at the whim of the employee. And only occasionally are jobs created because of the special knowledge or ability of a particular individual. It is the responsibility of the library administration to identify the tasks that are to be included in a job. The tasks, as indicated before, should be similar or related. That is, the tasks to be accomplished by a specific job should all require approximately the same level of education. One task should not be so excessively complex that extensive education is required, while the next task is so simple that it could be performed by an individual with much less education. Further, the tasks assigned to one job should require comparable experience. Some tasks can be performed only after extensive experience in a job, while others can be executed by novices with little or no experience. And, lastly, tasks assigned to a job should require comparable responsibility. Some tasks have end responsibility. There is no review. The action of the individual in a job having end responsibility is final. Such end responsibility is frequently found in reference services, book selection, and top administration. Other jobs require little or no end responsibility. Work is reviewed. Revisers in a catalog department may have end responsibility, while the catalogers whose work is revised have no end responsibility.

It can be said, therefore, that a well-defined job has assigned to it tasks that are 1) comparable in the amount of education required, 2) comparable in the amount of experience required, and 3) comparable in the degree of responsibility required.

Other elements are also to be considered in the development of a job. That the tasks assigned a job should be similar or related has been emphasized. Tasks should be similar in that they require comparable skills, knowledge, or abilities. Skill is defined as the capability of performing manual or routine activities, operating various types of equipment, or managing an organizational unit that follows established procedures.[4] Skills are here interpreted as those activities that require less education and less experience than other jobs and that have little or no end responsibility except, perhaps, the responsibility of accuracy. Knowledge is here defined as the specific body of facts and principles that are required in a job. The knowledge of filing rules, of the Anglo-American Cataloguing Rules, of a subject field, of personnel administration, or of techniques of public relations are examples of different kinds of knowledge. The education, experience, and end responsibility required of these jobs would be higher and greater than those required for skills performance. Abilities are here defined as the education and experience required to perform the most complex activities that usually entail full end responsibility. The term refers to the capability of synthesizing a group of facts and arriving at a decision. Likewise, analyzing community needs and planning and executing programs to meet those needs is an ability. Giving a speech, conducting a meeting, appearing effectively on television is an ability. Abilities require extensive knowledge but only an understanding of skills.

Tasks should be related to the accomplishment of a single function, process, or program, or should be related to the same subject field or type of material. In larger institutions, this is easily accomplished; in small institutions, however, tasks may have to be related to more than one function, process, program, subject, or type of resource. Nevertheless, even in small institutions, the number of unrelated tasks assigned to one job should be kept as low as possible.

A job, therefore, is a planned entity consisting of assigned tasks that are similar or related in skills, knowledge, or abilities. A job, however, should not be so restrictive that assigned tasks are quickly mastered and soon become dull, monotonous, and boring. In recognition of the fact that most jobs are too small in scope, a job should be made large enough to challenge and encourage employees to grow in skills, knowledge, and abilities. There are jobs in libraries that must be performed according to prescribed procedures in order to maintain uniformity or because of standardized methodologies. These jobs are generally low in the job hierarchy of the library. Nevertheless, every opportunity should be given the employee even at this level to be creative, to exercise initiative, and to vary the routines, as long as the established standards are maintained.

A LIBRARY PERSONNEL PROGRAM

If a library expects to make maximum utilization of its staff and at the same time to have a satisfied staff with good morale, then a clear, equitable library personnel program should be established. In most public institutions, school, academic, and public libraries, such programs are mandated by the parent institution—the municipality or county, the state college or university, or the school district. A personnel program is designed to guarantee that all employees, regardless of race, color, creed, or sex, are treated equally and fairly.

A library personnel program consists basically of five parts: 1) the development of written job descriptions, 2) the establishment of a process to audit the actual job being performed, 3) the formation of a program to evaluate the quality of personnel performance, 4) the maintenance of a current salary scale, and 5) the development of written personnel policies. All parts of a personnel program except the results of the performance evaluation are public and should be explained thoroughly to employees. The result of the performance evaluation is privileged information available only to the employee being evaluated and those supervisors who are involved in the process or who must use the evaluations to effect personnel action. Each part will be discussed in detail.

JOB DESCRIPTIONS

The use of job descriptions to identify tasks to be performed by a specific individual or group of individuals came into wide use during World Wars I and II. Frederick W. Taylor, of course, used job cards before this time to identify employee tasks and to prescribe the method of performing these tasks. But the concept of the job description as it is known today was somewhat expanded in World War I and to a great degree in World War II. Following World War II not only did the federal government initiate wide use of job descriptions, but state, county, and municipal governments began to require their use. Today, most government agencies and many businesses and industries require job descriptions for all employees.

A job description is a written statement prepared by the administration describing the tasks that an employee is to perform, defining the relationship of the job and the employee to other units of the institution, and setting standards of education, experience, and special skills required in the job. The term "job description" is used throughout this discussion even though some authorities use the term "position description" to designate jobs in the higher echelons of an organization. Such a designation seems to reinforce the popularly held concept of the bureaucratic hierarchy, so the vernacular term "job description" is preferred here.

There is no standard form for a job description. Individual institutions develop the form that best meets their needs. The following outline, however, indicates what information is needed in a job description:

1) name of institution, department, and sub-department to which the job is assigned

2) date

3) job title

4) purpose and scope of the job

5) specific tasks assigned the job

6) job requirements, including institutional standards as they apply to each job.

But it is not enough to present an outline. There are specific reasons that each element is important. A discussion of each part follows.

1) Since job descriptions are used for different purposes, a clear identification of the organizational unit in which the job is located is essential.

2) Jobs change, and as a result job descriptions change. Only the current job description is maintained; the date the job description was prepared indicates its currency.

3) In libraries there are no common job titles. Each library develops its own. The job title is designed to indicate the group (professional, associate, technician, or clerk) to which the job belongs and the level of the job within that grouping. Some libraries use for their professional grouping such terms as junior librarian, senior librarian, and supervising librarian. The current trend, however, is to use roman or arabic numerals to indicate levels of the professional group. The title "Librarian I" would be used to indicate the lowest level in the professional hierarchy of jobs. Librarian II and Librarian III indicate higher levels of professional jobs. If the same pattern is used to indicate levels in the clerical grouping, a Clerk I title can indicate the beginning level, while the term Clerk II shows that the job requires more education or experience or responsibility than the Clerk I job.

4) The statement of a job's purposes and scope includes: a) the primary responsibility of the job, b) the title of the person to whom the incumbent reports, c) the number of employees or the organizational unit supervised by this job, and d) internal and external relationships required by the job.

5) The list of specific tasks assigned the job is the most important part of the job description. It identifies for the employee the exact tasks for which he or she will be responsible. But it also indicates to the supervisor those tasks for which training must be given, tasks that must be supervised, and tasks that must be evaluated. Without this section of the job description the whole personnel program becomes meaningless, for neither the employee nor the supervisor knows what the employee is expected to do. The tasks assigned should, of course, be comparable in education, experience, and responsibility required and should demand similar or related skills, knowledge, and abilities.

6) Job requirements are established by each individual library. Requirements that are defined include: a) amount of education required for the job, b) amount of experience required, and c) special skills, knowledge, or abilities required.

Only for the beginning professional librarian is there a national standard, and that standard relates to education only. All other requirements are standards that an individual library wishes to establish. Under special skills, knowledge, and abilities the institution has the opportunity to identify capabilities needed. For example, a bookmobile driver must be able to handle heavy equipment and must hold a special driver's license; a typist must be able to type 60 words per minute with minimal errors; a professional must be able to read and speak a foreign language. These are examples of special capabilities that a library might identify as essential to a job.

It will be noted in the examples of job descriptions in Appendix 3 that tasks are generally defined. No standard of performance is indicated. Some libraries use the job description as a means of establishing standards of performance. The quality or quantity of performance expected is established in the job description through the use of statements similar to educational behavioral objectives. For example, it is inadequate to say, for a professional librarian, that one task is "to answer reference questions received from the public or by telephone." That task would be stated so that it could be measured: "To answer accurately reference questions received from the public or by telephone so that 80% of all questions received are answered to the satisfaction of the patron." The measurable factors are accuracy, quantity (80%), and patron satisfaction.

It is not difficult to measure activities that can be quantified, and many of the activities in a library can be. Even a cataloger using traditional methods might be assigned a measurable task: "To assign accurate classification and Cutter numbers and appropriate subject headings and to prepare a work slip for the typists not taking more than 30 minutes for each title." Accuracy could be measured as well as output. Tauber[5] once said that no cataloger should spend more than 15 minutes on one title, so the suggested 30 minutes is generous.

But it is very difficult to measure quality. In the example of the reference librarian, the supervisor could check accuracy by keeping a record of all questions asked and answers given. This is a time-consuming process, but perhaps it could be accomplished on a sampling basis. Patron satisfaction can also be sampled by brief questionnaires, and the 80% is a measurable factor. At the present time, much study is being given to the measurement of qualitative factors in librarianship. Ernest De Prospo and others are working on this type of performance measurement.[6] F. W. Lancaster[7] has summarized the methodologies and results of several hundred studies of library service in his publication *The Measurement and Evaluation of Library Services.*

The emphasis on performance emanates from the current emphasis on accountability. Librarians have performed too long without established standards against which to measure the quality and quantity of their performance. Lowell Martin[8] found, through a structured test conducted during his study of the Chicago Public Library, that many of the reference questions asked of branch librarians were inaccurately or incompletely answered. One suspects that this is not uncommon. Thomas Childers,[9] in his study of the Suffolk Cooperative Library System (New York), found that in the 57 libraries studied over a period of six months about 56% of the time actual answers were given in the form of a delivered document, a fact or a citation. "It was found that, when an actual answer was forthcoming, 84 percent of the time it was Correct or Mostly Correct."[10]

After all job descriptions are completed, they are arranged in a hierarchical order using required education, required experience, and the degree of end responsibility as the criteria. The job requiring the most education, experience, and responsibility will be highest in the hierarchical order, and the job requiring the least of the same three criteria will be at the bottom. The jobs are being classified and a Classified Personnel System is created. It is the job that is being classified and not the person who will hold the job. People are never classified.

The hierarchically arranged jobs are divided into the various groupings used in the *Library Education and Personnel Utilization* policy statement. All professional positions fall in one grouping, all associate librarians in another, and library technicians, clerks, and custodians into still other groups.[11] Within each group there will be a hierarchy level based on the same three requirements given above. A job title is assigned to each level; this is where roman or arabic numerals are recommended. Jobs requiring the same level of education, experience, and responsibility are given the same title even though the tasks may be different. For example, descriptive terms such as "art librarian" may be added to a general classification title. Figure 4-1 shows a hierarchy of professional positions and Figure 4-3 shows the relationship of professional and non-professional library positions to specialists. Specialists are placed at the same level of the professional group if their education, experience, and end responsibility requirements are comparable.

Figure 4-1
A Hierarchy of Professional Level Jobs

Job Title	Education	Experience	End Responsibility
Librarian IV	MA from an accredited library school plus an Advanced Certificate	10 years with 3 years in supervisory positions	Final responsibility for the operation of the institution
Librarian III	MA from an accredited library school plus subject specialization	5 years professional experience	Under general supervision and according to policies, end responsibility for a department
Librarian II	MA from an accredited library school	2 years professional experience	Under general supervision and according to policies, responsible for a unit of a department
Librarian I	MA from an accredited library school	0 years of experience	Under general supervision and according to policies, performs assigned task

The same procedure for the clerical level jobs might result in a hierarchical structure as shown in Figure 4-2.

Figure 4-2
Hierarchy of Group of Clerical Level Jobs

Job Title	Education	Experience	End Responsibility
Clerk III	High school plus business school graduate	3 years experience	Under general supervision, end responsibility for payroll
Clerk II	High school plus some business school	2 years experience	Under general supervision, end responsibility for verifying invoices
Clerk I	High school diploma	0 experience	Under close supervision, perform assigned tasks

There is no standard as to how many levels may be included in each level grouping. In larger institutions there will be many; in small institutions, only a few.

However, it is very necessary that job titles be assigned to each classification level. A library might end up with a list like that illustrated in Figure 4-3.

Figure 4-3
A Hierarchy of Jobs in a Classified Program

Librarian Lattice	Specialist Lattice
Librarian V Librarian IV Librarian III Librarian II Librarian I Library Associate II Library Associate I Library Technician III Library Technician II Library Technician I Clerk III Clerk II Clerk I	Personnel Officer Building Engineer Library Artist Key Punch Operator

This hierarchy of job titles eventually becomes the basis for the establishment of a salary scale. Each title in the Librarian Lattice indicates a different level of required education, experience, and responsibility. The specialists are placed opposite the librarian title that has comparable requirements and that would receive comparable pay.

Most job descriptions have a catch-all assignment at the end of the list of tasks. It usually reads "Other duties as assigned." The purposes of this undefined part of the job are 1) to permit flexibility in the job, and 2) to provide for emergency situations. Flexibility is necessary in a job description; otherwise the individual is frozen into a set pattern of tasks. Tasks can be assigned or removed in order to allow an individual to gain new experience or to function temporarily on a different job. Any change of tasks, however, must be carefully evaluated to be sure the tasks removed or added require education, experience, and responsibility comparable to the other tasks and the general level of the job. In emergency situations, employees might be requested to perform tasks completely foreign to their regular assignments. But this type of assignment is usually temporary, lasting for a very short time.

Job descriptions as described above fulfill several important administrative and personnel needs. A job description may be used in the recruitment of new employees. Not only does the recruiter know exactly the capabilities to search for, but the candidate also knows exactly what would be expected of him or her if the job were accepted. The job description should be made available to applicants for their study and review. After an individual has been hired, the job description becomes the basis for determining training needs and identifying job tasks that will require special effort before this employee can perform them well. Later, the job description becomes the basis for formal performance evaluation.

JOB AUDIT

Employees tend to de-emphasize or ignore tasks they do not like to perform and to expand and concentrate on tasks they like. Over a period of time an employee can change drastically the job that was originally established. It becomes necessary, therefore, to audit occasionally the jobs employees are performing to be sure that all assigned tasks are being performed.

An audit proving that all assigned tasks are being performed assures the institution that the employee is being fairly compensated. But if the audit shows that the employee has ceased doing essential tasks, the employee may be overpaid. The opposite is also true: if an employee has assumed new duties that require greater degrees of education, experience, or responsibility, then he or she may be underpaid. The audit will show the need for the reclassification of a job, upward or downward, and will identify jobs that need to be redefined and that thus need new job descriptions.

There are two methods of accomplishing a job audit. One method involves an interview between the employee and supervisor. The supervisor, using the job description as the basis for discussion, reviews the tasks assigned the employee. Progress achieved on each task and problems involved can be identified. The supervisor has the opportunity to recommend changes in methodology and emphasis. The supervisor must be very careful to conduct this interview in such a manner that the job audit is accomplished. This interview could become an evaluation interview, which is a completely different process conducted for a different purpose. However, the interview is not time consuming and does accomplish its purpose if the supervisor is skilled in interview techniques.

The other method of conducting a job audit is much more time consuming for both the employee and the supervisor. It requires that the employee complete a prepared form and that the supervisor analyze this information. The form usually includes the following data:

1) **General information.** Name of incumbent, title of position, department, name of supervisor, date, and job number (if any).

2) **A list of all tasks performed by the incumbent.** This list is to cover a larger period of time (three to six months) and may require that some form of diary be kept by the employee. The long time period is used so that the list does not overemphasize any special assignments or emergency situations.

3) **The percentage of time spent on each task.** By analyzing the amount of time spent on any one task, the supervisor can determine where the employee is placing job emphasis and which tasks are being neglected or overemphasized.

After the data gathered on the job audit form have been analyzed and compared with the job description by the supervisor, an interview is still required to redirect the actions of the employee.

This method of job audit is not undertaken very frequently because of the time involved. It would certainly not be accomplished more frequently than once a year, and perhaps less often than that. The verbal job audit, the first method described, could be accomplished weekly or monthly as normal supervisory conferences are held.

If a library decided to undertake a total reclassification of all positions, a written job audit would be required. It would identify all tasks performed within the library, thus providing a list of the tasks that could be grouped together because they were similar or related. A large library would certainly have to use special personnel or a management company to accomplish total reclassification. A medium-sized or small library might use the personnel officers in municipal or county government or in academic institutions.

PERFORMANCE EVALUATION

The rating or evaluation of one person by another is as old as mankind itself. It is a natural phenomenon in the sense that individuals continually judge others by what they say, what they do, and how they affect other people. This process applies not only to work situations but to all facets of life. Such personal judgments are generally private and are not communicated to the individual.

In work situations, however, the evaluation of an employee's performance must be communicated to the individual. Without this transfer of information and the development of remedial processes or plans, the total program of evaluation is worthless. This statement is meant to establish the fact that performance evaluations conducted secretly and not communicated to the employee are not only unfair but also achieve no improvement and no redirection in performance.

Performance evaluations have important functions to fulfill in a personnel program. Some of the benefits of a good performance evaluation are:

1) The employee's performance is measured against job requirements as set forth in the job description.

2) Performance evaluation is an important document if the employer's decision as a result of the performance evaluation is to terminate the employee.

3) The quality of performance provides a basis for personnel action such as promotion, demotion, and salary increases, and it may indicate the need for special training or retraining.

4) If properly conducted, the performance evaluation will give every level of management a better understanding of the individual's capabilities and potential within the organization.

5) The performance evaluation process should help employees establish personal goals that will enable them to grow and develop and that will further implement the institutional goals.

Each institution determines when performance evaluations will be administered. There should be a definite schedule, however, and that schedule should be public information.

In most libraries, newly appointed staff members serve a probationary period before permanent appointment is achieved. That probationary period may vary from one month for clerical positions or jobs in which there may be rapid turnover to one year for professional positions. A performance rating should be administered at the end of the probationary period. But a good supervisor will review with the new employee the job description and the quality of the employee's performance during the probationary period.

After the probationary period, performance evaluations are administered on a recurring basis. Some institutions accomplish all evaluations in January of each year, or some other designated month. To place such a heavy load on supervisors usually results in poorly prepared performance evaluations. Not enough time is allowed for thoughtful, careful evaluation. Other institutions carry out performance evaluations on each anniversary of the employee's appointment to permanent status. This timetable distributes the work load over the entire year and permits careful judgments to be made.

An organization that has a program of performance evaluation must be sure that it is strongly supported by top management, because this program is basically a line function. Top management must orient and train supervisors in systematic evaluation and convince them of its value. Most supervisors dislike the process of evaluating their employees and particularly try to avoid discussing employee deficiencies with the employee. But unless top management sees that these steps are accomplished, the program will be ineffective.

One of the major problems is to establish the standards of performance against which an employee's work is judged. Standards that need to be established fall clearly into three categories:[12]

1) **Quality-quantity standards.** How well does the employee perform the various tasks set forth in the job description, and how much of each task is actually accomplished?

2) **Desired effect standards.** Is work complete, accurate, and performed on time, benefiting positively the goals and objectives of the institution and users; are sound data gathered as a basis for judgments and decisions?

3) **Manner of performance standards.** Is the work accomplished in cooperation with others, without friction; can the employee adapt to new programs or processes?

Because no two supervisors will interpret these standards exactly the same, top management must define the standards. This is sometimes done by issuing a performance evaluation manual. Several libraries have prepared such written documents for the supervisor's guidance. If supervisors interpret standards differently or give greater weight to one standard over another, inequity in evaluation from department to department will result. A basic criterion in any organization should be "equal pay for equal work." This can be achieved not only through the use of good job descriptions but also through comparable judgment of performance, which might result in salary increases or promotions.

There are many pitfalls in performance evaluation. Some of the most common errors are described in the Denver Public Library's *Manual for Performance Evaluation*:[13]

1) **The error of the "halo effect":** Supervisors often evaluate the employee in terms of their personal mental attitude about the employee rather than by careful attention to the individual factors of work performance. He may be a "nice person", but still do poor work. (The opposite of the "halo effect" — down-grading someone you dislike but whose work is good — is also an error.)

2) **The error of "prejudice and partiality":** Not only is it an error of judgment but also a Constitutional violation to consider race,

creed, color, religion, politics, nationality and sex in evaluating work performance.

3) **The error of "leniency, softness, or spinelessness"**: This is the most common error — taking the easy way out. It occurs when supervisors can't face the unpleasantness that might arise from an unfavorable evaluation. "Spineless" ratings tag a supervisor as weak and therefore unfair to his really good employees. Effects of this error force ratings so drastically to the top of the scale that they are valueless to us and others in management. Such an error also creates an unrealistic feeling of success when improvement in performance is badly needed and often possible. Many supervisors believe that their bosses think that low ratings reflect poor supervision; thus, standard or above ratings may become defenses for the supervisor. He may presume that some supervisors do not rate honestly and that he must upgrade ratings to avoid penalizing his employees.

4) **The error of the "central tendency"**: On a normal distribution curve more people will be rated closer to the mean than to any other point on the scale. A rating which is near the norm becomes a central tendency error if it does not reflect true performance. It is most likely to occur when a supervisor is careless or lazy about the rating or does not know the worker well.

A standard rating for unusually good or poor performance is unfair — to the employee, his fellow workers and the Denver Public Library.

5) **The error of "contrast"**: Is this rating a measure of the work that this employee has actually accomplished or is it a measure of what I think he has the potential to do?

6) **The error of "association"**: In the process of rating, busy raters will sometimes rate factors at the same degree merely because they follow each other on the page. This may also happen when the supervisor is tired, or bored, and tries to make hurried judgments without all the facts.

There are no standard performance evaluation forms. Each institution usually prepares its own forms to meet its own requirements (*see* Appendix 4). Frequently staff committees are asked to develop the form by which they wish their work to be evaluated. In larger libraries, the personnel office is sometimes responsible for devising a form.

The first job of any group building a performance evaluation form is to determine the traits, characteristics, abilities, and skills on which they will be judged. The listing of all possible elements may indicate the desirability of having two forms — one for professionals and one for other classifications. But most institutions develop only one form, which lists all desirable elements but which provides a method to indicate those elements not appropriate to a particular job. Some elements that usually appear on evaluation forms are quality of work, quantity of work, job knowledge, cooperation, initiative, self-reliance, ability to get along with others, dependability, leadership, and appearance. Sometimes these broad elements are broken down into sub-elements. Dependability could be subdivided into 1) discharge of own job responsibilities, 2) regular and punctual attendance, and 3) self-control. Perhaps it is an understatement to say that it is easy to reach consensus on the basic elements to be included in the evaluation form. But consensus must eventually be reached.

The more difficult part of building an evaluation form concerns the manner in which the individual's performance of each element is indicated. Many forms use a horizontal line after each element with degrees of success indicated, as shown below:

Initiative: The ability to develop a new pattern of activity.

Poor   Fair   Average   Good   Excellent

The element being judged is given first, followed by a statement clarifying what is meant by that element. The horizontal line below the statement has words above it that describe varying degrees of success. The supervisor indicates the evaluation of the employee for that element by placing a check or X at the appropriate place on the horizontal line. But can any two people agree as to the meaning of average, or fair, or excellent? No matter how much training a supervisor is given, these terms will be interpreted differently to the detriment of employees. Nevertheless, many institutions, libraries, and other organizations, use forms based on this pattern.

In recent years the inadequacy of the horizontal line form has been recognized. A new pattern has developed which eliminates such words as poor, average, good. A short phrase is used to describe different levels of performance. The most difficult part is to develop a short phrase that cannot be misinterpreted, thus assuring comparable interpretation by various supervisors of the elements included on the performance evaluation. If *accuracy* were the element being evaluated, such phrases as the following might be used to show various degrees of accuracy.

Makes frequent errors

Makes more errors than average

Usually accurate

Unusually careful; almost always accurate

It does not make any difference how many levels of an element are defined, though generally four or five are given, as in the example above.

Another current trend in the administration of performance evaluations requires the supervisor performing the evaluation to prepare extensive written statements that show the quality of the employee's work. This requires the supervisors to clarify in their minds their own or institutional standards and to evaluate the employee's work in view of these standards. Such written comments must be prepared concisely and clearly so that the employee will know exactly what is meant by the evaluation. Usually an employee has the opportunity to answer these written comments.

Figure 4-4 illustrates these current trends in the performance evaluation form used by the Dallas Public Library.

Figure 4-4
Dallas Public Library
Municipal Library Department Performance Evaluation Form

DUE TO _____ BY _____   DUE IN PERSONNEL BY _____

MUNICIPAL LIBRARY DEPARTMENT
PERFORMANCE EVALUATION FORM   Division _____

Period in review _____

NAME _____   CURRENT GRADE _____ JOB TITLE _____

(YEAR)

(NAME)

Instructions:

Listed below are a number of traits, abilities and performance characteristics that
are important for job success. Enter an "X" mark on a rating scale in the place that
is most appropriate for the person being rated. Evaluations should take into consideration the person's performance achievements and contributions in relation to the
requirements of the position. Only factors which are directly related to the effective performance of the work should be considered. Personality traits should enter
into these ratings only insofar as they had an effect upon and were demonstrated in
actual performance of the job.

Carefully evaluate each of the qualities separately. A common mistake in rating is
the "halo effect," i.e., a tendency to rate the same individual high on every trait
or low on every trait based on the overall picture one has of the person being rated.
Each person has strong points and weak points, and these should be indicated on the
rating scales.

The following procedure is recommended for the use of this form:
(1) Both the employee and the supervisor will be provided with a copy of the form,
   which they are separately to fill out, the employee rating him or herself.
(2) Both forms will be sent directly to the appropriate manager by the date shown
   at the upper left.
(3) The manager will countersign the evaluation form filled out by the supervisor
   when it is approved, and both forms will be returned to the supervisor.
(4) The supervisor and the employee will meet to discuss the ratings and to attempt
   to come to a shared understanding of any discrepancies between them. The employee
   will be given an opportunity to comment on the form completed by the supervisor
   and will be asked to sign the form to indicate he/she has had a chance to see
   and respond to it.
(5) The two forms will be stapled together and both sent to Personnel to be placed
   in the employee's file.
(6) If, however, the box at the end of the form has been checked, both forms should
   be returned to the indicated manager after the evaluation conference between
   employee and supervisor has been completed. The manager will then forward the
   two forms to Personnel or back to the supervisor for a further conference with
   the employee.

ACCURACY is the correctness of work duties performed.

Makes frequent errors.	Makes more errors than average.	Usually accurate.	Unusually care-ful; almost always accurate.

Comments:

LEARNING ABILITY is the ability to grasp instructions, to understand the meaning and
implications of policies, to meet changing conditions, and to solve
problems in novel situations.

Limited.	Requires repeated instructions.	Grasps instruc-tions with average	Quick to under-stand and learn.	Exeptionally keen and alert.

Comments:

INITIATIVE is willingness to put forth effort without being told to accept personal
responsibility for performing job duties fully and for achieving job goals.

Lacking.	Shows average initiative.	High initiative.

Comments:

JOB KNOWLEDGE is the information and understanding which an individual must have for
job performance.

Limited.	Has minimum required knowledge.	Knowledgeable about all phases of work.

Comments:

QUANTITY OF WORK is the amount of work an individual gets done.

Does not meet minimum requirements.	Low production record.	Satisfactory.	Above average work production record.	Very fast and industrious; superior work production record.

Comments:

COURTESY is the quality of the personal relationships with either staff or public.

Often blunt; discourteous; antagonistic.	Sometimes tactless or irritable.	Agreeable and pleasant most of the time.	Polite and skillful at maintaining good will.

Comments:

ATTITUDE is demonstrated by cooperativeness and commitment to organizational goals.

Negative and uncooperative.	Cooperates reluctantly.	Usually cooperative.	Positive and constructive attitude.

Comments:

PERSONAL APPEARANCE (Consider cleanliness, neatness, and appropriateness of dress on the job.

Inappropriate.	Appropriate.

Comments:

ATTENDANCE is faithfulness in coming to work daily and conforming to work hours.

Not acceptable.	Poor.	Usually present and on time.	Prompt and has missed very few days of work for any reasons.

Comments:

PERFORMANCE AS A SUPERVISOR (when applicable).

Training and supervising efforts are failing to to meet minimum needs; a change to work not involving supervision is indicated.	Supervisory and training techniques need further improvement.	Handles routine supervisory and training tasks and problems adequately.	Can be depended upon to be effective in day-to-day supervisory and training activities.	An efficient and thorough trainer and a highly accomplished supervisor.

Comments:

ASSESSMENT OF THE ACHIEVEMENT OF GOALS ON THE LAST EVALUATION AND/OR FURTHER EXPLANATION
OF PERFORMANCE PROBLEMS:

GOALS FOR THE COMING EVALUATION PERIOD (CONSIDER HOW WEAKNESSES MAY BE STRENGTHENED AND
STRONG POINTS USED TO GREATEST EFFECT):

COMMENTS BY EMPLOYEE ON SUPERVISOR'S EVALUATION OR BY SUPERVISOR ON EMPLOYEE'S SELF-
EVALUATION.

Rated by _____   _____
               name   title

        (If not used as a self-evaluation form, the employee should sign
        below after conference.)

        A copy of this report has been given to me and has been
        discussed with me.

_____   _____
        signature of employee   date

_____   _____   _____   _____
signature of manager (supervisor's   date   signature of next level   date
supervisor)   manager when requested

☐ If checked, please return both forms to _____ after evaluation
   conference is completed.

The process of administering a performance evaluation program is not difficult.

1) An office is responsible for distributing to supervisors the evaluation forms according to the determined schedule. The office that has this responsibility varies according to the size of the organization. A personnel office, the librarian's office, or an administration assistant might be responsible. That office is responsible for identifying the individual whose performance is to be evaluated, the department in which the job is located, the name of the supervisor responsible for completing the form, and the date the form is due back in the initiating office.

2) The supervisor receiving the form now becomes the rater. The rater is the employee's immediate supervisor, who supposedly knows the most about the job being evaluated. It is the rater's responsibility to complete the form thoughtfully and carefully. Sometimes it is wise for the rater to base judgments on written notes or a diary kept over a period of time. The rater must have proof of evaluations given—particularly negative evaluations. Also, the rater should consider the employee's work from the last period of rating to the current time; evaluation should not be based on what happened last week or last month. But the rater must not be afraid to give negative ratings. Libraries have for too long a time been willing to tolerate incompetent employees. With today's emphasis on accountability and in view of the economic condition of most libraries, it is the rater's absolute responsibility to be accurate and truthful in the evaluation of an employee's performance. It not infrequently happens that a rater rates an employee as adequate or good only to request the employee's discharge or transfer a few months later. If the employee is bad, say so, but have proof; if the employee is good, mark the evaluation form accordingly.

3) Sometimes the rater is consciously or unconsciously prejudiced against an employee. Prejudice arises not only from race or creed but occasionally from such facts as color of hair, personality, physical characteristics, etc. In order to make sure that no prejudice or bias influences an evaluation rating, the rating should be reviewed by the supervisor's supervisor—the next person in the hierarchy. Together the rater and the next supervisor should review the proposed performance evaluation and come to a consensus on the accuracy of the evaluation.

4) Conducting the performance evaluation interview is probably the most difficult part of the process. At least it is the part most dreaded by employees and supervisors. Very specific steps should be taken to prepare for this interview. A specific appointment should be established with the employee by the supervisor, and the purpose of the appointment should be made clear. Before the meeting is held, the employee should receive the accomplished performance evaluation form. The

employee should have at least 24 hours to review the evaluation of his or her work and to consider its fairness and appropriateness. The supervisor also has to prepare for the meeting. Previous performance evaluations might be examined to review the employee's progress. Certainly the supervisor must plan how the meeting is to be structured. The accomplishment of these two steps eliminates two of the most prevalent errors in performance evaluation interviews, since 1) the employee has time to study the evaluation instead of being suddenly handed an evaluation without time to think about it, and 2) the supervisor plans the meeting instead of calling it on sudden impulse in an attempt to get it out of the way rapidly.

Because of the sensitivity of this interview, it is necessary for the supervisor to establish as informal and permissive an atmosphere as possible. Frequently supervisors eliminate the barrier and symbol of their authority by moving from their desk to an area having lounge furniture. Many supervisors do not realize the psychological obstacle a desk creates. Techniques of a good interview dictate that the supervisor ask questions or make comments that will encourage the employee to talk. The supervisor should not lecture the employee. If the employee is encouraged to talk, the discussion will naturally center on the performance evaluation. The employee has the opportunity to express concern or approval of the evaluation, the supervisor can explain why certain elements were rated as they were but should always lead back to the employee. Listed below are objectives that the supervisor hopes to accomplish through this interview:

1) to identify problems the employee has in performing any assigned tasks;

2) to plan methods or procedures by which these problems might be resolved;

3) to determine the employee's general level of satisfaction with the job, the institution, and the working environment;

4) to help the employee plan future personal programs and activities that will make him more effective in the job or that will help him prepare for advancement.

The last objective given above is particularly important. Together the employee and the supervisor are establishing current and long-range goals for the employee. Such goals (progress and objectives), after mutual agreement, are recorded on the performance evaluation form, and at the next evaluation interview progress toward these goals is measured. By signing the performance evaluation form, the employee indicates acceptance of the evaluation and proposed goals.

Of course, not all interviews will go as smoothly as indicated above. In some cases the supervisor may have to take such action as demoting or terminating an employee. But the supervisor should be able to anticipate when such action might be necessary and to be prepared for these situations. Previous evaluations and the current performance evaluation would provide one indication, and the known attitude and behavior of the employee would provide other signals that difficulty might be encountered. The smart supervisor is the one who is seldom caught unprepared for any direction the interview takes.

Performance evaluation is a necessary but difficult part of personnel administration. The rationale for it is that if employees are told where their performance is deficient, they will take steps to correct such deficiencies. But, as Gellerman points out, this is an oversimplification. He says that "it would be more accurate to say that most men would want to correct the deficiencies in their performance if they *agreed* that they were deficient and if there appeared to be enough *advantage* in correcting them to justify the effort."[14] The dichotomy of these two philosophies is the reason performance evaluation frequently results in resentment and tension between the supervisor and the employee.

Granted, performance evaluation may be an imperfect tool in personnel administration. Nevertheless, it can be made more effective if, as stated earlier, the program is strongly supported by top management. If it is viewed as a tool of second- or third-level supervisors it loses its clout. Then it encourages strife. But if it is given strong top support and if it uses objective standards for evaluation, it helps the employee to understand where he or she stands — and that is something all employees want to know.

SALARY ADMINISTRATION

The largest expenditure of most libraries is for employee salaries. Even though some libraries try to differentiate between "wages" for certain lower-level or hourly employees and "salaries" for upper echelon personnel, it is all money spent to compensate the people who make the library function. Since libraries, as compared to businesses and industries, do not operate for profit and therefore cannot offer annual bonuses, stock options, or other special forms of remuneration, salaries, which include fringe benefits, become the only method of compensating employees for their labor.

Most libraries receive their total salary fund from the institution to which they are attached. For public libraries, this funding comes from the municipality, the county, or other political structures. Academic libraries receive their funds from the parent educational institution, as do school media centers. A few libraries receive personnel funds from endowments, from federal or foundation grants, or, to a minor degree, from earned income. Funds received from federal or foundation grants are allocated for specific projects or programs on a one-time or temporary basis, and such funds are considered "soft" money as compared to funds for permanently authorized positions.

Private businesses and institutions are not required to make public the salaries paid any individual or group of employees. Indeed, in most industries salary information is a closely kept secret. Public institutions, on the other hand, are required to make salary information available to anyone. Some employees are not concerned that their salary is public information; others are concerned for they believe the amount of money they earn is indicative of their worth as an individual. Jealousies and insidious comparisons sometimes result from public disclosure of salary information.

In libraries, a salary administration program consists of three parts: 1) the determination of what salary to pay, 2) the development of a salary scale, and 3) the process of awarding salary increases.

Determination of Salary to be Paid

All institutions that pay personnel for services rendered must determine what is a fair and equitable compensation for the education, experience, and responsibility required in the job. It can be assumed that a job requiring more of each of these three criteria would receive more pay than a job that requires less. But that assumption is not necessarily true today because of the power of labor unions. Some professions in which a high degree of education is required receive less compensation than labor groups who have good manual skills and lower educational requirements. Perhaps this accounts for the present decline in college and university undergraduate enrollment.

Institutions that wish to recruit and retain highly qualified personnel must offer salaries that are competitive in the job market. Individuals who have specialized education, who have demonstrated capability resulting from successful work experience, and who are willing to accept responsibility are always in demand. But the compensation must be adequate to attract them to a job. While money may not be the major motivator for some people, it is still very important to most. Institutions that hope to obtain the best people and to retain their services will offer salaries higher than institutions that will accept less performance and anticipate turnover.

While it is generally considered that the salaries of professional librarians are competitive nationally, there are regional and local conditions which affect salaries. In large metropolitan centers such as the New York area, the cost of living is greater than in smaller communities. Factors of this nature will affect the level of salaries offered. The annual report of professional salaries received by current graduates of accredited library schools, usually published in the July issue of *Library Journal*,[15] shows the regional variation of beginning salaries as well as the national average and median salaries. It must be emphasized that this information is for the beginning or entry position into the field of librarianship.

In reality, the entry position is the only position for which the job requirements can be accurately described. While there are some exceptions, the entry position usually requires 1) five years of education beyond the secondary school with the fifth year culminating in graduation from an accredited library school, 2) no professional experience, and 3) minimal or moderate end responsibility in job performance. The requirements of other levels of professional positions will vary from institution to institution. Thus, many institutions use this entry level salary as the basis for their salary scale.

There are several ways to gather information on entry level salaries as well as on other professional level jobs. The annual article in the *Library Journal* has already been mentioned. But an institution may wish to gather this data by using a salary survey, or simply by evaluating salaries offered in advertisements in professional periodicals. Some state libraries issue salary data for all libraries of the state. Regardless of the method used, great care must be taken to assure that the data gathered are for positions that have the same job requirements.

If it is decided to conduct a salary survey to gather salary data, the following standards for the survey must be followed:

1) The libraries selected to be surveyed must be comparable in size.

2) The libraries must be located in communities or institutions with comparable population or enrollment.

3) The libraries selected must represent a geographic distribution covering the United States.

4) The job level for which salary information is being solicited must be clearly defined. As mentioned above, the entry level professional position is the only professional position that is comparable. However, other special positions, such as a personnel officer, can be described adequately to acquire comparable information.

When the data are received from libraries participating in the survey, the salaries are placed in rank order, with the highest at the top and lowest at the bottom. Taking into consideration such factors as competition in the job market, quality of personnel desired, and the ability of the local institution or political unit to pay, a decision must be reached concerning the salary figure to be accepted. The median of salaries identified through the survey might be accepted, or the average, or the average of the highest quartile, or the median of the lowest quartile. It is up to the governing body or institutional officials to make the decision. But a decision must be made. That figure then becomes the dollar value assigned to the position or positions surveyed.

The one danger of basing salaries on a survey is the fact that the survey reports salaries that are currently being paid, while the library making the survey is planning to use the figures for future salaries. The salaries of the surveying library, therefore, will be at least a year behind salaries being paid by those libraries included in the survey.

Salaries for library positions other than the professional grouping are usually determined by the going rate of pay in the community in which the library is located. Of course, careful attention has to be given to the requirements of each job to be sure the employee receives adequate compensation for the education, experience, and responsibility required by the job. Information concerning local salaries can be obtained from such agencies and institutions as the school system, local government, employment agencies, and sometimes Chambers of Commerce. If desired, a library can conduct a salary survey within a community. The standards for survey given above should be carefully observed.

Development of a Salary Scale

Only a few years ago it was not unusual for an employer to set a single dollar amount for job compensation. If that amount was changed, it was at the whim of the employer. As a result, unequal pay was given for comparable work. In many cases, employees were unfairly treated as adjustments in pay depended on the employer's attitude and feeling toward that employee. This practice still exists, particularly in small or medium-sized businesses that are owner operated.

But large industries, businesses, governmental agencies, and public institutions have been forced by employee and union pressure to develop more efficient and objective methods of salary administration. One method involves the establishment of specific salary scales for each job classification used in the organization. How classifications are established in libraries was discussed above, under the heading "Job Descriptions." Figure 4-2 above shows a hierarchy of jobs which might be used in a library.

A salary scale establishes the amount of money that will be paid for the accomplishment of duties designated in the job description. The scale has a minimum and a maximum amount that will be paid for that job. The minimum represents the beginning or entry level salary and the maximum amount indicates the value of the job to the institution when it is performed with maximum efficiency and thoroughness. The difference between the minimum and the maximum is known as the salary range for that job. In between the minimum and the maximum are steps on the salary scale, which designate salary increases awarded the employee as proficiency increases or as experience is gained. There is no standard for the number of steps to be included on a salary scale. It is common to find salary scales with six to eight steps, but some have as many as twelve. The dollar increase from one step to another depends on the institution—there is no standard. Generally, however, the difference from one step to the next ranges from three percent to five percent of the total salary. The more steps there are on a salary scale the smaller the percentage increase between steps. Once the percentage between steps is determined, it should be applied equally to all scales. Employers sometimes use a larger percentage between steps for salaries of the lower paying jobs and a smaller percentage increase for higher paying jobs. Such a practice results in a compression of the salary scale and is unfair to employees in higher salary brackets.

Some administrators and employers believe that salary schedules should not overlap. Figure 4-5 shows the relationship of non-overlapping salary scales. For each level of the clerk grouping, the minimum and maximum of the salary range is represented by the top and bottom of the vertical rectangles, and salary scale steps are shown between these parameters.

Figure 4-5
Relationship of Salaries in a Non-Overlapping Scale

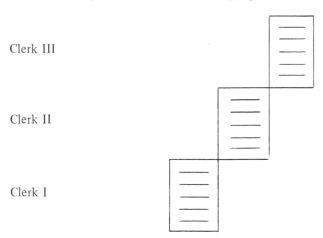

It is a more common practice, however, to have overlapping salary scales. Usually the last one-third of the first scale forms the first one-third of the next scale. The overlap philosophy is dictated by the assumption that an experienced, efficient employee in a lower classed job is more valuable to the institution than an inexperienced employee in a job with a higher classification. For the professional grouping shown in Figure 4-1 (page 94) an overlapping salary scale would have the following relationship.

Figure 4-6
Relationship of Salaries in an Overlapping Scale

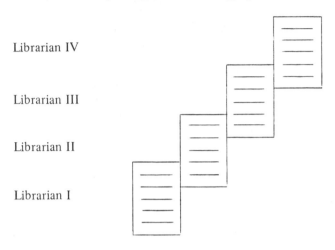

Librarian IV

Librarian III

Librarian II

Librarian I

A salary scale of six steps each for Librarian I and Librarian II jobs is shown in Figure 4-7. A five percent increment is used, but figures are rounded out to the nearest dollar value. Salary figures are illustrative and in no way constitute a recommendation for entry level salaries. The salary figures used represent monthly salaries. On a salary scale either monthly or annual salaries may be used.

Figure 4-7
Salary Scale

Step	A	B	C	D	E	F
Job Title						
Librarian II	1042*	1094	1149	1206	1266	1270
Librarian I	900*	945	992	1042	1094	1149

*Indicates entry level salary.

The same process carried out for all levels of the professional grouping shown in Figure 4-3 (page 95) would complete the salary scale for a library having five levels of professional jobs. But the salary scale, once established, is not a fixed and permanent personnel tool. Rather, it is a scale that has to be changed at least annually. As long as inflationary trends dominate the American economy, it can be anticipated that the findings of wage surveys will cause salary scales to increase. There may come a time, however, when they decrease. Regardless of the way they move, the principle of establishing a salary scale remains the same.

There are three principles that should be observed when administering a salary scale:

1) Not all employees are required to enter a salary scale at the first step. If it is the policy of the institution to recognize previous related work experience, a new employee might enter higher on the scale. The principle is that new employees should enter the scale at the same step as other employees who have comparable education, experience, and responsibility.

2) On Figure 4-7, if a Librarian I is at Step 4 of the salary scale and is receiving $1,042 per month is promoted to Librarian II, that employee should not be forced to take a salary cut because of the promotion. The principle is that an employee when promoted to a higher position should receive a salary increase. By this principle the promoted employee would receive $1,094. Some libraries have policies that permit the promotion but not the salary increase, but such policies are unfair because the employee is assuming more responsibility and should be so compensated.

3) If a new salary scale is adopted by the institution, the employee who has moved up the scale should remain at the same step. The principle is that if an employee because of quality service or length of service has advanced up the scale, he remains at the same step even if the scale changes, since otherwise his previous reward for meritorious or continuous service is withdrawn.

Awarding Salary Increases

Two philosophies dictate the basis for awarding salary increases. One philosophy holds that an employee is entitled to a salary increase because of continual service. The salary adjustment becomes automatic and is usually awarded on the anniversary of the employee's appointment. This philosophy is based on the assumption that continuous service means improved work. That assumption has not been proven true. Sometimes service over a long period of time permits the development of poor work habits and declining efficiency. Also, the employee's knowledge that a salary increase will be forthcoming if he maintains minimal performance creates a negative attitude toward the job. Despite this, many organizations operate their salary program on an automatic annual plan.

The other philosophy is based on the concept that salary increases should be awarded only for quality performance. It is assumed that awards in the form of a larger salary encourage employees to perform more efficient work. This assumption may be based on the findings of social scientists that money is a strong motivator. Money is a motivator at least for a period of time. If an organization follows this philosophy, only a part of the work force will receive salary adjustments. No award is made to those employees whose work is below standard.

Regardless of the philosophy that dictates an organization's salary program, some form of performance evaluation is needed. The function of the performance evaluation procedure in organizations giving automatic salary increases is to encourage the employee to set personal goals that will correct poor work habits and increase the quality of work. When the employee knows that average performance will result in increased pay, the possibility that the supervisor can motivate the employee to do better work is reduced. But when merit, as determined by the performance evaluation, becomes the basis for salary increases, the employee is much more concerned with work performance. The evaluation is important and the resulting rewards for good work are gratifying. The supervisor has a greater possibility of guiding the employee into good work habits and the production of good work.

Whether the salary program is based on service or on merit, nothing in a salary program limits the employee's movement on the salary scale to only one step at a time. For outstanding service and major contributions to an organization, an employee might be moved two or more steps on the salary scale at one time.

FRINGE BENEFITS

Most businesses and industries, including libraries, pay for a group of supplementary items called fringe benefits. The cost of fringe benefits is an additional cost to the organization, and most employees do not recognize that fringe benefits supplement their salaries.

Exactly which fringe benefits will be offered employees is generally determined by the organization's management. There are, however, a few that are required by federal and state laws as well as by labor contracts resulting from collective bargaining.

The Social Security Act of 1935, as amended, requires that employers collect through salary deduction a percentage of the employee's salary up to a designated amount. That sum, matched by a like sum paid by the employer, is paid to the federal government on a quarterly basis. In recent years both the percentage withheld from the employee and then matched by the employer and the salary amount on which the tax is imposed have continued to rise.

The Federal Unemployment Tax Act of 1935, as amended, requires employers of four or more employees covered by the Act to pay a percentage of the employees' salaries to the federal government to cover unemployment insurance.

Workman's Compensation, established by state laws, provides for payment to employees for injuries or diseases received or contracted as the result of job-oriented accidents or working conditions. Medical care, rehabilitation services, and death benefits are included. The employer bears the total cost of this program, though there are different methods from state to state of maintaining insurance programs to cover this cost.

State and federal programs cover more than 85% of salaried employees in the United States.[16] Hourly workers in small companies or workers doing domestic work are sometimes not covered. Also, some institutions maintain a separate retirement program and are not part of Social Security.

The Equal Pay Act has also had a strong impact on fringe benefits. This Act provides that it is "an unlawful employment practice for an employer to discriminate between men and women with regard to fringes."[17] This provision challenges programs that have different retirement requirements for men and women, different rules for the "head of the household" or "principal wage earner." Also under this Act, maternity leaves must be treated as temporary leave comparable to disability due to injury, surgery, or other incapacity.

In addition to the fringe benefits mandated by federal or state laws, institutions and organizations establish other forms of employee benefits. For some, the employer pays the full cost, while for others there is a shared payment. These can be grouped into four categories:

1) Supplementary health and insurance programs. Special group life insurance programs are frequently available, as are health and hospital programs. In some recent labor negotiations, dental insurance has been adopted.

2) Paid rest periods and lunch breaks.

3) Payment for time not worked includes vacations, sick leave, holidays, and leave because of State or National Guard duty, jury duty, death in the family, and personal business.

4) Other fringe benefits include special programs such as employee credit unions, service and suggestion awards, travel and moving expenses, and educational tuition refunds.

Most of the fringe benefits listed above are available in libraries — at least, in larger libraries. Employees tend to take fringe benefits for granted. They do not realize that fringe benefits are a significant part of the total labor cost of a library. Nor do they realize that fringe benefits add to their salary because of the contribution to these programs made by the employer. There are no studies of the cost of fringe benefit programs to libraries. Indeed, there is little information concerning fringe benefits in industry as a whole. Generally, when wage surveys are made no exploration of fringe benefit programs is conducted. Therefore, the dollar value of the fringe benefit program of any one institution cannot be compared to that of another.

On a percentage basis, however, the cost of such programs in recent years has been increasing substantially and more rapidly than basic salaries. The *Statistical Abstract of the United States*[18] for 1979 reports that for all domestic industries the cost of fringe benefits in 1978 was 18.22% of total annual wages and salaries, as compared to 11.48% for 1970. When fringe benefits paid in service industries are examined, the same publication reports the cost of 1978 fringe benefits as 13.16% of total annual wages and salaries, as compared to 8.28% for 1970.

Employees no longer view the library's fringe benefit program as a privilege, but rather as a right. It is believed that the years ahead will see an increase in such programs. Therefore, a library manager contemplating the establishment of a fringe benefit must carefully study the program to determine the future financial impact of the program on the institution. But even more important, after determining that the program is needed and desired by the employees, the manager must carefully define the program, establishing such policies, procedures, and rules as necessary to assure its fair and equitable implementation.

PERSONNEL POLICIES, PROCEDURES, AND RULES

As institutions grow, a body of policies, procedures, and rules develops. It was mentioned in chapter 3 that as an organization is structured, organizational policies are written so that organizational continuity is maintained. Likewise, as personnel programs are established, personnel policies, procedures, and rules are written 1) to guarantee program consistency, 2) to assure equitable and comparable interpretation of the program, and 3) to maximize the equal and fair application of the program to all employees.

A policy is defined as a statement that establishes a definite course or method of action to guide and determine present and future decisions. In no sense are policies engraved in stone and unchangeable. But they usually have a high degree of permanence.

Within the framework of the definition given above, it should be recognized that a policy is a broad statement of intent. The policy establishes guidelines for subordinate decision makers; it keeps all units of the organization moving in the same direction.

The preparation of policy statements can encourage participative management. Seldom does one person assume responsibility for policy determination. Rather, a group of supervisors or staff members might recommend the establishment or modification of a policy. Discussing, evaluating, and writing the policy statement can encourage the participation of those groups that will be affected by it.

Particularly in the field of personnel administration, clearly defined policies are needed. The employees of a library need to understand, through written policy statements, what the classified personnel program is, how it operates, why salaries are administered in a particular way, why and what the performance evaluation is, what fringe benefits are available, and all other factors that affect them personally.

A procedure is defined as a series of specific actions or operations that lead to a desired end. A procedural statement sets forth the steps essential for accomplishing a particular result. While there may be many statements of procedure throughout a library, there are not many in personnel administration. Only in programs that require comparable action are procedures necessary. Certainly a definite written procedure for receiving and handling employee grievances will be established, and the procedure for carrying out performance evaluations will be carefully determined.

The steps that many supervisors or staff specialists perform do not need to be described in public procedural statements. Those processes (such as the determination of the salary scale) are part of the abilities of the person accomplishing the task and need not be formalized in writing.

A rule is defined as a law, regulation, or prescribed guide for conduct of action or behavior. Rules can be considered as minimum standards of conduct which apply to a group of people. Rules tend to apply uniformity to the group of people concerned.

Libraries, like all other institutions, must have rules. Examples of rules are the number of hours to be worked each week, rest periods, and behavior before the public. Rules serve to ensure reasonable predictability of behavior so that the organization can achieve its goals and function without undue disruption.

As mentioned in chapter 3, an organization sometimes develops too many rules. Employees become frozen; they have no freedom of action. Some rules are necessary, but too many are detrimental. It is often thought that rules tend to be established for that small group of employees who do not conform—those who do not observe, for example, the authorized length of a coffee break. The total group should not be penalized because of the action of a few.

CIVIL SERVICE

U.S. Civil Service

The United States Civil Service Commission was created by act of Congress on January 16, 1883. Its basic task is to administer a Federal employment merit system, which includes recruiting, examining, training, and promoting people on the basis of their knowledge and skills, regardless of their race, religion, sex, political influence, or other nonmerit factors. Often called the "people agency" of government, the Civil Service Commission's role is to provide qualified people for government agencies and to ensure that the Federal government provides an array of personnel services to applicants and employees.

Decentralized operation of Commission programs is achieved by the establishment of 10 regional offices, under which are area offices—at least one in each state—located at major centers of population. The ten regional offices are:

Region	Address
I	Post Office and Courthouse Bldg., Boston, MA 02109
II	New Federal Bldg., 26 Federal Plaza, New York, NY 10007
III	Federal Bldg., 600 Arch St., Philadelphia, PA 19106
IV	1340 Spring St., NW, Atlanta, GA 30309
V	Federal Office Bldg., 29th Floor, 230 S. Dearborn St., Chicago, IL 60604
VI	1100 Commerce St., Dallas, TX 75242
VII	1256 Federal Bldg., St. Louis, MO 63103
VIII	Bldg. 20, Denver Federal Center, Denver, CO 80225
IX	Federal Bldg., 450 Golden Gate Ave., San Francisco, CA 94102
X	Federal Office Bldg., 916 Second Ave., Seattle, WA 98174

The human resources of government are the primary interest of this agency of the executive branch. The following activities of the Civil Service Commission show the range of programs designed to develop and support the effectiveness of the government employee.

1) Recruiting and examining applicants for positions in the Federal civil service.

2) Personnel investigations determining qualifications and suitability for employment.

3) Equal employment opportunity efforts seeking to eliminate nonmerit considerations such as race, color, religion, sex, national origin, or age from all aspects of Federal employment.

4) Employee development and training accomplished through a nationwide network of training centers.

5) The Incentive Award Program providing cash and honor awards to employees to encourage improvements in governmental operations.

6) Personnel management guidance offered to management throughout the Federal employment system.

7) Employee benefits, including health benefits, life insurance, occupational health, retirement, a system for appealing adverse personnel actions, and both protection from and prevention of prohibited political activity.

8) Intergovernmental personnel programs recommended to improve personnel management in state, local, and Indian tribal governments.

All libraries maintained by the executive branch of the Federal government are staffed by U.S. Civil Service employees. Therefore, libraries maintained by the Department of the Interior, the Department of Energy, the Department of State, etc. are staffed by Civil Service appointments. Nonmilitary personnel in libraries maintained by the Department of Defense, such as those operated by the Army, Navy, Air Force, and Marine Corps, are Civil Service appointments.

State and Local Civil Service

Many state, county, and municipal governments operate a form of civil service similar to that of the Federal government. Academic, county, and public libraries may be affected in their employment practices by such standards as the local civil service establishes. Standards for promotion, salary administration, job classification, fringe benefits, retirement, and dismissal are generally maintained by the civil service agency. Special libraries, other than those operated by the Federal government, and county and public libraries, which operate under an autonomous board, may not fall under the purview of the local civil service agency but rather operate their own civil service program. School libraries generally operate under the personnel rules established by the school district.

UNIONIZATION

The history of labor's attempt to get fair and equitable treatment and to have a voice in the decisions that affect their lives goes back to the earliest days of the American colonies. In 1636 a group of Maine fishermen protested the withholding of their wages. The first local craft union was formed in Philadelphia in 1792 by shoemakers. The first national organization of workers that has continued to the present day is the Typographical Union, founded in 1752.[19] Labor continued to strive for better working conditions, shorter hours, and better pay all through the 1800s and early 1900s. Some of the conflicts between labor and management were violent, and many people were hurt or killed.

The Federal government occasionally entered these conflicts through the establishment of Presidential Commissions that served as arbitrators or mediators. But only minor federal legislation was enacted until 1926, when the Railway Labor Act was passed establishing collective bargaining in the railway systems and procedures for the handling of grievances, arbitration, "cooling-off" periods, fact finding, and mediation.

But the real foundation of the American labor movement was laid in 1935, when the National Labor Relations Act, popularly known as the Wagner Act, was passed. This Act established the National Labor Relations Board and defined the right of workers to organize and to elect representatives to carry out collective bargaining. In the same year, the Social Security Act was established by congressional action. In 1936, the Public Contract Act, the Walsh-Healy Act, established labor standards on government contracts including minimum wages, overtime, compensation for time over 40 hours per week or 8 hours per day. The very important Labor Management Relations Act, better known as the Taft-Hartley Act, was passed in 1947; it amended some of the previously approved labor legislation, particularly the Wagner Act, but it also established certain union practices as unfair. The Taft-Hartley Act outlawed closed shops, jurisdictional strikes, sympathy strikes, and refusal to bargain. Also, it permitted states to pass "right-to-work" laws.

The Civil Rights Act was passed by Congress in 1964. Title VII of this Act prohibits discrimination in employment based on race, color, religion, sex, or national origin.

These, then, are keystones to labor relations today. After the passage of the Wagner Act in 1935, unions began to grow very rapidly. By 1970 union membership in the United States totaled 19,400,000. This membership constituted about 22.6% of the total work force and 27.4% of the employees in non-agricultural establishments. When employee associations engaging in collective bargaining are added, the figures increase to 21.3 million (24.7% and 30.1%, respectively).[20]

Historically, most union activities have involved the blue collar worker. The craftsman, manual worker, and assembly line worker are included in the blue collar category. White collar workers were not much involved until the late 1950s. There is no clear definition of a white collar worker, but the Bureau of Labor Statistics includes professional, technical, managerial, sales, and clerical workers in this category. Since 1956, however, the number of white collar workers included 17% of the total membership of national and international unions in the United States. When employee associations are added to unions, white collar membership rises to a total of 23%.[21]

Unions are presently focusing more attention on the white collar worker. Technological change in many industries has resulted in the reduction of the blue collar labor force. This has caused a slight decline in the number of union members. To compensate, many unions are concentrating on organizing the white collar worker. According to George Meany, the late president of the AFL-CIO, "organizing the unorganized" is considered the "greatest unresolved trade union problem."[22]

Because of the Taft-Hartley Act and some state right-to-work laws, unions find major problems in enforcing unionization. The closed shop (an industry or organization in which employers may hire only union members) is illegal, as is the union shop (where union membership is mandatory for all employees included in a bargaining unit). Because unions feel that individuals represented by the union should pay their share of union fees, maintenance of membership in a union is sometimes required during the period that the contract is in force, unless state right-to-work laws prohibit the practice. Also, unless prohibited by state law, "agency shop" provisions may require non-union employees to pay a contribution to the union representing some employees of a unionized unit. Usually that contribution is equal to union dues.

Unionization of an organization may be accomplished in several ways. 1) Union organizers may start talking to employees while they are off the job about the benefits of unionization. 2) If a union represents part of the labor force of a specific organization, members of the unionized group or union organizers may talk to employees of non-unionized units. 3) Employees of a non-unionized organization who are dissatisfied with the policies and practices of the organization may solicit the help of an organizer or may submit a petition signed by at least 30% of the employees of the unit to the National Labor Relations Board.

If the employees initiating unionization action are successful in obtaining signatures of the required 30% of all employees of the unit being unionized, an election is usually held to determine the desire of all the employees to unionize and to determine the agency that will be designated the bargaining agent. A vote is not mandatory if the organization agrees to recognize a union as the bargaining agent. But such action leaves the designation of the bargaining agent unresolved, and it is open to challenge by both employees and other unions.

Only a simple majority of all employees concerned must be obtained to effect unionization. The election is carefully supervised by representatives of the National Labor Relations Board and procedures are carefully observed by management and union representatives to be sure no unfair labor practices are carried out. A number of provisions of the Taft-Hartley Act (as amended by the Labor-Management Reporting Act of 1959, the Handrum-Griffin Act) control unionizing campaigns.

After a union or employee association has been certified as the exclusive bargaining agent for a group of employees or for a total company, management and the union must bargain collectively. This action is required by the Taft-Hartley Act. Matters that will be discussed in the bargaining sessions include wages, hours, and other conditions of employment. Agreement on these matters must eventually be reached and a contract prepared which both sides are willing to sign and abide by for a stipulated time.

Generally, an organization designates one person as its representative to carry out the bargaining process and to represent management after the bargaining process. That person may be the library personnel officer, an industrial relations specialist, or any other individual delegated to represent management. The individual must understand the bargaining process, which, while not described here, is complex, frequently frustrating, and exhausting.

The bargaining group also appoints an individual to represent them, and after the labor contract is signed, to monitor management's compliance with the contract. In industry this individual is known as the steward, or shop steward. It is this person to whom employees bring any complaints or grievances, and with whom management must work closely to maintain labor's cooperation.

White collar workers, particularly professionals, have historically been reluctant to join unions. But in recent years teachers, nurses, and professionals in municipal, state, and federal employment are more actively participating in collective bargaining. At the present time all types of libraries are being affected by the movement of professionals to unionize.

Historically, the main reasons for unionization have been to effect better wages, fringe benefits, and working conditions. But other factors are influencing the professional. Employees today are demanding a greater voice in the administrative decisions that affect their lives. They are objecting to jobs that are prescriptive and that fail to allow for individual growth and professional movement. In frequent cases, unionization is brought on by the inept or irresponsible action of management. Unionization is sometimes seen as a way to maintain personal integrity and to assure fair and just treatment for oneself. So not all unionization activities are based on the desire for increased wages.

Managers of libraries must recognize that unionization will affect their organization and their method of management. As a result of the bargaining process and the signing of a labor contract, the power and authority of management sometimes is greatly reduced. The degree of power and authority that management loses will depend on the bargaining process. Some libraries, using inexperienced and untrained representatives at the bargaining table, lose so much authority that it becomes difficult to manage the institution. Others, because of more skilled negotiators, retain the power and authority to effect program direction, job definitions, and quality personnel programs.

Library managers frequently respond to unionization movements in a very negative way. They feel that the employees are ungrateful for management's attempts to improve working conditions. Managers feel hurt and consider employees disloyal to the goals of the organization. Such reactions, while perhaps natural, must be overcome. Good labor negotiations can occur only when management faces the problems calmly and objectively. After the negotiations are completed and a labor contract signed, the institution can best move ahead if there is a cooperative attitude between management and the union representation. [Appendix 5 presents the labor agreements of the Library Board of the City of Minneapolis and the Board of Library Trustees of the Town of Watertown (MA)].

GRIEVANCES AND GRIEVANCE PROCEDURES

It was mentioned earlier that every library should have written personnel policies. These policies set forth standards for salary administration, promotion, transfer, demotion, termination, and other operational policies. In a nonunionized library, these policies are the guidelines for all supervisors. The statements are established to assure fair and equitable treatment of all workers. While personnel policy statements are formulated by management, the wise administrator will be sure not only that they are understood by the worker but also that the worker will understand why the policy has been established.

In a unionized organization, the personnel policies as modified by union-management negotiation become part of the union contract. A union contract usually spells out policies and procedures and workers' rights with respect to 1) wages and salaries; 2) hours of work; 3) holidays and vacations, demotions or force reduction, seniority, and policies of leaves of absence; 4) safety and health;

5) suspension and discharge; 6) training programs; and 7) the establishment of grievance channels.

Both the personnel policies developed by the organization and the policies and procedures established by a union contract are designed to guarantee fair treatment of workers. However, complaints and grievances will develop in spite of such precautions. Real or imagined unfair treatment of people will arise in any organization. Such feelings may vary from the supervisor's attitude toward an employee to the belief that promotion standards have not been fairly applied. Some workers harbor such feelings of unfair treatment within themselves. They are afraid to complain or express their unhappiness because of fear of reprisal by the supervisor. Other employees complain only to their immediate work group, thereby alienating the group from the supervisor. In either case, the individual or the group approaches the job with low morale and becomes a problem to the first-line supervisor.

One of the traditional ways of hearing and resolving employee grievances is the program known as the Open Door. This program is based on the assumption that when supervisors encourage employees to come to their offices voluntarily at any time to discuss their problems and complaints, they will feel free to do so. But this assumption is not completely sound. The Open Door policy works only when the supervisor has been able to instill in the employee a feeling of trust. The employee must feel that any problem or complaint will be objectively heard and fairly resolved and that the supervisor will not hold it against the employee or consider him or her a troublemaker. If the Open Door program works, it is because the supervisor is particularly skilled in human relations and sensitive to employee needs and feelings. But such a program does give the supervisor opportunity to explain why certain action was taken and to resolve the complaint or grievance through direct communication.

The Open Door program, while it can operate in a unionized organization, is more likely to function in a non-unionized organization. With the absence of a union contract, the supervisor has more freedom and more alternatives available with which to resolve problems. Factual problems are probably the easiest to resolve, since they involve working conditions, hours of work, or changes in methodology of the job. But problems involving sentiment or feeling are much more difficult to handle. Here, the supervisor must constantly ask himself, "Why does the employee feel this way?" The answer will depend on the supervisor's understanding of people.

Grievances in a unionized organization cannot be handled as directly as they are in the Open Door program. First, the union contract is the legal base for handling personnel grievances, and it must be adhered to. Second, a shop foreman is elected from the union membership. Although an employee of the company, the shop foreman is also the representative and spokesman for the union employees. Employee grievances are submitted to the foreman rather than to the supervisor. The supervisor is generally on the defensive and frequently has difficulty in determining the facts of the situation. This is particularly true if the complaint involves sentiment and feeling. The supervisor has little opportunity to probe for the reason for such feeling. The problem is couched in factual and legalistic terms, sometimes hiding the real situation.

In this era, when the rights of employees are carefully protected, it is essential that organizations have a written, public grievance procedure. In a unionized organization this procedure will undoubtedly be part of the union contract. But in a non-unionized organization, management must see that such procedures are established. A grievance procedure defines 1) the manner in which grievances are filed (written or oral); 2) to whom the grievance is submitted; 3) how the grievance proceeds through the organization's hierarchy; 4) where decisions of resolution can be made; and 5) the final point of decision. Usually the procedures identify action the aggrieved employee can take if he or she is not satisfied with the final decision (such as appeal to the union membership or court action).

It must be kept in mind that grievance channels are ways of removing the employee from the direct and complete control of the immediate supervisor. Grievance channels discipline supervisors and act as a guarantee to employees. They exist to assure employees that justice is available and can be properly dispensed.

EMPLOYEE DISCRIMINATION

The history of the American effort to prohibit discrimination against certain groups of employees goes back to the Civil Rights Acts of 1866 and 1870 and the Equal Protection Clause of the 14th Amendment to the United States Constitution. Recent presidents, including Eisenhower, Kennedy, Johnson, Nixon, Ford, and Carter, issued strong Executive Orders to prohibit discrimination in the United States Civil Service. President Eisenhower's Executive Order 10950 proclaimed "it is the policy of the United States Government that equal opportunity be afforded all qualified persons, consistent with law, for employment in the Federal Government." This was the first time the term "equal opportunity" surfaced. The concept of affirmative action was introduced in 1961. President Kennedy's Executive Order 10925 directed "positive measures for the elimination of any discrimination, direct or indirect, which now exists." President Johnson's Executive Order 11246 in 1965 introduced the significant charge of putting responsibility for government-wide guidance and leadership under the Civil Service Commission. President Nixon, soon after he took office in 1969, issued Executive Order 11478. This strong order made it clear for the first time that equal employment opportunity "applies to and must be an integral part of every aspect of personnel policy and practice in the employment, development, advancement, and treatment of civilian employees of the Federal Government." This Executive Order was considered a total integration of personnel management and equal employment opportunity in the Federal government.

This movement in the United States Civil Service had an impact on other employers. And Congress, recognizing the need to guarantee equal employment opportunity, took action by passing the Civil Rights Act of 1964 (Public Law 88-352). Title VII, Equal Employment Opportunity, provides the basis for fair employment practices. This Title prohibits discrimination based on race, color, or national origin in all programs or activities that receive federal financial aid. This Act also established the Equal Employment Opportunity Commission as the agency to enforce this law.

In 1972 Congress amended the 1964 law by passing a stronger Equal Employment Opportunity Act, which greatly strengthened the power and expanded the jurisdiction of the Equal Employment Opportunity Commission. As amended, Title VII now covers 1) all private employers of fifteen or more persons; 2) all educational institutions, public or private; 3) state and local government; 4) public and private employment agencies; 5) labor unions with fifteen or more members; 6) joint apprenticeship and training.

The Equal Employment Opportunity Commission requires that all businesses, industries, and institutions under their jurisdiction prepare and have approved an Affirmative Action program to meet the requirements of the 1972 law. Recurring reports are required to show action taken and progress made. The Commission sets forth the following requirements for the Affirmative Action program:[23]

A.   Issue a written equal employment policy and Affirmative Action commitment.

B.   Appoint a Top Official with responsibility and authority to direct and implement your program.
    1.   Specify responsibilities of Program Manager.
    2.   Specify responsibilities and accountability of all Managers and Supervisors.

C.   Publicize the policy and Affirmative Action commitment.
    1.   Internally: To managers, supervisors, all employees and unions.
    2.   Externally: To sources and potential sources of recruitment, potential minority and female applicants, to those with whom you do business, and to the community at large.

D.   Survey present minority and female employment by department and job classification.
    1.   Identify present areas and levels of employment.
    2.   Identify areas of concentration and underutilization. An area of concentration is one in which there is a significant number of minorities or females. Underutilization is defined as having fewer minorities or women in a particular job category than would be reasonably expected by their presence in the relevant job market.
    3.   Determine amount of underutilization.

E.   Develop goals and timetables to improve utilization of minorities, males and females in each area where underutilization has been identified.

F.   Develop and implement specific programs to achieve goals. This is the heart of the program. Review the entire employment system to identify barriers to equal employment opportunity; make needed changes to increase employment and advancement opportunities of minorities and females. These areas need review and action:
    1.   Recruitment: All personnel procedures.
    2.   Selection Process: Job requirements, job decriptions, standards and procedures. Pre-employment inquiries; application forms; testing; interviewing.
    3.   Upward mobility system: Assignments; job progressions; transfers; seniority; promotions; training.
    4.   Wage and salary structure.
    5.   Benefits and conditions of employment.

6. Layoff; recall; termination; demotion; discharge; disciplinary action.
7. Union Contract Provisions affecting above procedures.

G. Establish internal audit and reporting system to monitor and evaluate progress in each aspect of the program.
H. Develop supportive in-house and community programs.

Other federal laws also strive to prohibit discrimination. The Equal Pay Act of 1962 requires all employers subject to the Fair Labor Standards Act (FLSA) to provide equal pay for men and women performing similar work. In 1972, coverage of this Act was extended beyond employees covered by FLSA to an estimated 15 million additional executives, administrators, and professional employees including academic and administrative personnel, teachers in elementary and secondary schools, and outside salespeople. The Age Discrimination clause in the Employment Act of 1967 prohibits employers of 25 or more persons from discriminating against persons 40-65 years of age in any area of employment because of age, and President Carter signed into law April 6, 1978, a bill to raise legal mandatory retirement age for most workers from 65 to 70 years, effective January 1, 1979.

NOTES

[1]William D. Halsey, ed., *Collier's Encyclopedia* (New York: Crowell Collier Educational Corp., 1972), vol. 8, p. 172.

[2]*American Libraries* 6, no. 1 (Jan. 1975): 39.

[3]*Standards for Accreditation, 1972* (Chicago: American Library Association, 1972), p. 5.

[4]It is interesting to note that this concept of skills is similar to the one used by Peter F. Drucker in his book, *The Effective Executive* (New York: Harper and Row, 1967), chapter 1.

[5]Maurice F. Tauber and Associates, *Technical Services in Libraries* (New York: Columbia University Press, 1959).

[6]Ernest De Prospo, Ellen Altman, and Kenneth E. Beasley, *Performance Measures for Public Libraries* (Chicago: American Library Association, Public Library Association, 1973).

[7]F. W. Lancaster, *The Measurement and Evaluation of Library Services* (Washington, DC: Information Resources Press, 1977).

[8]Lowell Martin, *Library Response to Urban Change* (Chicago: American Library Association, 1969).

[9]Thomas Childers, "The Test of Reference," *Library Journal* 105, no. 8 (April 15, 1980).

10Childers, "The Test," p. 926.

11Note that, except for custodians, the levels identified are those included in the *Library Education and Manpower* policy statement of ALA.

12Denver Public Library, Librarian's Committee on Performance Evaluation, *Management Guide to Performance Evaluation* (1971), p. 1.

13Denver Public Library, *Management Guide*, pp. 3-4.

14Saul W. Gellerman, *Management by Motivation* (Chicago: American Management Association, 1968), p. 141.

15*See*, for example, Carol L. Learmont and Richard Troiano, "Placements and Salaries 1978: New Directions," *Library Journal*, vol. 104, no. 13 (July 1979): 1415-22.

16*The Report of the National Commission on State Workmen's Compensation Laws* (Washington, DC: GPO, 1972), p. 15.

17*Equal Employment Opportunity Commission Guidelines on Discrimination Based on Sex* (Washington, DC: GPO; amended April 4, 1972).

18*Statistical Abstract of the United States* (Washington, DC: GPO, 1979), p. 425.

19Wendell French, *The Personnel Management Process: Human Resources Administration*, 3rd ed. (Boston: Houghton Mifflin, 1974), p. 725.

20Bureau of National Affairs, *Labor Relations Yearbook — 1972* (Washington, DC: Bureau of National Affairs, 1973), p. 296.

21Bureau of National Affairs, *Labor Relations Yearbook*, p. 296.

22*Fortune* 75, no. 2 (Feb. 1967): 199.

23U.S. Equal Employment Opportunity Commission, *Affirmative Action and Equal Employment, a Guidebook for Employers*, vol. 1 (Washington, DC: Superintendent of Documents, 1974), p. 16.

5

DIRECTING

Directing is that complex function of getting workers to perform tasks efficiently and effectively so that the goals and objectives of the organization are fulfilled. Directing is therefore concerned with the relationship of a supervisor to the subordinate at all levels of the organization.

Historically, the picture of supervision practices is not a pretty one. Most workers, history shows, have performed duties because they were forced to. They were coerced into accomplishing what was desired by their "masters." Threat of harm, fear of punishment, or dependence on the ruler for protection, food, and shelter were the motivators used for centuries. Even when a strong and perhaps benevolent paternalism dominated the worker, that very attitude of paternalism reinforced dependence upon the father-figure and removed the power of making a decision, exercising judgment, or functioning as one's own master.

Since the beginning of the Industrial Revolution, managers have used negative methods of getting workers to work. Managers have tried to keep the worker economically dependent. The threat of dismissal or demotion, with the resulting loss of income, has forced workers to perform. The fear of losing special benefits, such as clean houses and schooling for children, as provided by Robert Owen's factory at New Lanark, dominated worker's thoughts. The total paternalism of Alfred Krupp lulled the worker into passive security. Economic dependence has been, and is today, a great motivator to get workers to work. In recent years managers have added a new dimension to economic dependence. A form of bribery has developed. If workers exceed established standards, they are "awarded" trips at company expense, vacations at company-owned resorts at reduced rates, or special bonuses or gifts. Worker motivation, it is assumed, is increased through special awards.

The worker, whether man, woman, or child, has been considered a commodity comparable to other resources utilized by an industry or organization. The labor factor has dominated the human factor.

In the early 1900s, however, this attitude toward workers began to change. Both Frederick W. Taylor and Henri Fayol emphasized the worker's importance to an enterprise and pointed out that the supervisor had to understand workers and their motivations. Both urged cooperative and harmonious relationships between the two groups.

Directing, or supervising, or managing, then, is the complex process of getting things done through people. It is a manager's greatest challenge today, because patterns of supervision are shifting rapidly due to extensive research by the social scientist, the labor relations expert, and the industrial psychologist.

THE SUPERVISOR

Whether at the lowest level or the highest echelon of the organization, the supervisor is the key to the employees' attitudes toward their jobs and to the quality and quantity of productivity. Subordinate supervisors sometimes adopt the supervisory style they perceive their supervisor to exercise. But more frequently the supervisory style demonstrated by any supervisor is the product of his or her own experience and attitude toward people.

Some supervisors want to be considered "good guys." They want to be part of the group they must manage. Recently a major supervisor said, "I like to be considered one of the team, to joke with and tease the employees. But that sure creates a problem when I have to discipline, correct, or fire an employee." That statement illustrates the problem of the "buddy" supervisor.

Other supervisors maintain both a formal and informal distance between themselves and their employees. There is no on-duty socialization and no outside contact except at official office or company affairs. To the employee, such a supervisor seems distant, cold, and uninterested in the employee's welfare. This supervisor probably feels that the responsibility of getting the department's work accomplished rests on his or her shoulders alone. No one else is concerned.

The two supervisors described above are extremes, it is granted. But both types are found in almost every organization. Both create problems for themselves and for the organization. Both cause trouble for their employees. An individual like the "good guy" changes when it is necessary to discipline an employee; the "distant" supervisor breaks his or her barrier of isolation at the Christmas party. The behavior of both becomes inconsistent with the previous supervisory patterns.

Consistency of behavior is an essential characteristic of good supervisors. Those who show friendship and humor today and distance and aloofness tomorrow confuse the employee and undermine the relationship of the two people. The supervisor who "blows up" and causes a tense situation quickly loses effectiveness as a supervisor. When an individual loses self-control, performs actions which he or she normally would not perform, or says things that should not be said, that individual is the loser — losing control in the fullest sense. Such a supervisor is inconsistent to the point that employees never know what to expect. But consistency is not the only positive characteristic of a good supervisor. Studies made over the last several years have identified other attributes of the good supervisor.

The term "supervisor" is being used here to indicate the leader of an endeavor; other terms are used to designate the same role in an organization. "Director" and "manager" are frequently used comparably. It is generally considered that these titles indicate positions of authority over the work of others and that this position has the power and responsibility to make decisions and establish policies. The power to establish policy is the greatest in top level positions and certainly the scope of a policy decision declines at each lower level of the organizational hierarchy. Therefore, a supervisor, director, or manager of a clerical pool or of a shelving unit in a library has the responsibility of directing the work of others, of making decisions regarding the functioning of that unit, and can even make policy decisions as long as those policy decisions are not in conflict with policies of other units in the organization or even with the organization as a whole.

The term "boss" is widely used to indicate that person who directs the work of others. *The American Heritage Dictionary of the English Language* defines "boss" as "An employer or supervisor of workers; manager; foreman. Someone who makes decisions or exercises authority." While "boss" might be used to show respect or even affection, it is generally believed to provide authority with a derogatory connotation.

Throughout history very little attention has been given to what a supervisor, manager, or director should do or to how his or her work should be done. Historically, there has been thinking about the manager's role, as the following examples from ancient Egypt and China show.

If thou art one to whom petition is made, be calm as thou listenest to what the petitioner has to say. Do not rebuff him before he has swept out his body or before he has said that for which he came.... It is not (necessary) that everything about which he has petitioned should come to pass, (but) a good hearing is soothing to the heart.[1]

If the words of command are not clear and distinct, if orders are not thoroughly understood, the general is to blame. But if his orders are clear, and the soldiers nevertheless disobey, then it is the fault of their officers.[2]

Only in the 1900s have studies been made which will help supervisors do their work more efficiently and which will enable them to understand better what motivates people to work and what discourages them. Some of the important studies in these areas are reviewed below.

The Hawthorne Studies

Between 1927 and 1932 Elton Mayo, of Harvard's Department of Industrial Research, made a study at the Hawthorne works of Western Electric Company in Chicago. This study has become a landmark in establishing in industry the modern concept of effective human relations. "The Hawthorne studies provide an excellent illustration of several important phenomena: restriction of output; informal work groups; the effects of the supervisor; and the so-called Hawthorne effect itself."[3]

As efficiency engineers at the Hawthorne plant were experimenting with various forms of illumination, an unexpected reaction from employees was noticed. When illumination was increased, productivity increased. That was not as surprising as the fact that when illumination decreased, production continued to increase. The same happened when the illumination was not changed at all. Mayo was asked to examine this paradox, and the "Hawthorne studies" resulted.

The study consisted of two parts. One involved special six-woman teams of workers. Working conditions for these teams were constantly changed to determine worker fatigue and worker production. Not only was the amount of illumination changed, but such factors as rest periods, shorter work days, coffee breaks, and other changes in standard working conditions were introduced. Employees had the authority to determine the timing of coffee breaks and could influence decisions relating to other changes. Mayo's conclusion was that "the singling out of certain groups of employees for special attention had the effect of coalescing previously indifferent individuals into cohesive groups with a high degree of group pride or esprit-de-corps."[4] When a group develops pride in their work and has some degree of authority over their work habits, productivity increases. This is the famous "Hawthorne effect," which now is widely recognized and is applicable to many work situations.

The second part of the Hawthorne studies involved interviewing approximately 20,000 different workers. Two things soon became apparent from the interviews: 1) work in the factory was dismal and dull at best, and most employees accepted it passively and with a feeling of futility; 2) informal groups of workers emerged through which the worker acquired a feeling of belonging and being welcome. Management frequently considered these groups to be threats (which they were in some cases, for one of the primary functions of these groups was to provide a safe retaliation for poor managerial techniques). Slowdowns in production, poor or careless work, and the forcing of all workers to comply with the group's behavior were within the power of the group. But Mayo believed that the group could become a positive force for increasing productivity if management changed its attitude toward the group and used it for positive action.

For the supervisor, the importance of the Hawthorne studies is significant: 1) employees respond to managerial efforts to improve the working environment; 2) they respond to being capable of making decisions that affect their work patterns and job behavior; 3) the informal group can be a positive unit helping management to achieve its goals; 4) the informal group needs to develop a sense of dignity and responsibility and to be recognized as a constructive force in the organization; 5) the worker must feel needed and welcomed by management.

Prudential Insurance Company of America

Soon after World War II, the University of Michigan established an Institute for Social Research. One of the companies this group studied was the Newark office of the Prudential Insurance Company of America.[5] The study, involving several large clerical departments, tried to identify supervisory styles of supervisors and their effect on employee productivity. It was recognized that supervisors usually had a fairly clear and constant concept of their jobs. Because of this, the researchers could have the supervisors describe their jobs, identify objectives and obstacles to achieving those objectives, and discuss their personal methods of reaching those objectives.

The analysis of interview data made it possible to divide supervisors into three groups: predominantly production-centered supervisors, predominantly employee-centered supervisors, and mixed patterns. Because no one person is always the same, the word "predominantly" is important. A production-centered supervisor was one who felt full responsibility for getting the work done; departmental employees were to do only what this supervisor told them to do. An employee-centered supervisor recognized that the subordinates did the work and that therefore they should have a major voice in determining how it was done. Coordinating and maintaining a harmonious environment was the supervisor's main responsibility.

The research results were surprising. Contrary to traditional management thinking, which emphasized that permissive supervision led to employee laxity and carelessness, the departments that had employee-centered supervisors had high production while those with production-centered supervisors produced less. The Michigan researchers had to make an assumption that was radical at the time and that is still surrounded by controversy: many workers like their jobs, they want to be productive, and they would be productive if given a share of control over their jobs.

Much research since the Prudential study supports the assumption made by the Michigan researchers, and the theory is applicable to many activities other than clerical activities. While it does not solve all supervisory problems, "the theory that workers feel responsible for productivity, and that employee-centered supervision is the best way to stimulate this feeling, has plenty of ... evidence to support it."[6]

The Likert Theory of Supervision

Rensis Likert[7] in his book *Patterns of Management* summarizes much of the research done at the Michigan Institute for Social Research up to 1961. It is a classic in the study of supervisory styles. Likert strongly rejects the theory that a concern for good human relations is a distraction to the primary function of management. He also rejects the theory that concern for good human relations reduces the efficient and profitable operation of an organization.

Likert recognizes that management's primary responsibility is to assure the best use of the organization's resources. Research has shown that strong centralized control of employees is not the best way to achieve operational efficiency or sustained productivity. A production-centered supervisory style may be detrimental to the organization's interest. There is no sentimentality involved in Likert's emphasis on human relations in supervision. He emphasizes that when management analyzes its operations, the appropriate supervisory style for the various operations can be determined. When the supervisor's style is attuned to the employee needs and job requirements, productivity is usually significantly higher and more constantly maintained. This is true for tasks that are worker-controlled; machine-controlled productivity jobs are dictated by the machine.

Likert in no way attempts to make a blanket prescription for employee-centered supervisory styles. He emphasizes that the supervisory methods used by supervisors in highly productive organizational units require "adaptability and adherence to a consistent appreciation of what the particular employees want and need rather than a doctrinaire insistence on being permissive."[8] Consistent productivity is the goal of any supervisor — not brief spurts of effort followed by a reduction of activities. Fluctuations in productivity frequently occur when employees receive pressure, threats, and constant watching by the supervisor. But this supervisory style brings its own destruction through the loss of morale and employee turnover. It encourages production slow-downs, resistance to new methods, and strikes. Likert believes that pressure and strong control may have to be used in emergency situations, but that continual use of such techniques will not build good morale, good productivity, and a team spirit in an organization.

Research at the Institute for Social Research has proven that a feeling of responsibility toward one's work is natural and is any employee's general tendency. Supervisors can encourage this attitude of responsibility by demonstrating sincere respect for the employee's trustworthiness, intelligence, and knowledge of the job. The employee readily discerns any artificial declaration of faith, and the resultant distrust of the supervisor reduces the employee's feelings of confidence and responsibility. But the supervisor who tries to reduce the number of restrictions placed on the employee, who is willing to consult with the employee about assigned tasks, and who makes sure the employee knows why a task is essential in the total flow of activity will strengthen that attitude of responsibility and develop good employees. Such a supervisor functions more as a partner in the activities of the organization than as a boss responsible for getting the job done.

The supervisor's success, then, will be determined by his or her supervisory style. Consistency in manner, a balance between over-friendliness and aloofness, a sincere respect for the employee's trustworthiness and intelligence, and a willingness to have the employees participate in making decisions that affect their jobs are attributes of the good supervisor. The good supervisor will not: 1) play favorites among employees, 2) apply rules and regulations differently to different employees, 3) develop in the employee a fear of the supervisor, and 4) make snap decisions with inadequate information.

MANAGEMENT PHILOSOPHIES

Any manager of people develops certain attitudes or philosophies about people in general and about workers specifically. This philosophy may develop from previous or current work experience, or because of the influence of the general work environment, and it colors the way in which a supervisor directs and evaluates workers. It determines the supervisor's opinion of what makes people work and what satisfactions, if any, they get from their jobs. The way in which a supervisor attempts to meet employee needs or to motivate employees is to a large extent determined by his or her attitude toward people.

These philosophies are probably assumptions about people and why they work. The assumptions are generally not provable; however, a number of social researchers have produced significant studies that need to be examined.

Maslow's Need Hierarchy

One of the important studies contributing to the understanding of people was accomplished by Abraham H. Maslow. He developed a hierarchy of human needs which, while not aimed primarily at work situations, is applicable to a work situation. The worker is viewed as moving from one level of need to another as his or her job develops. Maslow identifies five levels of need (*see* Figure 5-1).[9]

Figure 5-1
Maslow's Pyramid of Human Needs

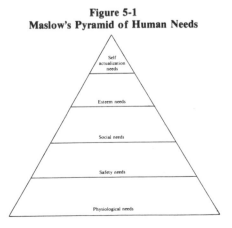

I.   Physiological needs
     The basic needs of any worker are food, water, shelter, sleep, which sustain life on its most minimal level.

II. Safety needs
     The worker needs an environment which provides an understandable, predictable and well-ordered situation. He needs assurance that the future physiological needs will be met. He is concerned about personal safety with security against theft, muggings, and attacks.

III. Social needs
     As other needs are met, the worker develops a need to belong, to love and be loved, to participate in activities which will create a feeling of togetherness.

IV. Esteem needs
     The worker desires respect from others, as well as having a high self-respect and self-esteem.

V.   Growth needs
     At the highest level the individual achieves self-realization by performing at his maximum potential and strives to become everything that he is capable of becoming. He reaches self-actualization.

In any community or organization in the community, one can identify individuals who are at various levels of this need hierarchy. The hourly worker striving to maintain the basic physiological needs, the people in the urban center striving to find safety, the "joiners" of clubs, churches or social organizations (including the company bowling team), the head of the company who accepts the chairmanship of the United Way, the community leader who is a primary decision-maker for the community—these are examples of workers at different levels of the need hierarchy.

Of course, not everyone rises systematically up the need hierarchy. Sometimes an individual never has to be concerned with physiological needs because of affluent parents; others never rise above this point. It is sometimes said that only a very few people in the world have reached the fifth level, self-actualization. Mahatma Gandhi, Eleanor Roosevelt, and Winston Churchill are sometimes credited as having reached full self-actualization. It is believed, however, that many people achieve this level of self-realization. It may be that they have passed through the need for esteem from others and the need to belong to groups. They have the ability to live fully to their maximum potential without the trappings of other levels.

To a supervisor, the importance of Maslow's need hierarchy is that it gives a guide to an individual's needs and desires. By identifying an employee's current location on the hierarchy, the supervisor has a better basis for guiding, counseling, and advising the employee to growth performance. The supervisor must recognize that a satisfied need is not a motivator.

Douglas McGregor's Theory X and Y

Another group of assumptions about workers was developed by Douglas McGregor.[10] X and Y are simply labels to designate contrasting management assumptions. McGregor does not imply that all assumptions in either Theory X or Theory Y are always right or always wrong. They may change according to the realities of a specific organization. However, unrealistic assumptions about people have caused many good plans to fail. If a planned activity flies in the face of human nature, its success will be only as great as the non-human factors can ensure. Not infrequently, when plans begin to fail management tightens controls and applies more pressure. McGregor found that such action only increases the potential for failure, for what is needed is a lessening of control and a freeing of initiative.

In 1960, McGregor defined Theory X as follows:

1) The average human being has an inherent dislike of work and will avoid it if he can.

    This assumption is deeply imbedded in management thought. Management sees itself as responsible for obtaining "a fair day's work," reducing or stopping restriction on production and slowdowns.

2) Because of this human characteristic of dislike of work, most people must be coerced, controlled, directed, threatened with punishment to get them to put forth adequate effort toward the achievement of organizational objectives.

    This assumption follows the concept of hard supervision as compared to soft (permissive-humanistic) supervision. The implication is that the dislike of work is so strong that more force than the promise of rewards must be exercised to get work accomplished.

3) The average human being prefers to be directed, wishes to avoid responsibility, has relatively little ambition, wants security above all.

    Rarely is the "mediocrity of the masses" stated so bluntly as in this assumption. This concept is not generally verbalized in American society. But it has been a concept held by some managers.

The knowledge about human behavior in many specialized fields, however, has made it possible to create another generalization about the management of human resources. McGregor called this assumption Theory Y.

1) The expenditure of physical and mental effort in work is as natural as play or rest.

    The average person does not basically dislike work, but may gain satisfaction from it or attempt to avoid it depending on past experiences.

2) External control and the threat of punishment are not the only means for bringing about effort toward organizational objectives. Man will exercise self-direction and self-control in the service of objectives to which he is committed.

3) Commitment to objectives is a function of the rewards associated with their achievement.

   Such positive rewards as ego satisfaction and self-realization are the most significant and can be direct products of efforts directed toward organizational objectives.

4) The average human being learns, under proper conditions, not only to accept but to seek responsibility.

5) The capacity to exercise a relatively high degree of imagination, ingenuity, and creativity in the solution of organizational problems is widely, not narrowly, distributed in the population.

6) Under the conditions of modern industrial life, the intellectual potentialities of the average human being are only partly utilized.

   These assumptions are much more challenging to management strategy. They are dynamic, not static. They indicate that human beings have the possibility of growing and developing. Most importantly, it makes management responsible for creating an environment that will permit the positive development of its human resources.

McGregor was the leading spokesman for the behavioral approach to management. He had both strong support for his philosophy and opponents to his concepts, and he persisted in expanding his assumptions about human beings. In 1966[11] he stated the concepts of Theory X in a slightly different way, but a way that still emphasizes the negative approach to supervision:

1) Management is responsible for organizing the elements of productive enterprise (money, materials, equipment, people) in the interest of economic ends.

2) With respect to people, this is the process of directing their efforts, motivating them, controlling their actions, modifying their behavior to fit the needs of the organization.

3) Without this active intervention by management, people would be passive — even resistent — to organizational needs. They must therefore be persuaded, rewarded, punished, controlled; their activities must be directed. This is management's task in managing subordinate managers and workers.

4) The average man is by nature indolent; he works as little as possible.

5) He lacks ambition, dislikes responsibility, prefers to be led.

6) He is inherently self-centered, indifferent to organizational needs.

7) He is by nature resistant to change.

8) He is gullible, not very bright, the ready dupe of the charlatan and the demagogue.

The human side of economic enterprise today is fashioned from propositions and beliefs such as these. Conventional organization structures, managerial policies, practices, and programs reflect these assumptions. However, this still seems a very pessimistic assessment of the average worker. It certainly is an unflattering one that many workers and supervisors would challenge. But the beliefs are stated as assumptions held by some managers. In some cases they may be true and in others false; assumptions as such have no proof. If they are true, then a supervisor with Theory X personnel would have to find a supervisory style that would get the work performed effectively. Whether he or she used a soft approach or a hard approach to supervision, there would be difficulty.

McGregor modified the Theory Y concept as follows:[12]

1) Management is responsible for organizing the elements of productive enterprise (money, materials, equipment, people) in the interest of economic ends.

2) People are *not* by nature passive or resistant to organizational needs. They have become so as a result of experience in organizations.

3) The motivation, the potential for development, the capacity for assuming responsibility, the readiness to direct behavior toward organizational goals are all present in people. Management does not put them there. It is a responsibility of management to make it possible for people to recognize and develop these human characteristics for themselves.

4) The essential task of management is to arrange organizational conditions and methods of operation so that people can achieve their own goals best by directing their own efforts toward organizational objectives.

While Theory Y is not diametrically opposed to Theory X, it still presents a much more positive picture of people. According to this assumption, people are the product of their past experiences, their behavior can be modified or changed, and they can be motivated to work and assume responsibility. Within the philosophy expressed in Theory Y, it is management's job to develop work assignments that are challenging to the worker and that help the workers to achieve their personal goals and objectives. At the same time, such work assignments must contribute to the accomplishment of management's goals and objectives.

If a supervisor accepts the assumptions set forth in Theory Y, his or her supervisory style will reflect a different set of values than would be demonstrated in Theory X. A greater respect for people as human beings would be demonstrated. Without exercising a soft or permissive form of supervision, the supervisor would be more participative in decision making and more cognizant of the workers' needs.

The Economic and the Social Man

Following McGregor, increased attention has been given to the study of man's behavioral patterns. New and more detailed studies have resulted in new assumptions about man. Schein[13] identifies four conceptions about man in the order of their historical appearance. Assumptions deduced from the concept of a rational economic man are:

1) Man is primarily motivated by economic incentives and will do that which gets him the greatest economic gain.

2) Since economic incentives are under the control of the organization, man is essentially a passive agent to be manipulated, motivated, and controlled by the organization.

3) Man's feelings are essentially irrational and must be prevented from interfering with his rational calculations of self-interest.

4) Organizations can and must be designed in such a way as to neutralize and control man's feelings and therefore his unpredictable traits.

It is not known when these assumptions about man were formulated. Schein does not identify those by whom they are held to be true. But the concept of the "economic man" is interesting and observable in modern society. Probably these assumptions were formulated before the Hawthorne studies, because assumptions coming from those important studies define man as a social creature.

The concept of the social man is:

1) Man is basically motivated by social needs and obtains his basic sense of identity through relationships with others.

2) As a result of the Industrial Revolution and the rationalization of work, much of the meaning has gone out of work itself and must therefore be sought in the social relationships on the job.

3) Man is more responsive to the social forces of the peer group than to the incentives and controls of management.

4) Man is responsive to management to the extent that management can help in the development of a subordinate's social needs and needs for acceptance.

Whether man is the indolent creature suggested by McGregor, an economically motivated creature, or a creature dominated by social needs is still a question. These are all assumptions about man's nature. A supervisor, whether in industry or in a library, must develop his or her own philosophy of human nature.

Koontz and O'Donnell recognize that people have superimposed an intelligence upon an animal nature and thus have modified behavior. The mind and a conceptual ability makes it possible for an individual to create an imaginative world, to exercise a degree of foresight, and to modify and direct his or her basic nature so that needs and satisfactions can be achieved. Koontz and O'Donnell[14] indicate that,

this view of the nature of man makes it possible to deduce certain conclusions that are of the utmost importance to the manager. These may be listed as follows:

1) The individual is the primary concern of man.
Man looks after himself both in the extremities of life or death and in the modern affluent society. It is he who wants preferment, who wants to win. He may very well enjoy the success of others after he has achieved, although his jealous and skeptical nature shows through. True, we do have our unselfish heroes, men who willingly have laid down their lives for others, the wholly unselfish mother, the man who will step aside for the benefit of others. The rarity of these people makes them subject to comment and to award.

2) The individual will work to satisfy the demands of his basic nature if the benefits exceed the costs.
It is often said that man enjoys work. This is certainly true if the effort is directed toward satisfying the demands of his complex nature. He is doing this even when he tinkers. As he approaches the point of marginal satisfaction, he scarcely has the will and verve to apply himself to the specific labor *for the same reason.* For instance, he may work at his bench with unusual productivity in order to save time at the end of the day to experiment with a new tool or a new method he has invented. In this view, the objective work may change for the worker several times a day.

3) The individual can be led.
Man responds to leadership. He can be persuaded through many devices to take the desired road, but the devices themselves must be selected, tuned, and timed to the individual's need to satisfy his basic nature. Appeals to pride, status, greed, and many other aspects of man's nature are sometimes successful. Ancient armies were led with promises of booty; modern armies would have none of this. The leader must be intuitive in identifying the persuasive device to which another, at a given time, will respond positively.

4) The individual wants to live and work in a social environment.
This seems to be true most of the time. There is a definite need for solitude, however; sometimes people cannot bear people; many scientists still work best alone. In general, these periods of time are much shorter than those when man desires group associations. Both aspects rest squarely upon man's basic nature. Man may be largely a social animal, but he is not entirely so.

5) The individual helps to create institutions to serve the needs of their memberships.
There are many needs that man alone cannot satisfy. He can achieve them only through cooperative effort. If they promise a surplus of benefits over costs, he is likely to accept the implied limitations upon his individuality. For these reasons man creates government, educational, religious, health, and many other institutions. His chief problem in

large-scale society is to retain his mastery of the institutions he has created and not become their slave.

6) There is no average man.

Attempts to take the square root of mankind, on the assumption that people are all alike, are bound to fail. People are not all alike. Natures are different and, for the individual, his nature may differ from time to time. Man does not, even as an individual, proceed to accommodate all aspects of his basic nature in the same degree at a given time. He exhibits priorities and these are kaleidoscopic.

7) The individual rises to the challenge of his full capabilities.

Man is impatient to use his abilities to their fullest extent. He resents the lack of opportunities to apply his knowledge and skills and to shoulder the responsibility for results. He becomes bored working at half speed, with routine. He is curious to learn the maximum level of his capabilities and he wants to operate at this level.

Maccoby's Managers

After extensive study, Michael Maccoby has identified four distinct types of manager.[15] While this applies primarily to large technical corporations, it has been observed that the same characteristics are present in managers of other endeavors. All four types have been seen in library managerial positions. Maccoby identifies these four types of supervisors as:

The craftsman. With his interest in the *process* of making something, the craftsman embodies the traditional work ethic, with his respect for people and his concern for quality and thrift. Leading a complex and changing organization is incompatible with his virtues of self-sufficiency and perfectionism.

The jungle fighter. The jungle fighter views his life and work in terms of winners and losers, with power as his goal. His psychic energy is directed toward defending himself.

The company man. The company man's goal is to be a functioning part of the organization. He views the integrity of the company in terms of mutual cooperation and commitment.

The gamesman. The gamesman is interested in the challenge and the competition of the game. His goal is to be a winner and he enthusiastically responds to life and work situations with innovative ideas, dynamic thinking and unbounded energy.

The Managerial Grid

In 1964, Robert R. Blake and Jane Srygley Mouton published *The Managerial Grid*.[16] That this theory of management has received widespread attention is demonstrated by the fact that this publication had gone through 20 printings by 1977.

The theory of the Managerial Grid involves three primary elements of an organization: 1) concern for production, 2) concern for people, and 3) the structure of the hierarchy. Organizations employ people to produce some item or service that represents the reason an organization exists. "Production," as used here "covers whatever it is that organizations engage people to accomplish."[17] The degree of concern for production by the manager might represent the manner in which the manager views the essentiality and significance of the organization. The manager's concern for people is demonstrated at a usual level by the maintenance of standard personnel procedures such as current salary scales and job descriptions, good working conditions and adequate fringe benefits. A greater concern for people would be reflected by the manager's willingness to solicit opinions and recommendations prior to making decisions and a willingness to make broad work assignments compatible with the goals of the organization while continuing to allow the employees to determine their own methods of work and procedures. The hierarchy is the managerial aspect represented by those assumptions, attitudes and philosophies which each supervisor practices in directing people. These managerial aspects of the hierarchy are demonstrated at every level of management whether it be the top and final decision maker, middle management, or a line supervisor.

The Managerial Grid, as presented by Blake and Mouton,

> shows these two concerns and a range of possible interactions between them. The horizontal axis indicates concern for production while the vertical axis indicates concern for people. Each is expressed as a nine-point scale of concern. The number 1 in each instance represents minimum concern.
>
> At the lower corner of the Grid is the 1,1 style. This has a minimum of both concerns; that is, of concern for production and concern for people. At the top left corner of the Grid is found the 1,9 style. Here there is a minimum of concern for production but maximum concern for people. In the lower right corner is 9,1. This style has a maximum concern for production and a minimum for human aspects. In the upper right corner is the 9,9 style, where concern for both people and production reaches maximum. Then, in the center is the 5,5 style, which is a "middle of the road" or an intermediate amount of both kinds of concerns.[18]

While there is a possibility of 81 "mixtures" of the manager's concern for people and production, it is doubted that such minute gradations can be made except by outside experts. However, objective managers at any level should be able to identify their degrees of concern for both production and people. The hierarchy is the means of linking people into the organization's production pattern.

THE SUPERVISOR AND MOTIVATION

Around the world people work. They expend effort to achieve some goal. The goal may be of little value or of high scientific or cultural significance, but energy is put forth to accomplish a task. If, as McGregor indicates in Theory X, work is unnatural and repugnant to man, why are millions of people involved in work?

In many cultures work is a group activity. Entire families or groups of families cooperate in growing and harvesting food. All of the men of the group participate in the defense of the group. The pressure of the group causes some people to work perhaps harder and more conscientiously than they would work alone, or perhaps slower and at the group's tempo. Group pressure is a strong motivating force, as identified in the Hawthorne studies. Not to be of the group is to lose social contact with one's peers. The social man, as discussed earlier, needs the group and the social contacts and safety it offers.

All organizations are composed of units established to perform specific tasks. While these units vary in size, each has its own supervisor. Each unit is in reality a group of workers striving to achieve specific goals and objectives. Many supervisors look at their subordinates as individuals, each of whom has his or her own problems and attitudes. They forget that these employees constitute a group and that the group can be used positively to help establish and achieve the unit's goals and objectives.

New theories of motivation place much emphasis on the power of groups to make workers want to work. Likert disagrees with the kind of organizational charts presented in chapter 4 and appendix 2. He believes that each organizational unit functioning as a group must interrelate with other groups until it becomes one large group all striving to achieve common goals.[19] Thus, the organization becomes an integrated whole. Likert says "an organization will function not as individuals but as members of highly effective work groups with high performance goals."[20] A supervisor following this philosophy should deliberately endeavor to build these effective groups, linking them into an overall organization by means of people who hold overlapping group membership.

It is this philosophy of supervision that has led to such developments as participative management, where the group has the power of decision making. Also, since the goals of the group are determined by group decisions, each individual tends to have a high degree of ego identification with the goals and will strive harder to achieve them. Motivation to achieve is increased. This is the psychological base for Gellerman's *Management by Motivation*.[21] Employees are motivated to work if they view their supervisors as supportive, fair, and constructive, and if they are able to maintain a sense of personal worth and importance.

For the group, Odiorne proposes that motivation can be accomplished by establishing, in cooperation with the group, specific objectives to be achieved.[22] But the process by which the objectives are achieved is not determined. Process is left to the group to determine—subject, of course, to quality control and to restrictions of space, time, and equipment. Odiorne's philosophy of motivation may be more easily applied to individuals, but numerous demonstrations, such as the Volvo experiment of worker groups responsible for the total assembling of a car, prove that it is applicable also to groups.

But not all individuals work in groups; many work as individuals even in large organizations. It is evident that their motivation is not primarily social but dominantly economic. At first, motivation may be the necessity of meeting those basic physiological needs identified by Maslow. The needs for food, shelter and clothing are recurring, constant needs. Hunger is a great motivator, causing people not only to work but in some situations to commit numerous and varied crimes.

But in America, the assurance of food, shelter, and clothing is not enough. This society, which is strongly materialistic, seeks more than the minimal creature comforts. Man seeks other things that require money—and money comes from work. Man strives to earn more in order to satisfy needs and desires beyond the physiological requirements. Money is a great motivator. Success is frequently measured according to the amount of money earned or accumulated.

Money itself is not the major motivator, however, according to studies accomplished by Frederick Herzberg and his associates.[23] In the book, *The Motivation to Work*, an extensive study is reported showing that an individual's morale affects his or her attitude toward work. High morale indicates a high job attitude; low morale indicates a low attitude toward a job. Morale can thus be defined as the attitude with which an employee approaches his or her job. Herzberg developed a questionnaire that required lengthy descriptive reports of events that made the worker feel good or bad. The answers were analyzed to identify the elements of high job attitudes. It is important to note that Herzberg's sample consisted of 203 engineers or accountants in middle management positions in industries in and around Pittsburg. The methodology of his study involved the writing of a story or sequence (critical incident) which affected the participant's attitude positively or negatively toward his or her position. These were carefully analyzed and interviews with each participant were conducted.

The analysis of data showed that the most frequent factor in a high job attitude is achievement. Success in the completion of a job created the highest job attitude. Beginning with achievement, factors that were identified are ranked here from high to low:

1) Achievement

2) Recognition by supervisors, peers, or customers and subordinates of work accomplished.

3) Work itself—aspects of the job that gave the worker personal satisfaction.

4) Responsibility—being able to work without supervision and being responsible for one's own effort.

5) Advancement—a promotion indicates growth, recognition, achievement, and more responsibility.

All of the five factors above relate to the job itself. They do not relate to other factors found by Herzberg to be characteristics of the context or environment in which the job is done. The other factors that influence high job attitudes are:

6) Salary

7) Possibility of growth

8) Interpersonal relations (subordinate)

9) Status

10) Interpersonal relations (superior)

11) Interpersonal relations (peer)

12) Supervision

13) Company policies and administration

14) Working conditions

15) Personal life

16) Job security

Herzberg emphasizes the differences between the first five factors, which relate to the actual job, and the last eleven, which describe the job situation and which he identified as hygienic factors. The factors that seem to have a long-range effect on job attitudes are work itself, responsibility, and advancement. However, achievement and recognition as factors for high job attitudes are of shorter duration. The combining of some of these factors (such as advancement and recognition) is a strong factor in developing a high job attitude.

For many people achievement alone creates a positive attitude toward work. To achieve—to complete a project or assignment—brings fulfillment and personal satisfaction. Even if there is no recognition for achievement, a worker knows within himself that he or she accomplished the job. Some recognition, even a verbal recognition or a pat on the back, will increase job satisfaction for a short time.

Herzberg's study reveals that a salary increase is a motivator, but one that lasts only a short time. The effect of a salary increase is soon dissipated. It does not have the long-range effect that achievement and recognition provide.

Since Herzberg's landmark study, many other studies on motivation have been conducted. Some, much to the surprise of the researchers, have shown over and over that money and security are the primary motivators for getting workers to produce. It is possible that motivators change as world and national situations change. Could it be that security becomes dominant when jobs are scarce and the holding of a job is vital? But when jobs are plentiful, security is not as strong a motivator. The same could be said about money as a motivator. Rising prices and inflation put an emphasis on money, while a stable economy removes the pressure of money as a strong motivator.

The supervisor must shape a supervisory style to include behavioral patterns that will motivate the worker to perform tasks efficiently. There is no prescription that can be offered to assure success. Rather, each supervisor has to evolve an individual pattern in view of his or her personality, managerial philosophy, and knowledge of the worker. The efficient supervisor will take advantage of the worker's personal and environmental reasons for working and will add identified additional inducements for working. Thus, a system of motivation emerges rather than a single source of motivation. Some inducements to work may be negative, but the majority will be positive. A system of inducements is not designed for across-the-board application but rather is designed to permit workers to select those inducements that provide the best motivation for them.

A sound motivational system is based on sociological principles, the policies of the organization, and the supervisor's philosophy of man's needs. Primary in any motivational system is the organization's responsibility to satisfy employee needs. This is difficult to accomplish because the needs of human beings not only vary greatly but also are flexible and subject to change. Perhaps the best a supervisor can do is to satisfy the most common needs of workers. Maslow's hierarchy of needs gives the supervisor a good guide of a range of needs, from basic life requirements to the social, ego, and creative needs. Likert and others emphasize the power of the group. Herzberg's studies show the need for recognition, achievement, advancement, and responsibility. Other studies emphasize the need for increased monetary rewards and job security.

The policies of the organization should be structured so that the capacity to do good work — work of growing significance — is not stifled. Good productivity reflects the quality of employee motivation. Frequently, the goals and objectives of an organization will spark an employee, who wants to be part of and contribute to their achievement. A high degree of achievement of its goals and objectives reflects well on the organization, creating a positive image of it. The worker is proud to be part of that organization and is motivated to promote its success through efficient work. Also vital to any system of motivation is the quality of worker selection and training. It is obvious that the capable and well-trained employee will be a more productive employee. The organization must plan a sound orientation and training program. Training is discussed in detail later in this chapter.

Any system of motivation, then, depends on the supervisors. The manner in which they apply their knowledge of employee needs and desires, the organizational environment that releases the capacity for work, the quality of training received by capable employees, and the pride of the employee in the organization for which he or she works establish the basic climate of the motivational system. It is the supervisor's responsibility to exercise sound judgment to make the system work. The system works when there is good productivity, high morale, a friendly, competitive team spirit, and a dedication to the organization's goals and objectives.

THE SUPERVISOR AND LEADERSHIP

Webster's dictionary defines a leader as a "guide, conductor, chief or head of a group." That definition implies that a leader is part of a group but is apart from the group because of leadership responsibilities. The leader always maintains an individual identity, though he or she acts to help the group achieve its goals and objectives. Carter gives five definitions of leadership:[24] 1) polarization of members of a group around some central person; 2) the person able to direct a group toward its goals; 3) the person selected by group members to lead them; 4) the person able to move a group along a specific dimension; and 5) the person possessing certain behavior patterns and capabilities.

In all definitions given above one person is designated the leader. This has been true historically for many centuries. Without one position that represents authority and gives direction, organizations tend to disintegrate. When two or more individuals try to fulfill the leadership role, the organization, because of conflicting direction, becomes formless and unable to act. Therefore, the basic concept of the superior-subordinate in an organization is established. The superior-subordinate group concept provides for the interlinking of groups through the scalar chain of authority of the organization. It is through this inter-linking of the superior-subordinate group that the leader can direct action, effect change, and depend on subordinates for effective supportive endeavors.

It is true that in some libraries in recent years experiments in management have been conducted to place the power of direction in the hands of committees or a group of supervisors. This is, of course, in violation of the superior-subordinate concept described above. As mentioned earlier, such managerial experiments have been called "participative management." The designated authority group makes the decisions that give direction to the institution.

In libraries, leaders at any level of the hierarchy are either promoted or appointed to their positions of leadership. The function of leadership assigned to an individual cannot be abnegated or eliminated. Though delegation of certain leadership functions might occur, the end responsibility for the direction of an organization or, at a lower level, of a group of employees, still rests with the one to whom the leadership role was assigned. Participative management is good in the sense that the leader seeks the advice and counsel of associates and then makes a decision in light of that advice. However, participative management in the sense that a group makes decisions is dangerous to the institution and represents a failure of the designated leader to accept responsibility.

Each leader must develop an individual style of leadership. Some leaders may be "soft" or extremely permissive. In this case, employees are given little direction and generally few decisions are made by the supervisor. The group of employees seems to "drift along." Social psychologists have found that some groups function well under this form of supervision, particularly if they know their jobs well and are dedicated to the accomplishment of their responsibilities. But most groups functioning under extremely permissive leadership tend to disintegrate. Their tasks are not fulfilled, and tensions develop because various members of the group want to deviate from established goals or processes. Occasionally a member of a group receiving this type of supervision will assume the leadership role, pulling the group back into a productive unit but relegating the assigned supervisor to an untenable position.

The opposite supervisory style is that identified as "autocratic." Here the leader functions as a total dictator, prescribing every action and activity. This "hard" leadership discourages creativity and communication. Employees generally respond in a retreat to silence, passivity, and resignation. They perform the tasks they have to, but no more.

These are, of course, descriptions of leadership roles at each end of the spectrum. Most leaders are somewhere in the middle of these extremes. The trend is for leaders to adopt a more humanistic attitude toward employees and to involve them in activities, studies, and decisions that affect their jobs.

A good leader of a library will develop a group of counselors or advisors who provide information. Such groups will include staff, the constituency, and governing boards. The complexities of a large library are so great that generally no one leader can anticipate all the ramifications and side effects individual decisions might have. So the wise leader will involve in the decision process those people who will be affected by decisions.

Decision making is expected of a leader. The subordinates expect and have the right to anticipate decisions that will affect them and their work. The constituency of a library has the right to expect the leader to make decisions concerning the quality of library service available to them. Decision making is a primary responsibility of the leader. But the process of making decisions is not easy. Snap decisions are usually bad or at best very risky because they are not based on fact. The gathering of all possible facts about a problem is the first step of decision making. Second, all possible solutions or alternatives must be identified. The wise leader evaluates each alternative in the light of possible reaction. As discussed in chapter 2, this process of attempting to forecast the effect of a decision is a vital step. Only after such careful studies does the wise leader make a decision.

The astute leader will establish short- and long-range goals for the institution, develop specific objectives to accomplish those goals, and develop programs and activities to meet the objectives. The leader will constantly be evaluating and restructuring the organization so that goals and objectives can be achieved. This responsibility, as creative as that of establishing goals, "means shaping the character of the organization, sensitizing it to ways of thinking and responding so that increased reliability in the expectation and elaboration of plans will be achieved according to its spirit as well as its letter."[25]

The leader of a library, while accomplishing the processes of planning, organizing, staffing, and controlling, will establish written policies for the guidance of subordinate supervisors. A policy is a written statement setting forth a decision that directs present and future action. Such policy statements maintain consistency and continuity. Policy statements should in general emphasize "what is to be done," not procedurally "how it is to be done." Such statements should be readily available to all staff members.

Emphasis has been placed on the role of the leader in the process of directing an institution, but the leader has other functions that are just as important. The manner in which the leader will fulfill the functions of being responsive to staff and constituency requests and of representing the institution locally as well as regionally and nationally will depend to a large degree on his or her personality and attitude toward people. But these functions are part of the responsibilities of a leader and must be fulfilled. To a large degree, the image an institution creates is determined by the leader who is the directing force of that institution.

Any leader working within an organization must be careful that his or her effectiveness is not dissipated by organizational restrictions. An organization is supposed, through the unification effort, to strengthen the effectiveness of a leader. But frequently organizational obstacles are placed in the leader's way. Drucker identifies four obstacles to a leader's effectiveness:[26]

1) The executive's time tends to belong to everyone else. (The leader has difficulty in controlling his time because of the organizational responsibility to be available to staff and constituency.)

2) Executives are forced to keep on "operating" unless they take positive action to change the reality in which they live and work. (Direct control of organizational units dominates the leader's time and prohibits him from functioning as a coordinator, motivator, and creator.)

3) The leader is pushed toward ineffectiveness because he is within the *organization*. (He is effective only when other people make use of what he can contribute.)

4) The leader is *within* the organization. (The organization is seen only from inside; the organization from the outside is seen only through distorted lenses. What actually goes on is seen only through reports, statistics, and second-hand information. The leader must get outside and view the organization as it really is.)

A leader who controls his or her time, contributes to the endeavor of the organization, and sees the institution in reality will undoubtedly be an effective, dynamic leader.

THE SUPERVISOR AND COMMUNICATION

Most supervisors spend a large share of their time communicating with other people. Indeed, some studies show that 60% to 100% of a supervisor's time is spent carrying out this process. It is apparent, then, that communication is an important element of supervision.

Communication between individuals and groups is as old as recorded history, yet is is only recently that the topic of communication has emerged in management literature. C. I. Bernard[27] was one of the first and best-known authorities to give serious consideration to problems of communication. He defined communication as the means by which people are linked together in an organization in order to achieve a central purpose. More recently the American Society of Training Directors has defined communication as the interchange of thought or information to bring about mutual understanding and confidence or good human relations. It appears, then, that communication is the exchange of words, letters, symbols, or messages in such a way that one individual or group receives information and understanding from other individuals or groups. It must be emphasized that the transfer of information is not nearly as difficult as the transfer of understanding. Understanding is achieved when the relevance of the transferred information is recognized as pertinent to the achievement of organizational goals.

Warren Weaver and Claude Shannon view communication as occurring in a system:[28] an information source (person or machine) selects a desired message from a set of possible messages; the selected message is then changed into a form to be transmitted over the communication channel to the receiver; the receiver changes the transmitted signal back into a message. Wolf simplifies this system with the following example: You ask a friend to open the door: your brain is the information source, your friend's brain is the destination, your vocal system is the transmitter, the sound waves serve as the principal channel of communication, and your friend's ear is the receiver.[29]

Actually, this sounds like a very simple system, but in practice it is seldom precise. The signal selected by the information source may be the wrong one, the signal transmitted may not give the intended information, the message may be distorted by unwanted additions or omissions while being sent or received. All such alterations in the transmitted signal are called "noise" in communications theory.

The majority of all communication involves symbols. The most frequent form of communication is carried on through a variety of codified symbols. Such symbols are languages—English, French, German, etc. Each consists of a plurality of signs that have a known meaning in written or oral form to a number of people, and the signs (written and oral) are capable of being reproduced. Written and oral communication based on a language is the most frequent form of communication used. However, actions, objects, and signs (since they, too, may have a known interpretation to a number of people and can be reproduced) often constitute communication languages. Jurgen Ruesch and Weldon Kees describe these languages as follows:[30]

> Sign language: "Sign language includes all forms of codification in which words, numbers, and punctuation marks have been supplanted by gestures; they may vary from the 'monosyllabic' gestures of the hitch-hiker to such complete systems as the language of the deaf."
>
> Action language: Action language "embraces all movements that are not used exclusively as signals. Such acts as walking and drinking, for example, have a dual function: on the one hand they serve personal needs, and on the other they constitute statements to those who may perceive them."
>
> Object language: Object language "comprises all intentional and nonintentional display of material things, such as implements, machines, art objects, architectural structures, and last but not least, the human body and whatever clothes cover it."

Through the use of these various languages, then, the supervisor communicates with subordinates, peers, and superiors. He or she writes memos, letters, and policy manuals, holds meetings with individuals and groups to discuss programs and problems, observes sign, action, and object language, and interprets the meaning of such language. And the good supervisor does one other thing in the communication process—listen. In oral communication the supervisor listens not only to the message being sent—what is being said—but also for the true meaning of what is being said. These other languages will occasionally help distinguish the true message from the false.

While an individual cannot resist being influenced by action, object, and sign languages, it is to verbal language—written and oral—that most attention is given. Most people, and certainly librarians, spend most of their day responding to verbal languages. Words (spoken, read, or thought) dominate.

Sometimes there are too many words. A supervisor must expect that there will be various forms of communication from subordinates. Specifically designed, required reports are needed for decision making. Suggestions, complaints, and commendations also come from subordinates. The supervisor in actual practice receives information not only from subordinates, but from superiors and from external sources. Sometimes there is too much information. No one yet has been able to answer adequately the question "How much information do I need?" But useless or unimportant information is noise in the communication process and distracts from the significant message.

In any organization communication is a two-way process. The good supervisor operates on the theory that the informed employee is a good employee. The supervisor assures the transmittal of information through the hierarchy according to authority lines. This formal channel of communication requires written memos, directives, and policy statements. It is hoped that these written statements not only answer "what" but also "why." The "why" gives understanding to the employee and the "what" gives the information. But written communication has numerous problems. Some may be poorly written and may not fully explain the action desired or completely define the scope of the problem. Employees are left with ambiguous instructions. Words used in written communications are frequently unclear and not defined. Every profession has its own vocabulary, and the same word may have several meanings; in librarianship, the word "system" has at least three meanings. Written communication allows no opportunity for feedback and clarification. The subordinate employee's perception of a written message is based on past experience and present needs.

Oral communication conducted through individuals or groups also has problems. Not all oral messages are clearly stated. There is still the problem of the ambiguous or misunderstood word. But in oral communication there is an opportunity for discussion — feedback — through which clarification can be accomplished. Frequently, oral communication is the best way to resolve conflict situations. Organizations should not be afraid of conflict situations if the issues are faced on an intellectual rather than an emotional basis. After oral communication has occurred between individuals or groups, it is not unusual for written communication to be prepared that summarizes the agreements, conclusions, or resolutions reached through the oral communication. Oral communication provides an excellent opportunity for the supervisor to observe the employee's use of object language, particularly as expressed by the body. Body language involves the use of gestures, tone of voice, facial expression, and, perhaps most important, eye expression and contact.

What has been discussed so far is the upward and downward formal pattern of communication in an organization. The messages are sent up or down the hierarchical lines of authority. However, a supervisor must recognize and encourage horizontal lines of communication. These informal channels through which peers communicate provide opportunities not only for clarification but also for coordination of effort. A supervisor should not fear these informal channels but should encourage them. Social events, coffee breaks, and informal staff meetings provide opportunities for such informal communication.

When formal communication is inadequate and events occur within an organization that are unexplained or hidden, it is not unusual for rumors and false information to enter the informal communication channels. The "grapevine" makes its appearance. Rumor tends to develop in an organization in proportion to the importance and ambiguity of its subject matter in the lives of the individual members of the group. While some rumors start as idle gossip or surface social communication, most rumors circulate because they provide an explanation for individuals and groups and provide a release for the emotional tensions felt by individuals. As rumors spread they tend to become shorter and more concise. Each individual involved in communicating a rumor injects into the rumor such falsification and distortion as is consistent with his or her feelings, thoughts, perceptions, and actions. Rumors can be stopped by clear, concise, complete communication through the formal communication channels.

Each supervisor must establish a program of communication. For the downward flow of information, the supervisor might use memos, letters, bulletin boards, staff newspapers, published reports such as annual reports, or employee handbooks and policy manuals. For the upward flow of information the supervisor might encourage suggestion systems, group discussions (listening carefully to grievances and the grapevine), face-to-face meetings with employees at different levels of the organization, and attitude surveys. Regardless of the methods selected, the message carried in communication must always be as clear and precise as possible and there should be provision for feedback.

THE SUPERVISOR AND EMPLOYEE TRAINING

Almost all practicing librarians have some assigned responsibilities that involve the training of other employees. The trainee may be a shelver or beginning clerical employee, or another professional. Regardless of the level, training must be accomplished. As a professional librarian assumes a greater role as manager, training will be one of his or her major responsibilities.

The concept of training can be limited to instructing an individual in specific steps that are essential for achieving a coordinated, uniform product. Or training can be on as broad a spectrum as a presentation of the philosophies and techniques essential to make a community analysis. Here, the term training is intended to cover the total gamut of instructing individuals, not only in how to do a job but also in why an assigned job is important. An employee performing a task without understanding why it is important and how it fits into the total endeavor of the institution probably will perform perfunctorily at best. If the employee understands and appreciates why a job is assigned, the task will probably be performed more efficiently.

In a library, as in any institution, there are many levels of training. Some training everyone receives; other parts of the training program are more individualized. The importance of training is based on the assumption that the informed employee is a good employee. With that assumption in mind the following training programs are suggested. Some libraries will be able to utilize all suggested activities, while others will use only a few because training is expensive in time. But over a period of time, the cost to the institution is returned in quality performance.

General Orientation

Soon after an employee has been hired, a general orientation meeting is held. This general orientation for all employees, regardless of level or place of employment within the institution, is designed to provide general information that all must have. Perhaps some of the information has been transmitted during the employment process. But it is wise to reinforce that knowledge. A general orientation can be planned so that two basic areas are covered—general information and the goals, objectives, and philosophies of the organization.

This part of the orientation covers rules and policies applicable to all employees, including information concerning pay periods, how vacation and sick leave are accumulated and how they can be used, requirements for reporting illness, and the use of time clocks. Many libraries have specific ways of answering telephone calls, such as requiring that the name of the library (or department) and the individual's name be given. The reason for this requirement should be explained. Many libraries require employees to wear name tags. Again, the reason for this is given. The overall policies and rules that affect all employees are interpreted—not in a manner of constraint but rather in a style that will make the new employee feel a part of the organization and sympathetic with general requirements.

Each employee, regardless of level or place of employment in the institution, needs to know the overall goals, objectives, and basic service philosophies of the organization. These are carefully and thoroughly presented by a major manager of the organization. If possible, the chief manager should make this presentation—not only because he or she best knows the philosophies, and goals and objectives of the institution, but also because the new employee is psychologically impressed and more readily accepts such information when it comes from the chief administrator.

Specific Job Training

As soon as the new employee reports for work, the immediate supervisor begins training on the specific tasks of the job. Sometimes this training is given by the person leaving the job. This practice of having the former incumbent of the job train the new employee is risky, particularly if that departing employee has in any way been a problem. Having the departing employee do the training perpetuates his or her work habits and patterns. It also frequently establishes attitudes and opinions toward the supervisor, the department, and the organization. For these reasons it is recommended that the immediate supervisor accomplish the training of new employees.

There are many ways of training. The worst way is to describe verbally in a few minutes the tasks to be performed. The new employee, already flustered by being in a new environment with new responsibilities, probably will hear little of the supervisor's remarks. Some employees are able to observe other employees, to figure out the job from the job description, and to learn the job on their own in spite of the supervisor. Others fail, and such failure is the fault of the supervisor. If the employee has not learned, to paraphrase an old saying, the supervisor has not taught.

Any training given an employee must be carefully planned. The following six basic principles guide a good trainer:

1) The simple tasks must be taught first.

2) The task must be broken down into its basic components.

3) Only the correct procedures should be taught.

4) Teaching cycles should be short and should be reinforced by practice.

5) Skills should be developed through repetition.

6) The trainee should be motivated.

During World War II the War Manpower Commission developed a widely used system of job training called Job Instruction Training (JIT). While it sounds as if it is limited to routine or clerical tasks, the principles of JIT can be successfully applied to any form of training. The JIT consists of four basic steps, which are carried out by the trainer after careful preparation. This information is taken from the Commission's *Training within Industry Report.*[31]

First, here's what *you must* do to *get ready* to teach a job:

1. Decide what the learner must be taught in order to do the job efficiently, safely, economically and intelligently.

2. Have the right tools, equipment, supplies and material ready.

3. Have the work place properly arranged, just as the worker will be expected to keep it. Then you should *instruct* the learner by the following *four basic steps*:

STEP I—PREPARATION (of the learner)

1. Put the learner at *ease*.

2. Find out what he already knows about the job.

3. Get him interested and desirous of learning the job.

STEP II—PRESENTATION (of the operations and knowledge)

1. *Tell, Show, Illustrate,* and *Question* in order to put over the new knowledge and operations.

2. Instruct slowly, clearly, completely and patiently, one point at a time.

3. Check, question and repeat.

4. Make sure the learner really knows.

STEP III—PERFORMANCE TRY-OUT

1. Test learner by having him perform the job.

2. Ask questions beginning with *why, how, when* or *where*.

3. Observe performance, correct errors, and repeat instructions if necessary.

4. Continue until you *know he knows*.

STEP IV—FOLLOW-UP

1. Put him "on his own."

2. Check frequently to be sure he follows instructions.

3. Taper off extra supervision and close follow-up until he is qualified to work with normal supervision.

REMEMBER—If the learner hasn't learned, the teacher hasn't taught.

Continuing Institutional Training

Periodically, following the initial orientation meetings described above, the institution provides continuing training programs for new employees and for selected groups of employees. The new employees need more orientation to the institution than just the general orientation. They need to have an understanding of the responsibilities of the various organizational units of the library. Such units as the personnel office, the public information office, and the various subject or functional departments are described so that the employees see their roles in the total organization. These training sessions are usually conducted by the manager of the unit being discussed. The techniques of using visual presentations and of permitting extensive discussion and questioning will make such sessions productive.

On a recurring basis, as specific training needs are identified, selected groups of employees are called together. These groups frequently consist of department managers and sub-managers. Training might cover such topics as how to prepare performance evaluation reports, how to conduct good performance evaluation interviews, how to prepare departmental budget recommendations, or how to do task analysis for job description revision. These training sessions concerning all units of the organization may be conducted by a specialist from within the institution or by an authority brought into the institution for this specific program.

All of the training programs described above are developed and presented by the institution. Many training and educational programs outside the institution must be available to employees. Attendance at local, regional, and national conferences and workshops provides opportunities for employee development and growth. But at the present time, when the role and responsibility of libraries of all types is changing, more structured forms of training or educational experiences must be made available. Many institutions provide tuition funds for employees who take formal courses that are job related. The necessity for an employee to do study beyond the first professional degree is increasing constantly as library operations become more complex.

Every library, regardless of size or type, needs a planned, continuing training program. Such activities are not haphazardly scheduled but are organized on a structured continuum. Such programs provide the means by which employees can grow on the job and be ready to advance as local opportunities become available. Through such programs employers are able to identify employees who are potential supervisors and to prepare them for such responsibility.

NOTES

[1]Claude S. George, Jr., *The History of Management Thought* (Englewood Cliffs, NJ: Prentice-Hall, 1968), p. 6.

[2]George, *History of Management*, p. 13.

[3]Saul W. Gellerman, *The Management of Human Relations* (New York: Holt, Rinehart and Winston, 1966), p. 27.

[4]Gellerman, *Management of Human Relations*, p. 28.

[5]Gellerman, *Management of Human Relations*, p. 32.

[6]Gellerman, *Management of Human Relations*, p. 34.

[7]Rensis Likert, *New Patterns of Management* (New York: McGraw-Hill, 1966).

[8]Gellerman, *Management of Human Relations*, p. 39.

[9]Abraham H. Maslow, *Motivation and Personality*, 2nd ed. (New York: Harper and Row, 1970), pp. 35ff.

[10]Douglas McGregor, *The Human Side of Enterprise* (New York: McGraw-Hill, 1960), chapters 3 and 4.

[11]Douglas McGregor, *Leadership and Motivation* (Cambridge, MA: M.I.T. Press, 1966), pp. 5-6.

[12]McGregor, *Leadership*, p. 15.

[13]Edgar H. Schein, *Organizational Psychology* (Englewood Cliffs, NJ: Prentice-Hall, 1965), pp. 49-63.

[14]Harold Koontz and Cyril O'Donnell, *Principles of Management*, 4th ed. (New York: McGraw-Hill, 1968), pp. 544-45.

[15]Michael Maccoby, *The Gamesman* (New York: Simon and Schuster, 1976).

[16]Robert R. Blake and Jane Srygley Mouton, *The Managerial Grid* (Houston, TX: Gulf Publishing Co., 1964).

[17]Blake and Mouton, *Managerial Grid*, p. 9.

[18]Blake and Mouton, *Managerial Grid*, pp. 9-11.

[19]Likert, *New Patterns*, chapter 8.

[20]Likert, *New Patterns*, p. 105.

[21]Saul W. Gellerman, *Management by Motivation* (Chicago: American Management Association, 1968).

[22]George S. Odiorne, *Personnel Administration by Objectives* (Homewood, IL: Richard D. Irwin, 1971).

[23]Frederick Herzberg, Bernard Mausner, and Barbara Bloch Snyderman, *The Motivation to Work* (New York: Wiley, 1959), p. 60.

[24]L. F. Carter, "On Defining Leadership," in C. G. Browne and T. S. Cohn, eds., *The Study of Leadership* (Danville, IL: Interstate Printers and Publishers, 1955).

[25]P. Selznick, *Leadership in Administration* (New York: Harper and Row, 1957), p. 63.

[26]Peter Drucker, *The Effective Executive* (New York: Harper and Row, 1967), chapter 1.

[27]C. I. Bernard, *The Functions of the Executive* (Cambridge, MA: Harvard University Press, 1938).

[28]Claude E. Shannon and Warren Weaver, *The Mathematical Theory of Communication* (Urbana, IL: University of Illinois Press, 1949).

[29]William B. Wolf, *The Management of Personnel* (Belmont, CA: Wadsworth Publishing Co., 1961).

[30]Jurgen Ruesch and Weldon Kees, *Non-Verbal Communication* (Berkeley, CA: University of California Press, 1956), p. 189.

[31]War Manpower Commission, *The Training within Industry Report* (Washington, DC: Bureau of Training, Training within Industry Service, War Manpower Commission, 1945), p. 195.

6

PRINCIPLES OF CONTROL

Some distinction must be made first between control and controls. The two are very much interrelated, effective control within an organization being dependent upon the types of controls that have been established. Control as a function is greatly emphasized in many organizations and by some schools of thought. Organizations that emphasize control view the manager as being ultimately responsible for the results of the organization, therefore the manager has to control carefully everything and everyone within the organization.The synonym of control, then, is direction, while a definition of "controls" might be measurement to provide information. The former, according to Drucker, pertains to an end while the latter is the means; the first is concerned with events and the other with facts; one is analytical and operational, concerned with what was and is, while the other deals with expectations.[1]

The concept of control is most evident in all types of libraries through their overall governing authorities. In academic libraries this direction is exercised through such regulatory groups as trustees and the chancellor or president and, to a lesser extent, by the faculty, through a faculty library committee, and the student, through a student library committee. The library is legally bound by the constitutional provisions, charters, articles of incorporation, and general or special laws applicable to the institution as a whole. In special or industrial libraries this function is exercised through one of the divisions of the organization—usually the research division, the sales division, or the manufacturing division. The controlling body is the corporate or company board of directors. Public libraries and school libraries are controlled by their city manager or superintendent, and the city council or school committee. These are all controlling agents for the library because of their total institutional charge and because of their funding responsibilities. Internal control of the library organization rests with the management—both the administration and the line supervisors within the library. Besides those bodies directly related to the controlling function within the organization, numerous outside groups are involved in such aspects as standards, certification, and accreditation of libraries and librarians. For example, the higher education accrediting bodies such as the North Central Association of College and Secondary Schools have an influence on the libraries of institutions they accredit; the American Library Association has influence both through the establishment of standards for different types of libraries and library services and through its Committee on Accreditation, which is responsible for setting standards for library education; state departments of education establish guidelines for the certification of school librarians or media specialists; and specialized interest groups, such as the Medical Library Association, set certification standards for their members.

Other laws include local, state, and national ones that regulate such aspects as planning, constructing, and maintaining library buildings through municipal ordinances and regulations, building codes, zoning, and fire regulations. Broader legislation includes, for instance, copyright and federal funding legislation, which places certain control on the operation of the library. These groups exist primarily to regulate the activities of the library and to measure, to one extent or another, the actions and output of the organization.

Other bodies that exert some external control on libraries include unions and political bodies. Through collective bargaining, unions can regulate hiring, salaries, working conditions, fringe benefits, etc., and political bodies can influence the appointments of individuals or the disbursal of funds within the library. Extreme pressures are often placed on libraries by outside bodies, both in the hiring of new staff and in issues relating to collection development, censorship and intellectual freedom, and library services and facilities. The "Friends of the Library" group is a good example of an organization that may expect to have some say in the directions the library will take in return for their charitable contributions.

REQUIREMENTS FOR ADEQUATE CONTROL

Controls are concerned with locating operational weakness and taking corrective action. Control implies the existence of goals and plans and the regulation of the organizations activities toward those predetermined goals; in fact, no organization can be effectively controlled without that element. The most effective control prevents deviations from those plans by anticipating that such deviations will occur unless immediate action is taken. However, other types of control are also necessary for the feedback process, and they naturally emanate from the planning process. Controls are important in any organization, but they are particularly important in a large organization to provide managers with facts in a comprehensible form and at the time when they are required. The term "controls," unfortunately, is often interpreted as restrictions or restraints to be forced on the system; in the strictly theoretical sense, however, they are guides for the organization and they indicate how effectively the organization is progressing toward meeting its established goals. At the heart of control is accountability, the obligation of reporting to a higher authority on the exercise of responsibility and authority in the organization. In these days of accountability library and information service managers are certainly expected to evaluate their institution's performance to make sure that the human and material resources are both effectively and efficiently employed toward achieving the goals of the institution.

Fayol's definition is still useful:

> The control of an undertaking consists of seeing that everything is being carried out in accordance with the plan which has been adopted, the orders which have been given, and the principles which have been laid down. Its object is to point out mistakes in order that they may be rectified and prevented from occurring again.[2]

To be effective, controls must be objective and must reflect the job they are to perform. The library should strive for control techniques that forecast deviations early enough so that corrections can be made before the problem occurs; at the least, the controls should point up exceptions at critical points. In addition, any controls system that does not pose corrective actions after deviations occur is little more than an interesting exercise. Controls, wherever they are found and whatever they control, involve three basic steps: establishing standards, measuring performance against standards, and correcting deviations.

Establishing Standards

Standards fall into two basic classes—those relating to material (including quality, quantity, cost, and time) and those relating to moral aspects (including ethical criteria that may be used to establish some sort of code of ethics). Standards are established criteria against which actual results can be measured. They may be physical and represent quantities of products, units of service, man-hours, etc., which can be evidenced through time and motion studies of library operations; they may be stated in monetary terms such as costs, revenues or investments, etc., which are evidenced through record keeping and budget preparation; or they may be expressed in any other terms that measure performance, such as performance rating systems. General standards, such as those proposed by the American Library Association, are important as guides but they do not provide meaningful evaluation for the individual library for a number of reasons. Hamburg points out this weakness:

1. Most of the standards are descriptive in nature ...
2. Most of the standards that prescribe quantitative objectives are arbitrarily formulated ...
3. The emphasis of the standards is directed toward evaluating the input resources of the library ...
4. The standards discourage experimentation with different programs and different allocations of input resources....[3]

Some standards are nebulous and almost impossible to measure, such as the loyalty of an employee to the library's objectives. If the scientific method is to be used, then standards must be measurable. In any case, to be effective standards should be acceptable to those whose performance is being regulated. The process should be explained and agreed upon rather than forced. If standards are forced some resistance will surely occur.

Measurement of Performance against Standards

There are many activities for which it is extremely difficult to develop sound standards and there are many that are hard to measure. Others—for instance, the number of titles cataloged in a month, or the number of volumes circulated—are easy to measure. What is important here is to keep accurate records of what is done. If records are not kept, if the output cannot be measured objectively, then it is difficult to assess the amount that the actual performance deviates from the planned performance. This feedback is an important factor in the controlling process. Controls which have been used in libraries to measure performance include: personal observation, statistical data, oral reports, and written reports. Personnel evaluation has been discussed at some length elsewhere in this volume. (*See* pages 97-106.)

There are two basic types of control—preventative and feedback. "Preventative control processes, as the name implies, attempt to prevent deviations from developing in the conduct of organizational behavior. Feedback control processes rely on information from actual performance and are designed to correct deviations after they have developed."[4] This process takes information about past performance and introduces it into decisions about adjustments that are needed for future actions. Such a process is just as important to an ordinary control process as it is to a more complex but automated one.

A simplified example of detecting deviations in libraries might be a monthly budget balance sheet that shows that in the month of July three-fourths of the amount budgeted for telephone for the year has already been expended and that unless corrective action is taken the library will go over the budgeted amount in that category. A decision must then be made on how to correct this.

Cybernetics, which has become increasingly important in the control feedback process, studies the interaction of communication and control as fundamental factors in all human activity and is now being applied to many large organizations including libraries. Cybernetics is basically a self-regulating method by which messages that the system sends to itself indicate deviations from the desired course. This may be expressed in a very simplified diagram (Figure 6-1), which shows how the information flow makes possible the self-regulation of the system.

Figure 6-1
Simplified Feedback Process

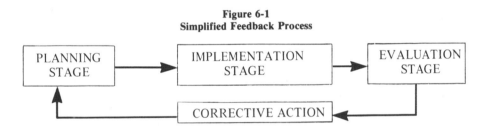

Communication is the most important aspect because it involves transmitting and receiving messages or information—in this case, data used to make the decisions that control the system's behavior. Again, a simplified diagram (Figure 6-2) illustrates the process.

Figure 6-2
Communications Process in a Feedback System

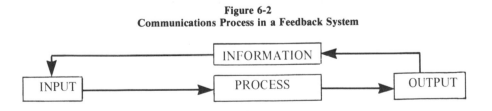

Correction of Deviation

Once standards have been agreed upon, some sort of analysis must be performed to measure the activity against the standard. Techniques, such as cost benefit analysis and time and motion studies, are often employed to measure against the standards of performance for operations. Such performance appraisal assures the organization that the individual is meeting the standard set and also reassures the individual that the contribution being made is significant. There has been some criticism of introducing techniques which may have strong control on personnel because it is maintained that although they may have short term benefits for the organization, such as higher output and economies, they may, in fact, be detrimental to the health of the organization because of deterioration of attitudes, motivation, and communication. Therefore, any such introduction must be done delicately and with full understanding of all involved. The next step is to correct any deviations from the norm which might be occurring. This correction can be achieved by exercising organizational prerogative in, for instance, the case of personnel, by reassignment or clarification of duties, by additional staffing, by better selection and training of staff, or by some other method of restaffing.

TECHNIQUES OF CONTROL

When one thinks of internal controls, mechanical controls come to mind first, including circulation control, automated acquisitions, etc. These technological controls are only one example of tools that are being used to measure library operations. The computer has become an invaluable aid to decision making, particularly for larger library organizations. It has been used effectively, although in a limited number of situations, in establishing models for library operations through decision theory, game theory, graph theory, queuing theory, and simulation exercises. Many more basic techniques and tools are being employed in the control process in the library, particularly as libraries become more "accountable" for their operations. These include such varying operations as cost benefit analysis, operational research, and budgeting. One might say that four aspects that can be controlled, to one extent or another, are time, cost, quality and quantity. Since some of these are rather sophisticated techniques, often applicable only to large library systems, they will be only briefly mentioned here.

Cost Benefit Analysis

The technique of cost benefit is simply one of choosing from alternatives when measurement in dollars or other specific measures may not be possible. Even in those cases, however, some measures can and should be established. For instance, if the objective is the improvement of referral service at the information desk, effectiveness can be measured by the number of personal and telephone inquiries answered or unanswered and the judgment of staff as to patrons' satisfaction with services offered. The emphasis of cost effectiveness is on output; each alternative is weighed in terms of effectiveness or costs against the objective that has been set. In some cases, cost models can be developed to show cost estimates for each alternative, or effectiveness models can be developed to show relationships between the alternatives and their effectiveness. Cost benefit analysis is often confused with cost-effectiveness but, as Lancaster[5] points out there is a subtle difference. One is concerned with the cost, the other with the value. One says "Which way is the best (least expensive) way of performing an operation?"; the other "This is what the service costs, is it worth it?"

Time and Motion Study

Motion study enables a library system to record in flow chart form the present method of doing something, to analyze its effectiveness, and then from this analysis to improve the method. The new method can then be timed to report the performance standard. Time studies complement motion studies in determining performance standards. The third element in this quantifying process is that of cost—that is, attaching a dollar figure to the activities of an individual. Both time and cost vary with the level of the individual performing the task and the institution in which the work is taking place. Many time and motion studies have been done in libraries, particularly relating to routine tasks such as pasting pockets in books, typing subject headings on pre-printed cards, preparing items for the bindery, etc.

Operations Research

Two terms which are closely related, and are often used interchangeably, are "operations research" and "systems analysis." Actually the latter emerges from the former. Operations research (OR) today is largely identified with specific techniques, such as linear programming, Monte Carlo (randomizing) methods, gaming and game theory, etc. It grew out of the military needs of World War II and occupies the interest of a number of different groups, particularly statisticians and mathematicians.

> The operations researchers soon joined forces with the mathematical economists who had come into the same area—to the mutual benefit of both groups.... No meaningful line can be drawn any more to demarcate operations research from scientific management or scientific management from management science.[6]

A working definition of operations research is that it is an "experimental and applied science devoted to observing, understanding and predicting the behavior of purposeful man-machine systems, and operations researchers are actively engaged in applying this knowledge to practical problems."[7] This definition can be further refined as: "the use of scientific methods to study the functions of an organization so as to develop better methods of planning and controlling changes in the organization. It can be viewed as a branch of management, engineering or science. As part of the field of management, its purpose is to assist decision makers in choosing preferred future courses of action by systematically identifying and examining the alternatives which are available to the manager, and by predicting the possible outcomes for such actions."[8]

During the late 1960s and early 1970s, applied operational research came into its own in the library decision-making process. This is primarily because in recent years decision making in general has emphasized the mathematical and statistical approach rather than an approach based on matter of judgment. This has been made possible primarily by technological development and the application of scientific methods, the major impact coming with the development of the computer, which is necessary for the manipulation of complex data. Conceptual "MODELS" for decision making are simply attempts to simulate reality. These are powerful means of testing various alternatives without changing the commitments involved in a typical decision. The primary approach of operations research consists of a broad view of the problem by the whole organization; this is succeeded by a team approach, using personnel with different backgrounds from different departments, with the team addressing the economic-technical aspects of the total system. The key components to the process, then, are application of the scientific method, using a systems approach to problem solving, and employing mathematical, probability, and statistical techniques and model building through the use of electronic computers.

As this technique relates to control, its major contribution has been in constructing models that can be used in the decision-making process. To accomplish this, a basic knowledge of systems analysis is necessary. Again, the important first step, as in most techniques, is to identify objectives and then to look at variables that might influence the objectives. These are then expressed mathematically to determine the best alternative in terms of the objectives set. The system currently in use is described. Based upon this analysis, a series of mathematical models are developed to describe the interrelationship within the organization. Data are then collected to measure the system or, if data are not available, assumptions or speculations are made. This information provides the basis for a working model for a new system. With this information in hand, the librarian is then able to make decisions based on the alternatives presented. The analytical statistical technique and the techniques of probability theory are employed. It has been pointed out that the utilization of OR in libraries is based on the application of the scientific approach to practical problems: "It normally operates in four distinctive stages: 1) Description of the system being considered, especially by means of mathematical models and computer simulations; 2) Measurement, using objective data wherever these can be obtained; 3) Evaluation, the presentation of relevant information to the system manager (here the librarian) to aid in making decisions between different courses of action; 4) Operational control, assisting the development of ways and means of achieving the objectives aimed for over a period of time."[9]

As Chen points out, "the greatest potential of the techniques of operations research lies in predicting the future by employing the mathematical models developed rather than in knowing the present by analyzing the past experimental data."[10] Because of the technique's complexity and its use of mathematics and computers, as well as the costs of modeling, most librarians have not yet reached the point of applying operations research to improve managerial control.

There are limits to this approach. The quantitative method can be no better than the assumptions and estimates used in reaching the solution. Its greatest limitation to use in libraries is that the quantitative analysis is not adaptable to all situations, some variables in libraries being very difficult to quantify, yet to be properly used all variables must be assigned quantitative weights either through amassed data or through estimates. Therefore, a great deal of judgment is required, first of all to know when to use it, and then to know how to estimate costs. This process can become very elaborate and costly. One criticism of the technique is that it does not emphasize human factors enough, since such factors are difficult to model mathematically. Also, this method demands some knowledge of mathematics and statistical concepts, and these are areas where librarians in general are at their weakest. We have relied heavily on non-librarians to provide this expertise. Finally, it should be remembered that use of quantitative tools concerns only one phase of the decision-making process. It is a kind of "management information" that is seldom used to identify the problem or develop alternatives.

One technique used by operations researchers is linear programming, though certain conditions must exist to make its use effective: "1) Goals must be stated in mathematical terms; 2) Alternatives must be available and stated; 3) Resources are usually limited; 4) Variables must be interrelated."[11] Sometimes the cost of such an approach outweighs the benefits, because it is often difficult if not impossible to quantify data. "Linear programming is concerned with optimizing a decision problem by analyzing interrelationships of system components and contributions of these components to the objective function."[12]

Other techniques are the Queuing Theory, or waiting-line theory (which could be applied in studying peak periods at circulation desks); the Monte Carlo technique, which is used to simulate an environment and then determine the results that certain decisions would provide within that environment; and the Decision Tree, which is part of the Decision Theory approach. Those interested in these and other techniques are encouraged to consult basic texts on those tools.

PERT

One other technique of control in the planning process, which is highly applicable to library operations, is that of PERT (Program Evaluation and Review Technique), developed by the U.S. Navy's Special Projects Office to plan the Polaris Weapon System. This system for planning and scheduling work, sometimes called Critical Path Method (CPM), involves: 1) identifying all of the key activities in a particular project; 2) devising the sequence of activities and arranging them in a flow diagram; and finally 3) assigning durations of time for the performance of each phase of the work to be done. This technique consists of enumerating events whose completion can be measured. "Most likely" times are then calculated for the accomplishment of each event, so that one can see how long it would take for the progression of events to be completed. This model-building network approach is most effectively used for major projects that are one-time *events*. An example would be the opening of a new branch library. Activities can be plotted to allow the librarian to determine the most expeditious route — or critical path — that can be taken to finish the event. Just as with other techniques already discussed, in PERT one must be able to state objectives, then activities must be enumerated and estimates must be given for the time required for each of these *activities*. An abbreviated two-path diagram serves to illustrate the concept (Figure 6-3).

Figure 6-3
Simplified Two-Path PERT Diagram

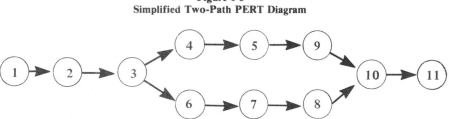

This would suggest that there are two paths to be taken—say, from the time the idea of a branch library is formulated until the building is ready for occupancy (○ represents events and➤represents activities). Times would be assigned for each activity (say, three weeks between events 4 and 5, while time between 6 and 7 may be one week). This suggests to the librarian that either path 1, 2, 3, 4, 5, 9, 10, 11 or path 1, 2, 3, 6, 7, 8, 10, 11 can be taken. If time is of the essence, the shorter route might be more desirable. At any rate, this technique allows one to analyze a project in depth before it is initiated. This not only gives the decision maker an idea of the time frame involved but also aids in identifying potential weaknesses.

The biggest disadvantage of PERT is its overemphasis on time and almost complete lack of attention to cost. This disadvantage has led to the development of PERT/COST, which introduces the *cost* factor into the process. When the system to be studied is complex and when a number of events are involved, it becomes very expensive to establish a cost for each event. PERT is used mainly in industry, but some library systems have begun to explore its value in their planning process, particularly if that operation is a complex and lengthy one.

This brief discussion in no way presents the importance or potential for these controls, and does not even begin to present all of the variations that those systems have produced. However, since volumes have been written on each of the topics, it would be almost impossible to cover their potential adequately in this volume. Readers interested in these subjects should consult those headings in the library literature for a fuller discussion. As mentioned earlier in this chapter, the computer is having great influence on the management of library operation. The effects of electronic data processing on circulation control, acquisitions of library materials, serials control, etc., are significant. In addition, computerized services such as online cataloging through OCLC, RLIN and other networks, and access to bibliographic data bases enable libraries to measure more adequately service output and costs.

BUDGETARY CONTROL

The budget is perhaps the best and most important control device in existence to measure programs and their effectiveness within the library. It is simply a stated program that reflects the goals and objectives of the library and defines the manager's authority to act. Funds for the organization's operation, depending on the type of library or information system, come from local, state, regional, or national sources, from foundation support or endowments, from tuition or gifts, or from a number of other sources. These funds may come to the library directly or to the parent organization, which then designates them for library use. Determination of that amount is usually based on expressed needs, which are justified by services offered or projected or, to a lesser extent, on standards that have been established for particular types of libraries—particularly ALA standards for public, school, junior college, college, and now university libraries. (These needs are often defined by the types of forms reproduced in Appendix 6.)

One good definition of budgetary control is that used by the International Management Institute, which defines it as a method of rationalization whereby estimates covering different periods of time are, by the study of statistical records and analytical research of all kinds, established for all and everything that affects the life of a business concern and that can be expressed in figures.

Budgeting in libraries, which is usually on a yearly cycle, is the primary means by which formulated plans can be carried out. More and more, as there is greater financial constraint, librarians find themselves spending greater amounts of time in budgeting review, analysis, and presentation. Many types of budgets are not really applicable to libraries, since libraries are not primarily profit-making institutions. However, several different types of approaches to budgeting are being used in libraries, and these will be discussed below.

One great danger in budgeting is the problem of disguised needs. Libraries are often accused of asking for much more than they actually need; indeed, they often do tend to base current budget justifications on past budgets. In other words, if a library spent a certain amount last year for equipment, that amount becomes this year's floor from which to work, even though the same kind and extent of equipment may not be needed this year. This kind of thinking often leads to automatic reductions in library budgets by those who hold the purse strings, whether they are city managers, college presidents, or school superintendents.

The budgeting process is often a time-delay process and is usually prepared one year — or in some cases two or three years — in advance. In those instances, it is extremely difficult to project what the needs will be three years from now, even if one has done some long-range planning. In most cases, a library must follow the budget system and budgeting cycle that has been adapted by the larger system, whether that is the university, college, city government, school district, or corporation. Usually, guidelines for the preparation of the budget come from the school committee, the state or local funding agency, or from the college or university administration or the corporation's fiscal officer.

The types of budgets discussed here are presented as unique; most often, however, a combination of budgeting systems is used. Although many libraries now have a separate staff concerned primarily with budgets and the accounting process, most libraries involve a number of employees in the budget-planning process. Budget requests for programs or units are frequently estimated by the supervisors most familiar with that aspect of the operation. A coordinating agent — either the director, his or her representative, or a committee — is responsible for pulling these budget requests into a total budget and presenting it to the funding authority so that they can understand and, it is hoped, support the budget. Timetables for budget preparation and presentation are essential so that wide impact can be gained.

The budgetary aspect of control becomes even more important as costs rise. With rising costs, librarians are forced to prepare comprehensive reports on the financial status so that effective allocation can be made, as well as accurate projections for future funding. This is the beginning of the formal process that is later magnified to the level of the whole town, district, university, or company. Most often, the librarian is required to make a formal budget presentation, which is then substantiated by back up documentation with things like an index of inflation for library materials, trends in higher education which effect libraries (continuing education students, specializations), etc.

Libraries are finding themselves forced to seek alternative routes for funding. These include federal and state funding, as well as private foundation and individual citizen funding. A new political role, with extensive public relations requirements, is being forced on libraries. See Appendix 6 for examples of budget forms, scheduling forms, justifications, etc. used in different types of institutions.

BUDGETING TECHNIQUES FOR LIBRARIES

Library budgeting techniques fall into several groups. These include both the traditional approaches used by many organizations and the more innovative techniques that have only recently found their ways into libraries. As these newer techniques are considered, it must be kept in mind that it is always costly to switch from one system to another. Therefore, the advantages of a different system must be clear before one decides to switch from the old system.

Line-Item

Probably the most common type of budget is that approach which divides expenditures into broad categories, such as salaries and wages, materials and supplies, equipment, capital expenditures, and miscellaneous, with further subdivisions within these categories. Its primary disadvantage is that items within these categories can be designated to such a degree that it becomes difficult, if not impossible, to shift them; thus, this system can be inflexible to innovation. For example, within the broad category of "materials and supplies" it may become desirable to add subscription money for new periodicals after the budget has been set. One might wish to accomplish this by transferring money from equipment, since it has now been determined that one can do without an additional typewriter. This kind of transfer is usually frowned upon by budgeting authorities, however; if it is not completely discouraged, it is often made very difficult to accomplish because of the paper work and red tape involved. It is also sometimes called "incremental budgeting" since the object is usually to "add on" to existing figures and to assume that all currently existing programs are good and necessary.

There are several advantages to the line-item approach. For one thing, line-item budgets are easy to prepare. Most are done by projecting current expenditures to next year, taking cost increases into account. This type of budget is also easy to understand and to justify, since it can be shown that the allocated funds were spent in the areas for which they were budgeted. A request to open a new position or to increase the supplies budget by 10% because that is the average amount that postage, telephone charges, etc., went up last year, can be understood by the funding authority. The greatest disadvantage to the line-item approach is that there is almost no relationship at all between the request and the objectives of the organization. Using the line-item approach simply projects the past and present into the future. An example of a line-item budget is given in Figure 6-4.

Lump Sum

A commonly used and much more primitive variation on the traditional approach is the lump sum approach. In this form of budgeting, a certain dollar amount is allocated to the library, and it becomes the responsibility of the library to decide how that sum is broken into categories that can be identified. These categories are usually the same ones mentioned under line-item budgeting: salaries and wages, materials and supplies, equipment, capital expenditures, and miscellaneous or overhead. This might seem more flexible than line-item budgeting, but it still does not relate the objectives to services. Libraries using this technique are forced to develop programs within the dollar figure allocated, instead of the other way around.

Figure 6-4
Line-Item Budget Summary Sheet

BUDGET REQUEST FORM 1

SUMMARY

Department or Program: Library

Department No.: 02876

For Fiscal Year: 1976-77

Control No.	Expenditures	Actual Prior Year 1974-75	Budget Current Year 1975-76	Budget Request Next Year 1976-77	Budget Approved Next Year 1976-77
100	Salaries	138,000	139,000	150,000	
102	Wages	11,000	11,500	12,000	
103	Staff benefits	20,700	20,850	22,500	
108	Contracted Services	3,500	3,500	4,000	
109	Telephone Services	5,700	5,800	6,000	
111	Office Equipment	1,000	1,300	1,200	
112	Office Supplies	7,800	8,000	8,500	
113	Travel	2,800	2,800	3,000	
114	Instructional Supplies	90,000	93,000	96,000	
	TOTAL	280,500	$285,750	$303,200	

Formula Budgets

Formula budgeting uses some predetermined standards for allocation of monetary resources. Such an approach has been adopted by several large library systems with the thought that once the criteria have been established they can be applied across the board to all units within the library system. Allen surmises that the reason for the popularity of formula — over a Planning Programming Budgetary System — is:

1. Formula is mechanical and easy to prepare.
2. Because of its application to all institutions in the political jurisdiction, there appears to be justification for monies requested.
3. The governing bodies have a sense of equity because each institution in the system is measured against the same criteria.
4. Fewer budgeting and planning skills are required to prepare and administer a formula budget.[13]

These formulae, which are usually expressed in terms of a percentage of the total institutional cost, focus on input rather than activities. For instance, the budget-related standard of the Standards for College Libraries states that "experience has shown that library budgets, exclusive of capital costs and the costs of physical maintenance, which fall below six percent of the college's total educational and general expenditures, are seldom able to sustain the range of library programs required by the institution."[14] Other formulae have applied a fixed dollar figure per full-time equivalent student and faculty, or have attached collection and staff figures to programs offered.

Formula budgeting in libraries probably had its impetus with the Clapp-Jordan formula,[15] which developed a theoretical model for measuring the adequacy of library resources. Other formulae have developed since then — most notably the Michigan system formula,[16] the California University formula,[17] and the Washington State formula.[18] Perhaps the most recent one is that developed by the Standards for College Libraries,[19] which relates to Holdings (Formula A), Staff (Formula B), and Facilities (Formula C). The formulae that have developed vary in their degrees of sophistication. Some functions cannot be related to those formulae and must receive separate justification. Perhaps the biggest fallacy in such an approach is that it assumes a relationship between the quantity being expressed and the quality of service. Several state systems now use or contemplate using some type of formula budget.

Program Budgeting

A relatively new concept in budgeting for libraries is the idea of program budgeting, which is concerned with the organization's activities, not with individual items or expenditures, which were the concern of the approaches discussed above. Such a budget is presented so that the library's activities are emphasized, and dollars can then be assigned to programs or services provided. For example, if a public library system provides bookmobile service for the community, the cost of that service (staffing, materials, overhead, etc.) is calculated. In this way one can see just what the bookmobile service is costing. Based on the total program, one can decide whether to continue, modify, or delete the service. An example of a Program Budget is given in Figure 6-5.

Figure 6-5
Program Budget Sheet

Organization: County Library	

Program: Bookmobile Service	

Objective: This service is offered to county residents who reside more than three miles from a public library. Specific services offered include providing basic reference collection of encyclopedias, dictionaries and handbooks and a rotating collection of circulating materials on a variety of subjects for all levels of readers. Makes two stops per day, covers seven miles, five days per week.

Costs:	**Personnel Service**	
	Librarian	$12,500
	Driver	9,500
	Stock boy (to load, unload truck, 4 hrs. per week @ $3.25 x 52 weeks)	676
	Benefits	4,620
	SUB-TOTAL	$27,296 (1)
	Materials	
	Books (2,000 collection x $12 average + $5.10 processing costs)	34,200
	Periodicals (15 subscriptions @ $12 each)	180
	SUB-TOTAL	$34,380 (2)
	Other	
	Vehicle depreciation	1,200
	Maintenances, gasoline (30 mi. per week x 52 weeks x 20¢ per mile), oil, insurance, etc.	612
	SUB-TOTAL	$ 1,812 (3)
	TOTAL (Sub-totals 1 + 2 + 3)	$63,488

Performance Budgeting

A technique similar to program budgeting is performance budgeting, which bases expenditures on the performance of activities and emphasizes efficiency of operations. This approach requires the careful accumulation of quantitative data, over a period of time. Techniques of cost benefit analysis are required to measure the performance and establish norms. Performance budgeting has been criticized because in it the economy aspect overshadows the service aspect. This approach is sometimes called function budgeting, because costs are presented in terms of work to be accomplished. A good example of this would be processing materials — from submission of an order until the time that the volume is on the shelf and the cards are in the catalog. All activities involved (verifying the author, title, etc.; ordering, receiving, cataloging, and classifying; providing book pockets, call number, and catalog cards; filing cards in the catalog and placing the volume on the shelf) can be analyzed as to average time for the activity and average cost per item. Therefore, careful cost and work measurements can be applied to each activity. Fixed costs of building maintenance, heating, lights, equipment used, etc. — which are variable but are directly related to the work being done — must also be added to the final cost. This approach measures quantity rather than quality of service.

Planning Programming Budgeting System (PPBS)

PPBS is a technique originally developed by Rand Corporation and introduced into the Department of Defense by Robert McNamara in 1961. President Johnson directed all principal government agencies to implement it, and by 1965 it was being used by all of these agencies. Many complex organizations, of which libraries are a part, are now using PPBS or some modified form of it. These include state and local governments, college and university systems, and industry.

PPBS combines the best of both program budgeting and performance budgeting. The emphasis in this approach is on planning. It begins with the establishment of goals and objectives, just as in program budgeting, but the controlling aspect of measurement, which is paramount in performance budgeting, is also part of PPBS. It emphasizes the cost of accomplishing goals (programs) set by the library instead of stressing objects, which the more traditional budgets highlight. This approach forces one to think of the budget as a tool to allocate resources rather than to control operations.

The steps important in PPBS are:

1) Identifying the objectives of the library.
2) Presenting alternative ways to achieve those objectives — with cost benefit ratios presented for each.
3) Identifying the activities that are necessary for each program.
4) Evaluating the result so that corrective actions can be taken.

This is a re-emphasis of the desired steps in the control process already discussed. An example might be given of a particular library's preliminary development of a PPBS approach (see Figure 6-6).

Figure 6-6
Library Service Measurement Framework (LSMF)*

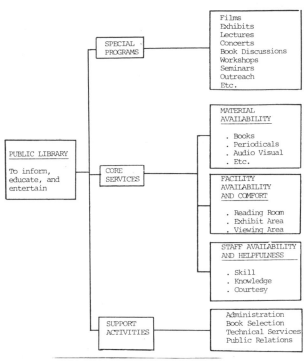

(Model developed by Dr. Robert DeNoble on the basis of
work done at Peat, Marwick, Mitchell & Co., Boston)

*Reproduced with permission.

In essence, this scientific approach to budgeting improves the decision-making process, which calls for systematic analysis of alternative ways of meeting objectives. The crux of the PPBS system is the selection of appropriate criteria for evaluating each alternative against relevant objectives; it combines the functions of planning (identifying objectives), translating that to a program (staff and materials), and finally, stating those requirements in budgetary terms (financing). Headings for a PPBS Summary Sheet are shown in Figure 6-7.

Figure 6-7
PPBS Summary Sheet Headings

County of: Operating Budget: (Year)	PROGRAM SUMMARY
Program: (Title of Program)	
Goal: (Brief operational goal)	
Description: (Brief description of Program)	

Such an approach allows the librarian to enumerate programs and assign costs to those programs. It also allows funding agencies to place programs into perspective and to evaluate the effects of cutting monies from or adding monies to the budget.

A good example of a modified PPBS approach is the Vigo County Public Library (Indiana) summary of activities, which indicates eight program categories (*see* Figure 6-8).

Zero Based Budgeting (ZBB)

One new technique of budgeting, which has been used primarily in industry and government but also in all types of libraries, although in a very limited number of cases, is Zero Based Budgeting. The current national interest began to develop in the early 1970s, starting with the Texas Instruments Company and further popularized by President Carter when he was Governor of Georgia. However, before that time, the U.S. Department of Agriculture used it as early as 1962.

Basically, ZBB is not concerned with what happened previously but rather with what is required in the future. In this approach and in its development ZBB is very similar to PPBS; therefore it requires careful analysis of activities that should take place in the library and further requires justification for each unit of work identified. It forces each unit manager and the unit workers to identify priorities within that unit of the organization. Doing this and by stating it in terms of cost, forces the unit to answer the questions: "Is it really worth it?" and "Are there alternatives to achieving this objective?" ZBB also requires that justification for each program will start from point "zero" in the discussions each year. Of course, once a decision unit has been identified, that particular unit does not need to be reidentified the next year and needs to be further described only if changes occur, although it still must be considered in the list of priorities and costs must be recalculated.

Two important steps can be identified in ZBB:

1) **Identification of "decision packages."** The "package" identified should be the lowest unit for which budget can be prepared. It requires a description of each activity within that management unit. This process requires the identification of goals and objectives, a statement of alternatives, the reason for the activity, consequences of not introducing the package, detailed measurement of performance, and the costs of the activity. Of course, the size and complexity of the organization will determine the number of units identified. A unit may be described along functional lines (i.e., circulation); or by smaller units in larger organizations (i.e., reserve function of circulation); or as a special program of the organization, such as a new building. Care must be exercised so that decision units are large enough to reflect major portions of a person's time; smaller distribution would probably be meaningless since it might eliminate a small fraction of a full-time salary, for instance. Once a decision unit is identified, a series of decision packages are identified, each including goals and objectives, etc. Such a process focuses on the "best way" of doing things, either through cost savings or efficiency of service.

Figure 6-8
Community Use of a Public Library*

Community Use of the Vigo County Public Library for the Six Months' Period January to June 1969

Input Cost	Service Category	Program Objective	Output Totals	Cost per Output
$92,866	SELF SERVICE	Provide facilities, library materials and equipment.	203,587 persons	$ .45
$77,524	LENDING SERVICE	Lend library materials for home and office use.	324,481 items	$ .24
$42,398	INDIVIDUAL SERVICE	Furnish information, reader advisory, and reference assistance.	40,301 persons	$ 1.05
$ 7,878	ALERTING SERVICE	Promote awareness of the library and use of its resources.	908 productions	$ 8.67
$ 5,202	OUTREACH SERVICE	Provide library materials for the physically or environmentally handicapped.	10 stations	$520.20
$14,288	CONTROL SERVICE	Maintain control of materials through registration of patrons and overdue reminders to borrowers.	12,173 persons	$ 1.17
$20,106	GROUP SERVICE	Provide specialized services to groups, agencies, and organizations.	459 groups	$ 43.80
$ 3,720	RESEARCH SERVICE	Perform research service for public officials, ministers, business and industry managers, labor and other civic leaders.	150 researchers	$ 24.80

*Reprinted by permission of the American Library Association from "Toward PPBS in the Public Library," Edward N. Howard, *American Libraries*, April 1971, p. 391, copyrighted © 1971 by the American Library Association.

Of course, once alternatives have been suggested, quantitative measures must be established to monitor output, which is usually expressed in financial terms. Once all the packages have been developed, using the objectives as guides, they are ranked in priority order and are presented for approval or rejection, the decision being based on level and affordability.

2) **Ranking "decision packages."** This setting of priorities within each unit of the organization forces decisions to be made as to the most important activities within that unit of the organization. Priorities of all the units are then amalgamated into one pool and the process is repeated in light of the importance to the total organization. At some point in these priorities there is a cut off level, those falling below it are not funded. Since this reordering at the organization level involves every unit within the organization, clear guidelines for ranking must be established. As Chen points out, the process of priority formulation "assists the manager to delete their support of those functions and activities which have lost their significance through obsolescence, inefficiency, or change of policy and objectives."[20]

It is assumed in the Zero Based Budgeting mode that the sum of those units receiving top priority status is less than the current budgeted amount and that a cut off will occur at some point. This attitude allows for a "reduced level" at which activities can be carried out to meet the essential objectives of the organization. Figures 6-9 and 6-10 illustrate, at a very abbreviated level, the process involved in establishing a decision package statement and then how that package might fit into the priorities of the total organization.

Figure 6-9
Form for Decision Package Statement

Prepared by: Martha Wyatt
Date: 1 / 15 / 1980

Program Name: Children's Division	**Priority Rank:** 1
Department: Public Services Department of Westdale Public Library	**Level** 1 of 3

Statement of Purpose (Goals and Objectives — what is to be accomplished):
Provide library services to children (pre-schoolers to teen-aged years)
Work in conjunction with town's school department to offer comprehensive services to children of the town.

Description of Activity: 1) Direct summer reading program for children of the town; 2) Offer story hour and puppet shows for pre-school through 2nd graders; 3) Select children's materials for the public library collection; 4) Interpret questions of informational, educational, and recreational nature; 5) Coordinate library services for children in the community.

Benefits/Desired Results: Enable children to explore, with guidance, good literature; aid in providing informational services to school children both in their school work and in their quest for knowledge; encourage children to explore areas of interest on their own.

Related Activities: School library service in the elementary schools of the town.

Alternatives/Other Options (to achieve same or partial results):
1) Let schools assume full responsibility
2) Public Services (general) assume responsibility for limited services

Consequences If Activity Is Not Approved/Is Eliminated:
Service to children would be seriously curtailed, thereby abrogating one of the original charges from the town to the library.

Costs/Resources Required	Prior Period	Budgeted Period
Personnel:		
Professional (3/4)	9,500	10,500
Para-professional (1/2)	4,000	4,400
Hourly Wages (9 per week)	1,500	1,600
Secretarial Staff (1/4)	1,800	1,980
Operations:		
Supplies	800	800
Equipment	200	580
Travel	-	-
Contracted Services	-	760
Other	150	180
Total:	$17,950	$20,800

Approved by: Myra James
Title: Director of the Library
Date: 2 / 2 / 1980

Figure 6-10
Ranking System Form

Level of Effort	Rank within System	Package Name	Current Year Commitment	Planned Addition/ Deletion to Current Commitment	Projected Additions to Commitments	Cumulative Expenses
1	1	Administrative Services	$ 20,200	$ 2,600		$ 22,800
1	2	Public Services (general)	23,300	2,350		25,650
1	3	Technical Services	45,750	3,800		49,550
1	4	Children's Division	17,950	2,850		20,800
2	5	Branch Library (North)			$ 13,400	13,400*
2	6	Young Adult Division			9,300	9,300
3	7	Bookmobile Service			26,500	26,500
3	8	Branch Library (East)			13,400	13,400
3	9	Music & Art Division			11,200	11,200
TOTAL			$107,200	$11,600	$ 73,800	$192,600

FISCAL YEAR 1981-82

Organization: __Town of Westdale__
Department: __Westdale Public Library__
Prepared by: __Myra James, Director__
Date: __2 / 10 / 1980__

*Note: Example indicates that, in addition to current unit commitments with increases, the town has agreed to fund second priority level unit which is ranked number 5 in the priorities for the library. This means that the budget for the fiscal year 1981-82 will be $132,200, an increase of 23.32%. (It should be remembered that this example is given to show a priority system and not to indicate "next year" potential funding of all priorities. One can see that the extent of priorities listed in this example and the costs involved are certainly long-ranged. For this reason individual managers would be discouraged from preparing such "ideal" priority lists using the ZBB mode because the time involved in establishing such an extensive list would be prohibitive.)

ACCOUNTING AND REPORTING

The final aspect of budgeting is that of keeping accurate records of what has been disbursed, what has been encumbered, and what remains. This is usually achieved through monthly records prepared by the accounting office — either as a part of the library or as a part of the larger organization, such as the city government. These monthly statements can act as benchmarks to tell the library staff how they are progressing toward the objectives, if they have been stated, or simply to tell the library staff how much remains of the budget figure. This monthly summary statement, or balance sheet, is the procedure used in most organizations. Since accounting is a separate function, many large libraries employ accountants, in "staff" positions, whose primary responsibilities are to report facts as they exist or have existed. That person is not normally responsible for making decisions that affect the operations of the library. However, the accountant is most helpful in collecting relevant cost data for anticipated decisions and in making cost studies that might be keys to decision making.

Along with accounting goes the important element of reporting — reporting to the funding authority, reporting to the staff, and reporting to the community. These reporting procedures can take a variety of forms — formal written reports with detailed statistical documentation, or informal reports (through memos, staff meetings, newspaper articles, etc.). It is at this point that the librarian's public relations responsibility becomes most evident. Only through a conscientious, positive approach of selling the library and its services can the librarian hope to maintain a level of activity and funding; and it is to be hoped that the approach can be so convincing that the support for those activities will even be increased. Public relations for librarians, then, is an art through which information and persuasion solicit public support for the causes that have been set forth in the goals of the library. Public relations is an integral part of the goals and objectives and the budgeting procedures in a library. More specifically, the publicity aspect (to staff, students, faculty, the public at large, and particularly benefactors) must be attractive and to the point. This is the library's primary means of gaining and holding the support necessary to develop programs.

NOTES

[1]Peter F. Drucker, "Controls, Control and Management," in C. P. Bonini, R. K. Jaedicke, and H. M. Wanger, eds., *Managerial Controls: New Directions in Basic Research* (New York: McGraw-Hill, 1964), p. 286.

[2]Henri Fayol, *Industrial and General Administration* (Geneva: International Management Institute, 1929), p. 77.

[3]Morris Hamburg et al., *Library Planning and Decision-Making Systems* (Philadelphia, PA: University of Pennsylvania, 1974), pp. 38-39.

[4]W. Jack Duncan, *Essentials of Management* (Hinsdale, IL: Dryden Press, 1975), p. 408.

[5]F. W. Lancaster, "Operations Research and Systems Analysis," in F. W. Lancaster and C. W. Cleverdon, eds., *Evaluation and Scientific Management of Libraries and Information Centers* (Leyden: Noordhoff, 1977), p. 131.

[6]Herbert A. Simon, *The New Science of Management Decision* (New York: Harper and Row, 1960), p. 15.

[7]"Guidelines for the Practice of Operations Research," *Operations Research* (Sept. 1971): 1138.

[8]Ferdinand F. Leimkuhler, "Operations Research and Systems Analysis," in F. W. Lancaster and C. W. Cleverdon, eds., *Evaluation and Scientific Management of Libraries and Information Centers* (Leyden: Noordhoff, 1977), p. 131.

[9]A. Graham Mackenzie and Michael K. Buckland, "Operations Research," in H. A. Whatley, ed., *British Librarianship and Information Science, 1966-70* (London: The Library Association, 1972), p. 24.

[10]Ching-Chih Chen, *Applications of Operations Research Models to Libraries* (Cambridge, MA: MIT Press, 1976), p. 3.

[11]Richard I. Levin and Charles A. Kirkpatrick, *Quantitative Approaches to Management*, 2nd ed. (New York: McGraw-Hill, 1971), p. 161.

[12]Sang M. Lee and L. J. Moore, *Introduction to Decision Science* (New York: Petrocelli-Charter, 1975), p. 90.

[13]Kenneth R. Allen, *Current and Emerging Budgeting Techniques in Academic Libraries* (Washington, DC: U.S. Department of Health, Education and Welfare, Office of Education, 1972), ED 071-726, p. 18.

[14]"Standards for College Libraries," in *College and Research Library News* 9 (Oct. 1975): 298.

[15]Verner W. Clapp and Robert J. Jordan, "Quantitative Criteria for Adequacy of Academic Library Collections," *College and Research Libraries* 26 (Sept. 1965): 371-80.

[16]Robert E. Burton, "Formula Budgeting: An Example," *Special Libraries* 66 (Feb. 1975): 61-67.

[17]University of California, Office of the Vice President for Finance, *Library Workload Measures* (Berkeley, CA: University of California, 1963), pp. 1-20 (mimeo).

[18]University of Washington, Office of Interinstitutional Business Studies, *Model Budget Analysis System for Program 05 Libraries* (Olympia: University of Washington, 1970), pp. 1-16 (mimeo).

[19]"Standards for College Libraries," pp. 277-79, 290-301.

[20]Ching-Chih Chen, *Zero Based Budgeting in Library Management* (New York: Gaylord Professional Books, 1980), p. 36.

7

CHANGE—ITS IMPACT ON
LIBRARY MANAGEMENT DEVELOPMENT

Many of us have a vague "feeling" that things are moving faster. Doctors and executives alike complain that they cannot keep up with the latest developments in their fields. Hardly a meeting or conference takes place today without some ritualistic oratory about "the challenge of change." Among many there is an uneasy mood—a suspicion that change is out of control.[1]

THE CHANGE PROCESS

Certainly this feeling exists in many libraries and information centers today. The acceleration of change, in technology, in mobility, in urbanization, in international relations, in economics, all have affected libraries. Drucker maintains that major changes that have affected many organizations are those relating to: 1) introduction of new technologies, which will create new industries and render existing industries obsolete; 2) emergence of a world economy that involves a world market or global shopping center; 3) development of a changing political and social matrix involving much disenchantment with our major institutions; and 4) creation of a "knowledge economy" in which about half of our American dollars are spent on procuring ideas and information and in which knowledge has become the central "factor of production."[2] In libraries and information centers one is acutely aware of some "change" forces working, such as cooperation and networking, which were either not desirable or not feasible in the past. Talk of such cooperative efforts as a National Periodical Center, cooperative cataloging via computer networks, inter-library loan via computer networks, and other cooperative efforts have forced libraries to assess new technology as it develops.

Staff participation in the decision-making process, unionization and collective bargaining efforts, and decentralization of library services has also influenced change and has had an impact on how managers spend their time. In addition, only a few short years ago managers in libraries spent little time on external matters, while today a major portion of their time is spent on such external matters as civic organizations, library trustees meetings, collective bargaining sessions, friends of libraries group meetings, and meetings with higher administration and funding agencies or authorities in defense of the budget or other matters. As Beer so aptly put it, "the whole world is by now a richly interactive system."[3]

This interactive system finds organizations that previously had informal group structures now more organized into formal hierarchical structures, bureaucracies as Weber would call them. Libraries have not been immune to this development. Such a structure has a tendency first of all to remove top management from everyday contact with all individuals while at the same time increasing the number of people in the organization who are involved in the management process. This phenomenon in libraries is primarily of World War II origin, the beginning of a milestone for organizational development. In addition to forces already mentioned, the introduction of highly specialized staff has affected the approach to library management. Employees are more sophisticated, more articulate, and less willing to settle for the lower level needs that Maslow so well describes. Although change is sometimes forced upon an organization by outside influences, it most often comes from within as a calculated effort on the part of people working in the organization. For instance, redefinition of work roles among levels of staff working in libraries has been demanded and welcomed, but this has also brought about tension and conflict. In addition to these and other inside pressures, change in libraries has come from a variety of other sources, from pressures of the external environment (patrons and governing authorities), from changes in directions (goals and objectives), from technology, and from modification of the physical plant. All of these have had an impact on libraries and are causing changes in the structure, the individual's attitudes, and the individuals themselves, both as managers and as workers. Negative forces, such as poor management, which can cause organizational decay, have forced change, just as positive forces, such as expansion and growth, have caused change. Many feel that learning to manage change is the prime requirement for any successful library manager. One way change has come about in libraries is through employment of "change agents," either individuals in the organization — self-appointed or management-appointed — or brought in from outside the organization with responsibilities for adapting the organization's structure to a changing environment, control the speed and direction of organization change, and management of conflict. The cycle of change is best illustrated in Figure 7-1.

This internal environment, which fosters change, includes the organizational structure itself, the decision-making process, and the process of communications, all of which are management controlled. In addition, modification of attitudes and/or behavior of individuals, a much more delicate process and one that is not management "controlled," is an important factor in the internal environment.

The external environment also influences the attitudes, habits, and values of those persons working in the organization, as well as the organization itself, on the social, technical and political levels. Library legislation enacted during the New Frontier and Great Society days of the 1960s, for example, had a tremendous impact on the resources and organization of many libraries, on their technological development, and on access to their resources. The question of "fee'" based services versus "free" services in public libraries also is a societal impact question which influences individuals working in libraries as well as the total operation. Therefore, libraries may need to change internally to respond to external pressures.

It is generally recognized that there are several variables that can either change organizations or can be changed themselves, including: 1) direction — the purpose of the library and its responsibility to its larger community; 2) people — the most important resource, including attitudes and motivation; 3) structure — of the whole organization; and 4) technology — with its influence on the operations. All components must be considered as a whole since each one affects and interacts with all of the others. Stated another way, the library is basically an open system which receives input from the outside, transforms that information, and then outputs to the environment, and it has a number of subsystems that respond to this change cycle: 1) Goals and Objectives are determined, to an extent, by that larger system, and if the library is to be successful it must depend on that outside input to be able to produce usable output;

Figure 7-1
Model of Organizational Change and Innovation

(From: *Innovations and Organizations* by G. Zaltman, Duncan and
Holbek, © 1973. Used with the permission of John Wiley & Sons, Inc.)

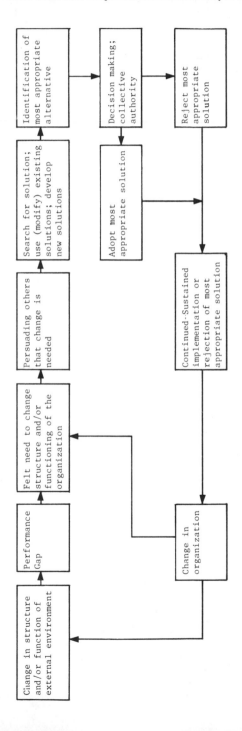

2) the Psychosocial subsystem is formed by individuals and groups each interacting in the system; 3) the Structure determines the way assignments are divided, and they are reflected in such documents as organization charts, policies and procedures manuals, etc.; and 4) the Technical subsystem is shaped by the specialized knowledge and skills required, the types of machinery and equipment involved, etc. Each of these subsystems interact in both informal and formal ways within the system. This interaction is reflected in the total Managerial Subsystem which encompasses parts of the entire organization and which is subject to greatest change. Figure 7-2 illustrates the interrelationships.

Figure 7-2
Organizational System

(From: *Organization and Management* by F. E. Kast and J. E. Rosenzweig,
© 1974. Used with the permission of McGraw Hill Book Company.)

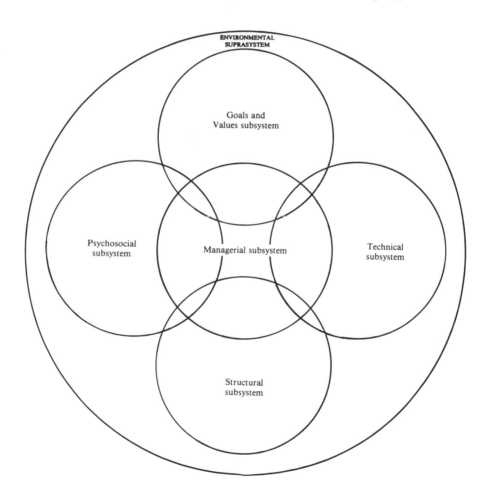

The environment is described by writers on organizational structure as either placid or turbulent.[4] Either state can reflect organizational change, although when it does occur, whether or not the occurance is planned or unpredicted, it is almost always with tension, anxiety, resistance, and conflict. Greiner points out that change is often effected unilaterally by the hierarchy where the "definition and solution to the problem at hand tends to be specified by the upper echelons and directed downward through formal and impersonal control mechanisms."[5] This attitude and approach is one of the major causes of resistance to change. Resistance can occur because:

1) People do not understand or do not want to understand. Also, certain types of people resist change more than others. It has been said that people who have been in an organization longer are more resistant to change because they have more time and money vested in the status quo. People who have less time invested have no strong commitment to the old way and are more adaptable to new situations.

2) People have not been fully informed. Communication is the key, and it is management's responsibility to see that everyone is kept fully informed. Unfortunately, information about change is sometimes restricted, thereby causing resistance. Filley points out that not only will "providing opportunities for individuals to have influence over and participate in the change process" lessen resistance to change, but also providing continuing involvement after the initial change effort "will produce significant increases in motivation, satisfaction, and performance."[6]

3) People's habits and securities are threatened. At least they feel their basic assumptions, personal values, sources of security, or friendship relationships are being threatened.

4) People do not care and are happy with the status quo. When groups of individuals are comfortable together group norms and pressures influence attitudes toward change.

5) People have vested interests and definite perceptions of what is needed or wanted, although they may agree that change is necessary. With the increase in size of organizations, there comes a greater disparity of backgrounds, attitudes, and values, thereby allowing greater chance of individual or group resistance.

6) Finally, rapid change, or rather the speed with which change occurs, causes greater strain on the organization. Such strain forces "consensus" on groups and places much greater reliance on the managers as coordinators, negotiators and arbitrators, as well as motivators.

Changes that affect libraries and resistance to those changes, either on the part of library managers or other librarians, follow the same pattern as changes in society in general. A historical glance at library management development will indicate changes that have taken place in management attitudes and actions over the last 100 years.

LIBRARY MANAGEMENT DEVELOPMENT

Library management, as might be expected, shows no identifiable characteristic that would serve to set it apart from other organizational management. Trends, theories, and techniques introduced in management literature have slowly found their way into libraries. This development can be traced through a brief look at library literature.

In 1887 F. M. Cruden, then librarian of the St. Louis Public Library, stated that "the duties of a chief executive of a library differ in no essential way from those of a manager of a stock company ... the librarian may profit by the methods of the businessman."[7] Arthur E. Bostwick, addressing the New Zealand Library Association in 1911, advocated adoption of the methods of business efficiency in the operation of the library.[8] A number of other librarians, including Charles C. Williamson, emphasized the value to libraries of industrial methods, pointing out that "no one has attempted yet to treat comprehensively the principles and philosophy of library service or library management."[9] This was the period of development of the scientific management school, whose theories were applied to a number of industrial situations but not yet to libraries. It was not until the 1930s that particular attention was paid to the application of scientific management to libraries. Donald Coney emphasized the "new" approach by stating that " ... scientific management furnishes library administrators with a useful instrument for orientating their activities."[10] Twenty years later, in 1954, Laurence J. Kipp published an article[11] that discussed the application of scientific management to library operations for the period of 1920 to 1950. Kittle, in his dissertation, points out that scientific management did not receive serious attention in libraries until after World War II.[12]

Ralph R. Shaw began his leading studies of the scientific management of library operations in the late 1940s and early 1950s. In one study he analyzed two trends in library management — specialization and integration of specialties into a functional organization.[13] These two conflicting trends, which he termed micromanagement and macromanagement, are still evident in library organization today. In 1954 Shaw, writing as editor of an issue of *Library Trends*, noted "a trend toward the application of scientific management techniques to public and research libraries, on time-and-motion studies, on standardization, and on management surveys."[14] Dougherty and Heinritz, students of Shaw, published the first full treatise on the application of scientific management to libraries.[15]

The influence of the human relations school on libraries also became evident in the early 1930s; the problems of people became as important as the mechanical procedures, and preparation for library administrators took on the personnel relations approach. An article by Danton[16] emphasized the trend toward analyzing the human side, where "personnel administration" became paramount to the democratization of the library organization. This was further expounded in a 1939 volume[17] on personnel administration. Among the recommendations were: greater attention to personnel administration; greater consideration of basic organization directed toward the simplification and coordination of activities; greater staff development; and better working conditions.[18]

The McDiarmids, in their writings of the late 1930s[19] recognized two paramount problems in libraries — the need to delegate authority to the level of responsibility, and the need to define library objectives and their influence on the administration. Amy Winslow, in her 1953 paper, emphasized staff participation in "democratic organization."[20] Reese's article, directed to library administration, notes, among other things, an increase in staff participation in management of libraries.[21]

With respect to the social systems school, several works cited the development of library management in relation to the larger institution and the community the library serves. Joeckel, a pioneer in the field of library management, suggested that "library administrators will do well to seek models from comparative study in the fields of public administration, in business, in industry, and in education."[22] The Library Institute at which Joeckel's paper was presented was, perhaps, the landmark event in the analysis of library administration. Twenty years later, Wasserman supports Joeckel's contention that " ... in a very real sense library administration is only an extension of public administration."[23]

Stone's survey has shown a tendency toward "emphasis upon theory and principles and basic functions, bringing with it corresponding de-emphasis upon specific technical skills."[24] This is substantiated when one examines the volumes that have been published in the last several years on organization and administration of specific types of libraries—academic, public, school, and special. In this regard, the Association of Research Libraries, through funding from the Council on Library Resources, has developed its Office of Management Studies, which is responsible for a number of projects relating to library management. One primary activity has been the issuing of "SPEC KITS" on such topics as goals and objectives, collective bargaining, acquisition policies, etc. That office has also developed the self-study guide called "Management Review and Analysis" (MRAP), for larger academic libraries, and, on a trial basis, an Academic Library Development Program for smaller academic libraries. Through task forces both guides, aimed at improving productivity and staff morale, examine planning and control processes, organizational development, and personnel needs and relationships in individual libraries.

Finally, one must look at the quantitative or mathematical school and the influence it has had on library operations. During the late 1960s and into the 1970s managers of libraries began to use applied operational research in their decision-making responsibilities.[25] Since that time, an original group of researchers, led by Philip Morse at MIT, and a later group, headed by Ferdinand Leimkuhler at Purdue, have continued to study library problems using the operations research mode. Two reports from other sources illustrate this trend. In 1972 the Wharton School at the University of Pennsylvania finished a report that had been supported by a federal grant to design and develop a model for management information systems for universities and large public libraries.[26] That report classified library functions into seventeen categories, and it proposed that those categories be used as a basis for program budgeting systems in libraries. More recently Chen, in her dissertation, has demonstrated how operations research techniques can be used by library administrators in their everyday decision-making process.[27]

Issues of major research journals and monographs on librarianship make it clear that management "topics" are receiving increasing attention. The proceedings of the first Association of College and Research Libraries national conference present the thoughts and concerns of academic and research librarians in several major areas, including "Administration and Management."[28] A 1971 issue of *Library Trends* addresses itself to the dilemma of "How we can optimally integrate the technical and human resources that we manage toward achieving the library's service mission and, at the same time, manage working arrangements and role relationships so that people's needs for self-worth, growth, and development are significantly met in our libraries."[29] On that same topic, Stone researched a commissioned study for NCLIS,[30] and the issue of participative management has been addressed in research studies.[31] An example, drawn from a number of volumes on the subject of personnel in libraries, is a report done for the Illinois State Library, which identifies the kinds of activities that are typical of the training and background of individuals working in libraries.[32] Another important and timely view is presented by Conroy in her examination of staff development and continuing education.[33]

Other special issues of *Library Trends* have been on "Effective Resource Allocation in Library Management," which addresses the issue of accountability in libraries;[34] "Evaluation of Library Services," which examines "evaluative techniques and procedures used by librarians to determine the effectiveness of their programs (e.g., surveys, cost accounting, systems analysis, operations research, PPBS, MBO, PERT)";[35] and "Systems Design and Analysis for Libraries," which views systems analysis as a management tool to be used in "seeking out the fundamentals of a situation and applying to this study rigorous scientific methods, with the aim of finding an optimal solution to the problems facing managers."[36] The importance of measurement and evaluation of library services continues to receive attention as is evidenced by major works on the topic.[37]

Works on networking give the state of the art: one, "Resources and Bibliographic Support for a Nationwide Library Program,"[38] was commissioned by NCLIS; a second, co-sponsored by NCLIS, addresses the structure and governance of networks;[39] another, now somewhat dated, "Library Networks: Promise and Performance,"[40] emphasizes the need for developing networks that include all types of libraries; and the latest, *Networks for Networkers*, takes what is probably the most comprehensive view, to date, on problems and potentials of library networking.[41]

Perhaps the unit that is contributing the most, on a continuing basis, to the study of library management is the Association of Research Libraries. Through its University Library Management Studies Office it publishes "Occasional Papers" on relevant topics, and through its Management Studies Office it publishes SPEC (Systems and Procedures Exchange Center) flyers which have already been mentioned. Another analytical study of note is the one for Columbia University Libraries.[42]

Finally, but most importantly, the issue of women and minorities as managers is developing. Although the profession is a female profession, at least in numbers, the majority of top management positions are held by males, mostly white males. The causes for this are being discussed in institutes, such as *Library Management Without Bias*,[43] in group activities of organizations, like the Status of Women in Librarianship Committee of the American Library Association, and through research studies, which are ongoing. The outlook has been gradually changing as the "mentor" system, as opposed to the "old boy network," begins to function and as individuals are hired based on their abilities and qualifications and not necessarily on other variables.

It is evident that the theories developed by the different schools (scientific management; human relations; quantitative) are being applied to library operations today. The continued use, development, and refinement of those thoughts and techniques will result in more efficient and effective library service.

NOTES

[1]Alvin Toffler, *Future Shock* (New York: Bantam Books, 1970), p. 19.

[2]Peter F. Drucker, *The Age of Discontinuity: Guidelines to Our Changing Society* (New York: Harper and Row, 1979).

[3]S. Beer, "The World We Manage," *Behavioral Science* 18 (1973): 198.

[4]F. E. Emery and E. L. Trist, "The Causal Texture of Organizational Environments," *Human Relations* 18 (Feb. 1965): 21.

[5]L. E. Greiner, "Patterns of Organization Change," *Harvard Business Review* 45 (1967): 120.

[6]Alan C. Filley, R. J. House, and S. Kerr, *Managerial Process and Organizational Behavior* (Glenview, IL: Scott, Foresman and Co., 1976), p. 491.

[7]Gertrude G. Drury, *The Library and Its Organization* (New York: H. W. Wilson, 1924), pp. 83-84.

[8]Arthur E. Bostwick, "Two Tendencies of American Library Work," *Library Journal* 36 (1911): 275-78.

[9]Charles C. Williamson, "Efficiency in Library Management," *Library Journal* 44 (1919): 76.

[10]Donald Coney, "Scientific Management in University Libraries," in G. T. Schwennig, ed., *Management Problems* (Chapel Hill, NC: University of North Carolina Press, 1930), p. 173.

[11]Laurence J. Kipp, "Scientific Management in Research Libraries," *Library Trends* 2 (Jan. 1954): 390-400.

[12]Arthur T. Kittle, "Management Theories in Public Administration in the United States," Ph.D. dissertation, Columbia Univerity, 1961.

[13]Ralph R. Shaw, "Scientific Management in the Library," *Wilson Library Bulletin* 21 (Jan. 1947): 349-52.

[14]Ralph R. Shaw, "Scientific Management," *Library Trends* 2 (Jan. 1954): 359-483.

[15]Richard M. Dougherty and Fred J. Heinritz, *Scientific Management of Library Operations* (Metuchen, NJ: Scarecrow Press, 1966).

[16]J. Periam Danton, "Our Libraries—The Trend Towards Democracy," *Library Quarterly* 4 (Jan. 1934): 16-27.

[17]Clara W. Herbert, *Personnel Administration in Public Libraries* (Chicago, IL: American Library Association, 1939).

[18]Herbert, *Personnel Administration in Public Libraries*, pp. xiii-xiv.

[19]E. W. McDiarmid and John M. McDiarmid, *The Administration of the American Public Library* (Chicago, IL: American Library Association, 1943).

[20]Amy Winslow, "Staff Participation in Management," *Wilson Library Bulletin* 27 (April 1953): 624-28.

[21]Ernest J. Reese, ed., "Current Trends in Library Administration," *Library Trends* 7 (Jan. 1959).

[22]C. B. Joeckel, ed., *Current Issues in Library Administration: Papers Presented Before the Library Institute at the University of Chicago, August 1-12, 1938* (Chicago, IL: University of Chicago Press, 1939), pp. vii-ix.

[23]Paul Wasserman, "Development of Administration in Library Service: Current Status and Future Prospects," *College and Research Libraries* 19 (Nov. 1958): 288.

[24]Elizabeth W. Stone, *Training for the Improvement of Library Administration* (Urbana, IL: University of Illinois, Graduate School of Library Science, 1967), p. 15.

[25]Don R. Swanson and Abraham Bookstein, eds., *Operations Research: Implications for Libraries* (Chicago, IL: University of Chicago Press, 1972).

[26]Morris Hamburg et al., "Library Planning and Decision Making Systems," USOE Final Report, Project no. 8-0802 (Philadelphia, PA: Wharton School, University of Pennsylvania, 1972). (Monograph published by MIT Press.)

[27]Ching-Chih Chen, *Applications of Operations Research Models to Libraries* (Cambridge, MA: MIT Press, 1976).

[28]Robert D. Stueart and Richard D. Johnson, eds., *New Horizons for Academic Libraries* (New York: K. G. Saur, 1979).

[29]Elizabeth W. Stone, ed., "Personnel Development and Continuing Education in Libraries," *Library Trends* 20, no. 1 (July 1971): 3.

[30]U.S. National Commission on Libraries and Information Science, *Continuing Library and Information Science Education*, submitted by E. Stone et al. (Washington, DC: ASIS, 1974).

[31]Maurice P. Marchant, *Participative Management in Academic Libraries* (Westport, CT: Greenwood Press, 1976).

[32]Myrl Ricking and Robert E. Booth, *Personnel Utilization in Libraries: A Systems Approach* (Chicago, IL: American Library Association, 1974).

[33]Barbara Conroy, *Library Staff Development and Continuing Education* (Littleton, CO: Libraries Unlimited, 1978).

[34]H. William Axford, "Effective Resource Allocation in Library Management," *Library Trends* 25, no. 4 (april 1975): 547-72.

[35]Sarah R. Reed, "Evaluation of Library Services," *Library Trends* 22, no. 3 (Jan. 1974): 255.

[36]F. Wilfrid Lancaster, "Systems Design and Analysis for Libraries," *Library Trends* 21, no. 4 (April 1973): 463.

[37]Ernest R. DeProspo, E. Altman, and K. E. Beasley, *Performance Measures for Public Libraries* (Chicago, IL: American Library Association, 1973); Lowell Martin et al., *Library Response to Urban Change: A Study of the Chicago Public Library* (Chicago, IL: American Library Association, 1969); F. Wilfred Lancaster, *The Measurement and Evaluation of Library Services* (Washington, DC: Information Resources Press, 1977).

[38]U.S. National Commission on Libraries and Information Science, *Resources and Bibliographic Support for a Nationwide Library Program*, submitted by Vernon E. Palmour et al. (Rockville, MD: Westat, 1974).

[39]Allen Kent and Thomas J. Galvin, eds., *The Structure and Governance of Library Networks* (New York: Marcel Dekker, 1979).

[40]Leon Carnovsky, ed., "Library Networks: Promise and Performance," *Library Quarterly* 39, no. 1 (Jan. 1969): 1-108.

[41]Barbara E. Markuson and Blanche Woolls, eds., *Networks for Networkers: Critical Issues in Cooperative Library Development* (New York: Neal-Schuman, 1980).

[42]Booz, Allen and Hamilton, Inc., *Organization and Staffing of the Libraries of Columbia University* (Westport, CT: Redgrave, 1973).

[43]Ching-Chih Chen, ed., *Library Management Without Bias* (Greenwich, CT: JAI Press, 1980).

A.   Dallas Public Library. A number of documents exist in regards to planning and stating institutional goals. Excerpts follow:

1.   Long Range Plan for Public Library Service (City of Dallas publication no. 77-1085).

Summary:

Objective: To prepare a document which would help direct Public Library planning for the City of Dallas during the next 25 years.

Methodology: A self-study under the direction of the Municipal Library Department staff was proposed to the City Manager and accepted by the City Council in November, 1976; staff solicited critiques of present programs and suggestions for new ones from citizens through neighborhood meetings, librarians in other libraries, professional associates in fields basic to long-range planning, and City of Dallas personnel.

The Plan: Based upon an analysis of the data in Chapter I, this document presents programs, plans, and projects which will provide a foundation upon which Dallas can build excellent Public Library service for its citizens in the years ahead; inasmuch as the preparation and contents of this Plan may be of interest to a national library audience, some background materials, such as the History and Philosophy of the Dallas Public Library and the various appendices, are included.

(The document then details those plans, programs and projects.)

2.   Library Service Goals 1972-1982 for the Dallas Public Library (printed 1972).

The five areas defined by goals, include: User-Oriented Service; Materials Collection and Selection; Organization of Materials; Staffing; and Management and Communications. The first area is presented here as an example:

USER-ORIENTED SERVICE

General Goal: Provide the highest quality user-oriented public library service which will effectively contribute to the development of our major urban area through the utilization of the broad range of contemporary media and technology.

Specific Goals:

1. Emphasize service to those library users whose needs are not the primary responsibility of other institutions in this major urban area.

2. Identify the informational and material needs the Library can fulfill and, when appropriate, provide referral service to other agencies.

3. Take the lead in planning cooperative endeavors with all institutional, organizational, industrial, and private libraries in this major urban area to assure the development, availability, and accessibility of resources in all subject areas in which all share proportionately the economic burdens and benefits.

4. In order to develop maximum, efficient, and economic Library service, participate in cooperative informational services, networks, and systems on local, state, regional, national, and international bases.

5. Determine methods and urge implementation of adequate remuneration for services rendered and services received between the Dallas Public Library and other governmental entities and private organizations.

6. Develop a plan for specialized services, such as in depth bibliographic searching, which will be made available on a cost-per-job basis to individual and corporate patrons.

7. Recognizing the public library as the logical center for independent and self learning, determine the public library's responsibility to students enrolled in educational institutions at all levels in our major urban area.

8. Develop a diversified public relations program which will generate increased library usage, support all facets of library service, and result in increased understanding and good will.

9. Develop a Reference-Research Center to provide in depth resources and services to meet the identified specialized reference and bibliographic needs of Dallasites, as well as those needs generated through cooperative networks such as the Texas State Library Communications Network and the Northeast Texas Library System.

10. Continue to extend public library services into the community through a system of branch libraries, mobile units, and individual and group related services and programs.

11. To assure that each branch library, mobile unit, and special service will identify with its community, develop each unit with a uniqueness corresponding to the particular characteristics of its community.

12. Continue to work with staffs of community agencies to make library services and materials available through those staffs to the citizens served by those agencies.

(Used with the permission of the Dallas Public Library, City of Dallas.)

B.   Minneapolis Public Library and Information Center, "Goals and Objectives Statement," updated 8/24/79.

This statement identifies nine goals with objectives for each one. These fall into broad categories of: materials; physical resources; staff; services; technology; cooperation; access; public relations; and management. The first goal is presented here as an example:

> **Goal:** Provide a vital collection of books and other materials; an adequate number of staff for guidance in its use; and access at hours convenient to the public, as funds permit and the seasons dictate.
>
> **Objectives:**
> 1.   Develop an alternative schedule for hours of operation of Central and Community Libraries to adjust to changing fiscal conditions by Oct. 31, 1979.
> 2.   Investigate the physical conditions of the microfilm holdings of the Minneapolis newspapers by December, 1979, weeding and recommending replacements as necessary.
> 3.   Develop a system for conservation and preservation of old, valuable, and rare materials by June 30, 1980.

(Used with the permission of the Minneapolis Public Library and Information Center.)

C.   New York State Library "Program and Action Document."

This document is developed in five sections: 1) Fifteen *Assumptions* upon which plans and assignment of responsibility are based; 2) *Mission and Goals* statement; 3) Twenty-four *Service Imperatives* of the New York State Library derived from the mission and goals; 4) *Unit Responsibilities*, which details assignments made to major units in order to accomplish the service imperatives; and 5) *Unit Action Plans*, to be developed in each of the units in consultation with library management. Only the Mission and Goals statement is included here as an example:

> **Mission:** The New York State Library, a "public library for the use of the government and people" of the state, has as its mission to provide reference, informational and loan service to the legislative, executive and judicial branches of the government and to ensure that every resident of the state has convenient free access to essential library services.
>
> **Goal A:** To maintain a collection of materials which will meet the needs of state government and serve as a major research resource for the people of New York State, to provide a full range of library services for the blind, to identify the needs

of user groups, to organize and provide the materials and staff required to meet these needs, and to make these resources available through on-site services, the New York State Interlibrary Loan (NYSILL) network and other appropriate means.

Goal B: To develop coordinated library service to all the citizens of the State, including the handicapped, the disadvantaged, and the institutionalized at every appropriate level — local, regional, and state — so that all persons may have direct and easy access to a system which will provide them with the needed or desired information and library materials and services for the pursuit of their own social, cultural, and educational growth.

(Used with the permission of the New York State Library.)

D.   Duke University Libraries.

This document, in addition to stating the Mission already cited, presents both guiding principles and objectives upon which planning is based. Those are presented in their entirety here as examples:

Guiding Principles:
1.   To recognize that the Library is not an autonomous body but operates within a larger organizational framework;
2.   To support the University commitment to concerns beyond the institution proper;
3.   To participate in inter-library cooperation in both the spirit of sharing information and in making most efficient use of finances and other resources;
4.   To view the Library as a dynamic system, in need of constant evaluation and adjustment, in order to maintain the necessary flexibility to accommodate changing environmental and patron demands;
5.   To strive toward maximal organizational efficiency and effectiveness, in order to best utilize material and human resources;
6.   To aim for an internal working environment that will produce personal satisfaction in the attainment of Library goals;
7.   To resist attempts to censor information;
8.   To respect individual patrons and to guard their rights to privacy;
9.   To acquire and preserve recorded knowledge for future generations as well as provide tools for ongoing teaching and research;

10. To maintain flexibility in meeting patron needs, whether planning services, applying regulations, providing resources, or some other activity;

11. To maximize access to information and use of the collections so that the greatest number of patrons can be satisfied, yet recognizing unique demands of individuals; and

12. To recognize that patron service is the ultimate goal of all Library activities.

Objectives: The basic objectives of the Perkins Library System is to facilitate access to information, and to Library materials and services for members of the University community through a common endeavor on the part of the entire staff to acquire, process, service, and preserve Library materials. In an effort to achieve the basic objective it is incumbent upon the Library staff to:

1. Develop the collection both current and retrospective based upon a thorough knowledge of the instructional and research needs of the University community;

2. Develop and establish more effective collection control through improved circulation service, increased security, and collection preservation including proper attention to materials requiring special considerations;

3. Study and effect means of improving access to Library materials and information through staff awareness and development, user education and the utilization of expanded and non-traditional library services;

4. Improve and expedite the processing of Library materials through both innovative and traditional methods to provide necessary bibliographic control and access;

5. Continue to study, ascertain and appraise the Library's responsibilities and ability to serve others beyond the University community;

6. Develop cooperative programs for resource sharing in light of the University's obligations to this University community, to other libraries, and to researchers and scholars nationally and internationally;

7. Systematically examine space problems and needs to ascertain the best possible arrangement of materials, services and staff for maximum effectiveness and efficiency in Library operations;

8. Maintain and further develop a highly capable Library staff through systematic programs of national recruitment, career development and effective utilization of individual talents;

9. Establish and maintain an effective liaison between the Library's staff and its primary clientele to assist in the planning and development of Library programs and services to meet the changing needs of the University;

10. Utilize the widest number of avenues of communication possible both internally and externally to insure the clearest understanding of Library policies and programs;

11. Continue to review the above objectives and develop new objectives as appropriate.

(Used with permission of the Long Range Planning Committee, Duke University Library.)

New York State Library
State Education Department Organization Chart
January 16, 1979

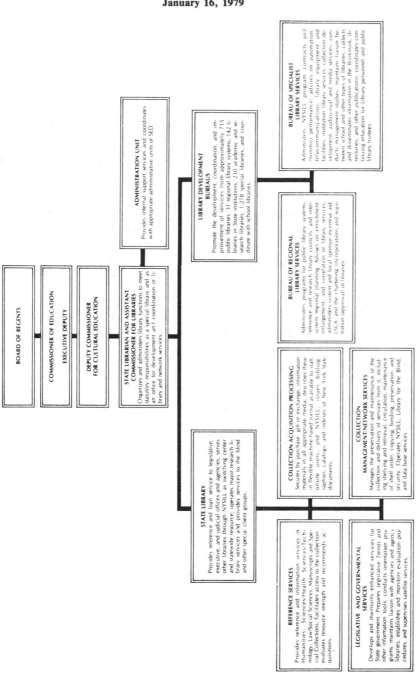

BOARD OF REGENTS

COMMISSIONER OF EDUCATION

EXECUTIVE DEPUTY

DEPUTY COMMISSIONER FOR CULTURAL EDUCATION

STATE LIBRARIAN AND ASSISTANT COMMISSIONER FOR LIBRARIES
Organizes and administers library functions to meet statutory responsibilities as a special library and as an office for development and coordination of library and network services.

ADMINISTRATION UNIT
Provides internal support services, and coordinates with appropriate administrative units of SED.

STATE LIBRARY
Provides reference and loan service to legislative, executive, and judicial offices and agencies, serves other libraries through NYSILL as switching center and statewide resource; operates major research library services and provides services to the blind and other special client groups.

COLLECTION ACQUISITION PROCESSING
Secures by purchase gift or exchange, information materials in all appropriate media, describes these in flexible machine-based format available to staff, onsite users, and NYSILL; issues bibliographies, catalogs, and indexes of New York State documents.

COLLECTION MANAGEMENT/NETWORK SERVICES
Manages the preservation and maintenance of the collection and delivery of services from it, including shelving and retrieval, circulation, maintenance of shelf order, copying, binding, preservation, and security. Operates NYSILL, Library for the Blind, and data base services.

REFERENCE SERVICES
Provides reference and information services in Humanities; Sciences/Health Sciences/Technology; Law/Social Sciences. Manuscripts and Special Collections. Facilitates access to the collection evaluates resource strength and recommends acquisitions.

LEGISLATIVE AND GOVERNMENTAL SERVICES
Develops and maintains enhanced services for State government. Prepares *Legislative Trends* and other information tools; conducts orientation programs, maintains liaison with agencies and agency libraries, establishes and monitors evaluation procedures, and supervises satellite services.

LIBRARY DEVELOPMENT BUREAUS
Promote the development, coordination, and improvement of services from approximately 715 public libraries 31 regional library systems, 142 libraries in State institutions, 210 academic, and research libraries, 1,278 special libraries, and coordinate with school libraries.

BUREAU OF REGIONAL LIBRARY SERVICES
Administers programs for public library systems, reference and research library councils, and intersystem regional planning. Advises on enrichment enlargement, and correlation of library services, administers system and local sponsor incentive and LSCA and the chartering incorporation and registration approval of libraries.

BUREAU OF SPECIALIST LIBRARY SERVICES
Administers NYSILL program contracts and monitors performance; advises on automation telecommunications, library equipment and facilities, institution library services, collection development audiovisual and media services, conducts management studies; maintains liaison between school and other types of libraries, collects and disseminates information in the *Bookmark*, directories, and other publications; coordinates continuing education for library personnel and public library trustees.

Cornell University Libraries Organization Chart
(Reprinted by permission from the Cornell University Libraries)

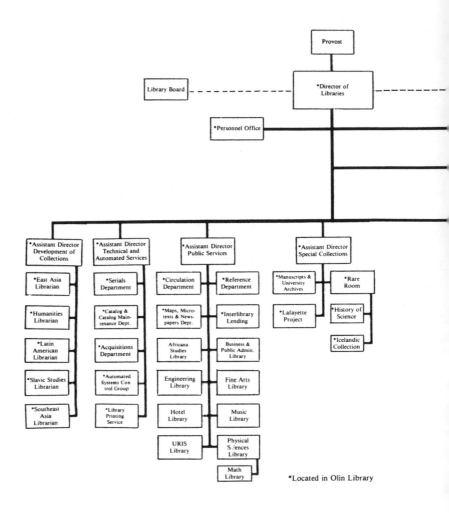

Cornell University Libraries Organization Chart (cont'd)

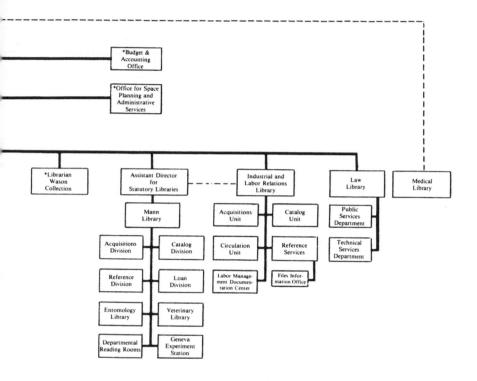

January 1977

Municipal Library Department
City of Dallas
Organization Chart
1979-80
(Reprinted by permission from the Dallas Public Library,
City of Dallas)

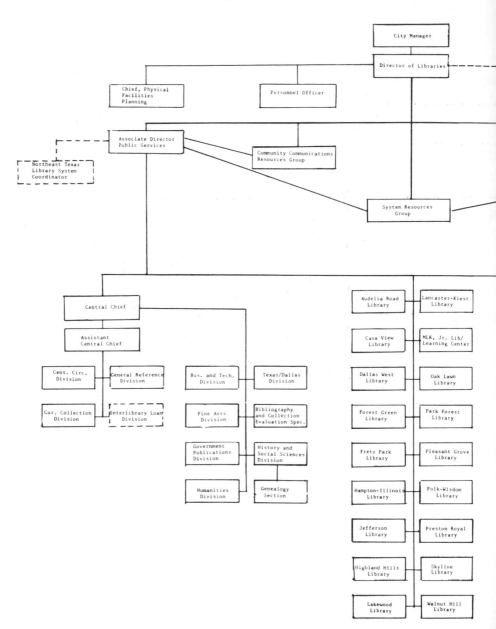

Municipal Library Department (cont'd)

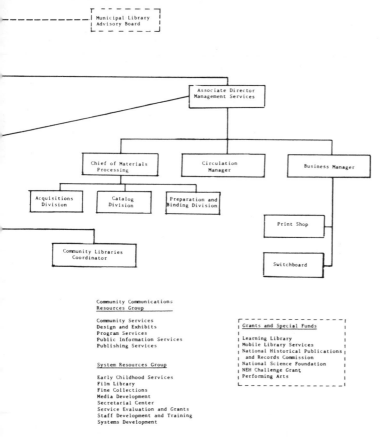

Municipal Library
Advisory Board

Associate Director
Management Services

Chief of Materials
Processing

Circulation
Manager

Business Manager

Acquisitions
Division

Catalog
Division

Preparation and
Binding Division

Print Shop

Community Libraries
Coordinator

Switchboard

Community Communications
Resources Group

Community Services
Design and Exhibits
Program Services
Public Information Services
Publishing Services

System Resources Group

Early Childhood Services
Film Library
Fine Collections
Media Development
Secretarial Center
Service Evaluation and Grants
Staff Development and Training
Systems Development

Grants and Special Funds

Learning Library
Mobile Library Services
National Historical Publications
and Records Commission
National Science Foundation
NEH Challenge Grant
Performing Arts

Municipal Library Department
City of Dallas
Organization Chart
1979-80

Organization of The University Library
The University of Michigan
Ann Arbor, Michigan

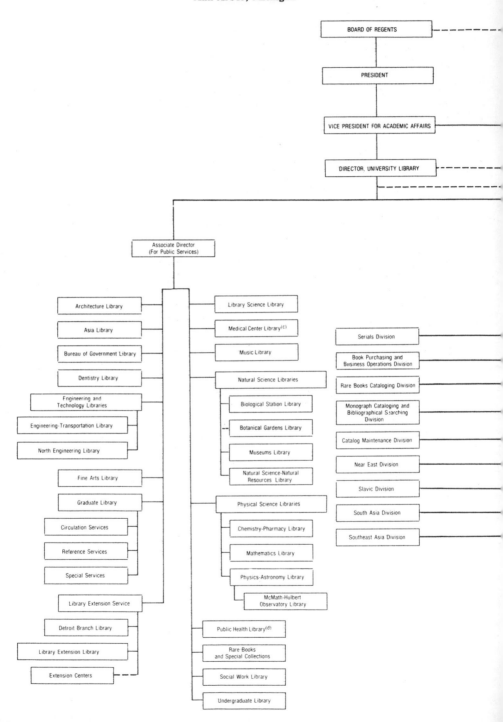

Organization of The University Library (cont'd)

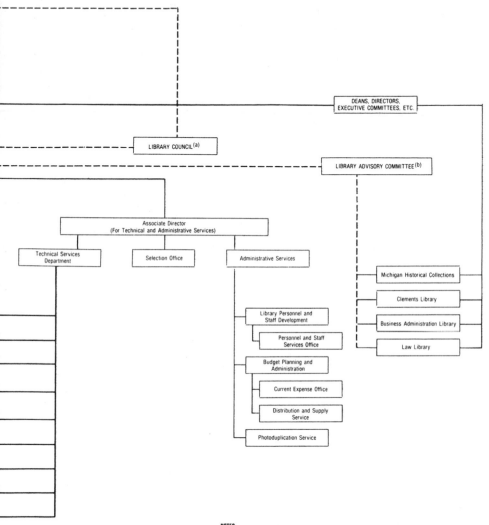

NOTES:

(a) Consists of 8 members of the University Senate appointed by the Regents. The Director of the University Library serves as Chairman. The Council assists the Director of the Library in allocation of funds, in formulating the policies of the University Library, in developing the educational values thereof, and in cooperating with the several schools, colleges, and other units within the University.

(b) Serves as a medium of discussion and advice respecting matters of common interest to the several libraries on the campus. Consists of the Director of the University Library (Chairman), the Law Librarian, the Director of the Clements Library, the Director of the Michigan Historical Collections, and the Head of the Business Administration Library.

(c) Serves Medical and Nursing Schools and University Hospital.

(d) Includes Public Health Practice.

Organization of the University Library
The University of Michigan
Ann Arbor, Michigan
Assistant for Library Personnel and Staff Development

**ASSISTANT FOR LIBRARY PERSONNEL
AND STAFF DEVELOPMENT**

Under the general supervision of the Associate Director (for Technical and Administrative Services) of the University Library, has general responsibility for policies, procedures, and services in the area of personnel, including recruitment and orientation programs, and general responsibility for intralibrary communications.

**PERSONNEL AND
STAFF SERVICES OFFICE**

Conducts the personnel program of the University Library, including recruitment and orientation of full-time non-librarian and part-time staff. Maintains payroll and personnel records, salary and wage allocations, and expenditure and accounting controls on the salary budget. Participates in the preparation of the annual salary and wage budget. Provides monthly and annual reports of salary expenditures. Responsible for special personnel programs such as College Work Study Program, Student Employment Program, Tuition Refund Program, and University Staff Development Programs. Provides substitute service for all units.

    1   Administrative Associate I (Head)

SECRETARY

Serves as receptionist; provides secretarial services; assists in maintaining personnel files and records; assists in implementation of special personnel programs.

    1   Secretary C-5

**NON-LIBRARIAN EMPLOYEE
INTERVIEWING**

Recruits and interviews applicants for non-librarian positions, obtains references, refers applicants to supervisors for interview.

    4   Supervisor

**REGULAR NON-LIBRARIAN AND
LIBRARIAN PERSONNEL RECORDS**

Processes all appointments, resignations, and leaves of absence; maintains records of vacation, sick leave, and payrolls; maintains bookkeeping records on the salary budget and funds allocated to Library units for hourly help; maintains personnel files of all Library employees. Handles tuition refund records.

    1   Supervisor
    2   Principal Clerk C-5
  54   H

Organization of the University Library
Assistant for Library Personnel and Staff Development (cont'd)

Assistant for Library Personnel and Staff Development
Chart No. 5
December 1, 1977

PART-TIME HOURLY EMPLOYEE INTERVIEWING
Recruits and interviews applicants for part-time hourly positions: refers applicants to supervisors for interviews.

3	Supervisor
1	C-4

SUBSTITUTE SERVICE
Provides substitute service during absence of library personnel; supplies staff for special projects when substitute service is not needed.

2	Supervisor
1	C-5
1	C-4
1	GSSA

DALLAS PUBLIC LIBRARY
City of Dallas
(Reprinted by permission)

CLASSIFICATION SPECIFICATION

Classification: Librarian 14   Class Code:

Class Type: Unclassified

Grade: 14

Distinguishing Characteristics:

This is difficult, responsible professional librarianship in the administration of units or special services of the municipal library, requiring administrative experience in library or related professional fields.

Employees in this class administer and direct units or special services of the library within broadly defined departmental service policy and specifically defined City-wide and departmental operational policy. Professional duties and administrative responsibilities may be in the areas of public service, interlibrary loan service, technical processes, community service, or research. Employees perform as first level line officers, supervise professional and clerical employees, and are responsible for the operation of units or special services of the library. Responsibilities include development of materials collections, interpretation of service policies, efficient and effective use of staff, streamlining of work methods, and participation in research and studies. Employees work with only general guidance from a superior. Continued experience and proven ability provide opportunity to assume more responsibility.

Typical Duties:

1. Administers and guides the development of a subject or technical processes department, branch, or special service of the library.

2. Provides direction and opportunities for development of staff members in the areas of professional growth, improved services and service methods, and professional activities.

3. Establishes and maintains communication and cooperation with other units of the library and with outside agencies, organizations, institutions, and groups.

4. Prepares monthly and annual reports, annual budget requests, and special reports as required.

5. Participates in the selection of professional and clerical staff members and makes recommendations for promotion, reassignments, dismissals, and other personnel actions.

6. Performs related professional duties as assigned.

(Classification Specification continues on page 205)

Dallas Public Library
Classification Specification (cont'd)

Classification: Librarian 14   Code:

Education:

Master's Degree in Library Science

Experience:

Two years progressive professional library administration or special service experience.

Acceptable Equivalency:

Master's Degree in a related field (for those positions of special services) and two years special service experience in a related field.

Abilities Required to Perform Work:

Thorough knowledge of the philosophy and techniques of library service and of the administrative/supervisory and/or specialty skills as these relate to the unit or special service concerned.

Thorough knowledge of the principles of personnel management, library management, and budget preparation as these relate to the unit concerned.

Thorough knowledge of departmental policies and procedures.

Particular skill in establishing and maintaining effective working relationships with other employees, with subordinates, and with the general public.

Must have very high level of verbal ability, social skill, and adaptability.

Working Conditions and Hazards:

Normal library conditions including work shifts that include night and weekend duty. Normal traffic hazards when visiting other libraries, schools, and institutions/agencies/organizations in normal course of work.

Promotes from:

Librarian 12

Promotes to:

Librarian 16

Advertising Specification:

Master's Degree in Library Science and two years experience.

Approved: Date:

MASSACHUSETTS INSTITUTE OF TECHNOLOGY
(Reprinted by permission of the
Massachusetts Institute of Technology Libraries)

CLASSIFICATION DESCRIPTION CLASSIFICATION CODE

FLSA DESIGNATION

EEO CODE

ISSUED

SUPERSEDES

TITLE   LIBRARIAN II   GRADE

BASIC FUNCTION AND RESPONSIBILITY

To perform professional library work of a difficult nature, requiring originality and independent judgement, or be responsible for a small unit.

CHARACTERISTIC DUTIES AND RESPONSIBILITIES

Establish classification and subject entries; examine, verify, classify and catalogue printed materials requiring originality and independent judgement.

Create, proofread and revise card files and records; establish and maintain information retrieval system; prepare and maintain inventory records.

Supervise the processing of library materials, circulation activities and collection maintenance.

Compile bibliographies, conduct searches and research, plan and prepare displays and exhibits.

Assist unit heads in planning, administering department policies, procedures and operations.

Prepare memoranda, reports and correspondence as required.

Advise, instruct, lecture, train supporting staff and students in a subject area or in the application of professional library skills.

Supervise lower ranking librarians and supporting staff in completing work assignments, including planning, scheduling and reviewing work.

May be responsible for the selection of materials to be purchased, acquired or discarded; contact vendors to discuss and order materials.

Assist students, faculty and other users of the library in locating information; interpret and communicate library policies and procedures, provide information, reference and resource services.

Attend and participate in department, Institute and professional activities, meetings, conferences and the like to contribute to individual professional growth and competence.

Participate in related functions that contribute to the individual's professional growth and competence.

Participate in discussing, advising and consulting with academic department heads, faculty, administrative staff on the selection and acquisition of printed materials and other media.

This description is intended to indicate the kinds of tasks and levels of work difficulty that will be required of positions that will be given this title and shall not be construed as declaring what the specific duties and responsibilities of any particular position shall be. It is not intended to limit or in any way modify the right of any supervisor to assign, direct and control the work of employees under his supervision. The use of a particular expression or illustration describing duties shall not be held to exclude other duties not mentioned that are of similar kind or level of difficulty.

rev. 7/17/74

MASSACHUSETTS INSTITUTE OF TECHNOLOGY
Classification Description (cont'd)

LIBRARIAN II

SUPERVISION RECEIVED

Supervision is received from a senior ranking librarian or the administrator of a functional library unit or division.

SUPERVISION EXERCISED

Functional supervision is exercised over biweekly staff and/or assistant librarians.

QUALIFICATIONS

A Master's degree in Library Science is necessary.

Reasonable demonstrated knowledge of library skills gained through employment as a professional librarian is necessary.

A reading knowledge of one or more foreign languages may be necessary.

A degree in a specific subject discipline may be necessary.

MINNEAPOLIS PUBLIC LIBRARY AND INFORMATION CENTER
JOB DESCRIPTION

Library Assistant
History and Travel Department

Grade: Library Assistant
Title: Library Assistant, History and Travel Department
Reports to: Department Head, History Department

Description: Is responsible for assisting with the indexing project and other professional work in the department; functions in accord with goals and objectives for Central Library Services; maintains standards for public service and internal professional activities; indexes local newspapers; assists when needed in providing person to person reading guidance and reference assistance, works with and supervises classified staff assisting with the indexing project and at the reference desk; increases knowledge and background in indexing and in the subject areas of the department.

Requirements: Bachelor's degree with a major or a minor in library science.

4-77

NEW YORK STATE LIBRARY

Occ. Code 3601200

ASSISTANT LIBRARIAN, GRADE 14

New York State Department of Civil Service

Classification Standard

NATURE OF WORK

Assistant Librarians select, acquire, classify, catalog and circulate books, periodicals, tapes, etc., and provide reference and bibliographic assistance services in the State Library or in a general library servicing an institution's clients or residents or in a reference library supporting technical and professional agency programs. In the State Library, incumbents provide such services within an assigned subject matter or technical specialty. In other agencies or institutions, an incumbent performs these tasks and may either be the highest level librarian or assist a Senior level librarian as a general assistant or as an assistant in charge of a major section such as Technical Processes or Reader Services.

The largest number of positions in this class are found in the Education Department in the State Library; many positions also exist in the institutions of the Departments of Mental Hygiene and Correctional Services and in the Main Offices of several State agencies.

CLASSIFICATION CRITERIA AND DISTINGUISHING CHARACTERISTICS

Positions in this class are characterized by the performance of a full range of professional librarian activities such as the selection, acquisition, classification, cataloging and indexing library materials and providing bibliographic, reader assistance, and research services to the library clientele. The classification of individual positions is dependent upon the size of the library and the responsibilities of higher level librarians in the organization. There are three typical organizational situations which support the classification of an Assistant Librarian.

First, in the State Library, under the supervision of a senior level librarian, Assistant Librarians perform the full range of library services as appropriate to any one of the following specialties—Law, Legislative References, Manuscripts and History, Rare Books, References and Technical Processes. In each major section of the library, Senior level librarians plan, coordinate and supervise the technical phases of the activities of the section under the overall direction of an Associate Librarian who has responsibility for policy, planning, coordination, budgeting review and evaluation of library services in a major division of the Library.

Second, in an agency or institution library of less than 15,000 volumes, periodicals and tapes or in a library with between 10,000 and 15,000 volumes, tapes and periodicals with an annual circulation of less than 10,000, an Assistant Librarian not only performs the full range of professional activities as noted above but also administers the library services as the highest level librarian.

Finally, in an agency or institution library supporting a Senior Librarian (see standard code 3601200) an Assistant Librarian may be classified to provide general support in the operation of the entire library or in accordance with workload demands to provide professional support in a major section of the library.

(Classification Standard continues on page 210)

NEW YORK STATE LIBRARY
Classification Standard (cont'd)

The Assistant Librarian class is distinguished from the Clerk (Library) series in that incumbents in positions of Assistant Librarian must possess a knowledge of theories, objectives, principles, and techniques of library science. The Clerk (Library) series requires incumbents to possess only the ability to apply standard library methods and procedures and a basic knowledge of the functions and services offered by the library.

TYPICAL ACTIVITIES, TASKS AND ASSIGNMENTS

Assistant Librarians in the State Library or those who act as a general assistant or as an assistant in charge of a major section in an agency or institution library perform all of the following activities but the emphasis varies according to the assigned specialty and type of library.

Selects and acquires library materials.

- Reviews available publisher's material, critical reviews, books, periodicals and tapes; screens those best suited to meet library needs.
- Prepares basic collection list of materials to meet library needs.
- Acquires material from lists by purchase, loan, exchange or gift according to budget restrictions, library priorities and expected usage.
- Checks ordered material on receipt to insure correct edition, proper condition and price of material.
- In the State Library oversees clerical functions related to computer based system for check-in and control of materials.
- Examines material in library to determine if it should be replaced, discarded or placed in storage according to established guidelines.

Classifies, catalogs and indexes materials.

- Assigns material to proper places using established classification system such as the Dewey Decimal System or Library of Congress System.
- Catalogs material using established rules and reference works to identify its unique features, to describe it bibliographically and to integrate it with the rest of the collection.
- Assigns subject headings by determining material dealt with and selecting standard subject headings which best indicate subject matter.
- Indexes special collections or material of special interest to the library clientele to provide a more detailed listing of the contents of the material.
- In the State Library oversees and reviews clerical input of bibliographic data into machine readable system.
- May verify the work of other Assistant Librarians to insure their work agrees with the established systems.

Provides reference, searching, bibliographic and reader assistance services to library clientele using card file systems or automated information data bases.

- Explains physical layout of library, types of material available and procedures for obtaining material.
- Explains the use of various library tools such as the catalogs, indexes, bibliographies and standard reference books.
- Answers questions from clientele which require the searching of material within the library and from outside sources.

NEW YORK STATE LIBRARY

CLASSIFICATION STANDARD (cont'd)

- Compiles bibliographies at the request of clientele ranging from a short list of material pertinent to subject matter to a long list of technical material with annotations describing and evaluating material.
- Maintains bibliographies in areas of special interest to clientele or agencies.
- Informs clientele of newly acquired material which may be of special interest to them.
- Conducts group activities such as talks on books, readings, or tours.

In addition, Assistant Librarians functioning as the highest level librarians in a small library perform some of the tasks listed in the Senior Librarian standard in support of the following activities:

- Plans and develops services for library clientele.
- Manages and evaluates services provided by the library.
- Supervises and trains subordinate staff, including paid, volunteer and/or resident workers.

RELATIONSHIPS WITH OTHERS

Incumbents of positions in this class have extensive face-to-face oral communications with the library clientele which may include residents of Mental Hygiene and Correctional Services institutions, program staffs in institutions and State agencies, legislators, legislative staffs and the general public. This communication involves providing information and answering questions concerning library services and the availability of material. Incumbents may also prepare bibliographies and written answers to questions which require research activities as requested by the clientele.

Where positions in this class are the highest level positions in the library, incumbents have occasional oral and written communications with program and administrative personnel. They prepare written budget requests and justifications, discuss the nature of library services to be offered, negotiate the amount of space for the library and negotiate the need for paid resident and volunteer staff. They also prepare written work reports concerning activities within the library such as circulation of data, bibliographic requests, etc.

Face-to-face oral communication is an integral part of Assistant Librarian positions, but is not a major factor in the classification of a specific position.

NATURE OF SUPERVISION

Assistant Librarians in the State Library or in a large institution or agency library receive assignments from a Senior Librarian with general guidance related to library policies. The Assistant Librarians independently perform specific assignments which are spot checked at their completion for adherence to library guidelines.

As the highest level position in a library, Assistant Librarians function independently setting overall library policies, selecting material and performing reader and technical services. They are supervised by a higher level administrative or education position who discusses the type of services and materials to be offered and the annual budget for the library with the Assistant Librarian. They do not review the work of the Assistant Librarian but they do make suggestions regarding services and material offered based on written requests received from program personnel or institution residents and evaluate the overall services provided by the library.

NEW YORK STATE LIBRARY
CLASSIFICATION STANDARD (cont'd)

Assistant Librarians may supervise a subordinate clerical staff. They explain services to be offered, assign work according to qualifications and insure work is completed on time. In an institution library, the clerical staff may include resident and/or volunteer workers.

JOB REQUIREMENTS

- Good knowledge of the theory, objectives and principles of library science.
- Good knowledge of procedures and techniques for classifying and cataloging material for use in the library.
- Good knowledge of the procedures, techniques and tools used in bibliography, reference and research services.
- Working knowledge of available interlibrary loan networks such as New York State Interlibrary Law Network.
- Working knowledge of sources for the purchase of material for use in the library.
- Working knowledge of agency, institution or library mission and programs.
- Working knowledge of the needs and interests of library clientele.
- Ability to use standard reference, indexing, cataloging and classifying tools and systems.
- Ability to effectively communicate with a wide variety of clientele in an agency or institution.
- Ability to prepare written reports.

As required:

- Working knowledge of the functions and characteristics of computer based library systems.
- Basic knowledge of the principles and practices of supervision.
- Basic knowledge of budgeting techniques and procedures used by employing agency.
- Ability to supervise a subordinate staff consisting of paid, volunteer and resident workers.

MINIMUM QUALIFICATIONS

Possession of a Public Librarian provisional certificate issued by the New York State Department of Education.

STATE OF WASHINGTON

EMPLOYEE PERFORMANCE EVALUATION
(Reprinted by permission from the Washington State Library)

How to Complete the Participative Performance Evaluation Process

The State's policy is that every employee will be evaluated at least once each year, preferably on the employee's anniversary date of employment. The forms provided for evaluation require that both supervisor and employee rate the employee's performance, then discuss independent ratings with a goal of coming to mutual understanding on the final evaluation. It is the process of communication that is important; the form only provides the vehicle whereby this communication takes place.

The evaluation process includes the following steps:

1. Both employee and supervisor review the employee's current Classification Questionnaire (CQ) and meet to discuss and come to mutual understanding upon the content of the CQ. If a new CQ is necessary, it should be prepared following the normal procedures.

2. Both employee and supervisor independently rate employee performance for the rating period by completing the rating and comment spaces under performance dimensions A through E in Section I on their respective WORKSHEETS. The rating should be centered upon the employee's overall accomplishment of the various elements of each performance dimension — the actual relative importance of which will vary from job to job. NOTE: The rating should be done on the basis of results achieved on the job as described in the CQ, and should not focus upon the employee's personality traits. Employees and supervisors can add additional elements under any performance dimension if the characteristics of the individual CQ require special attention to performance elements not listed. In the space after each element (e.g., Quantity of Work —) the supervisor and employee are required to write-in a brief "Comment" on their respective WORKSHEETS which describes the employee's performance during the rating period.

3. The supervision should arrange to have a full discussion of the ratings with the employee at a mutually convenient time and in a private office if possible. This discussion is the heart of the evaluation process and requires that both employee and supervisor be willing to discuss with frankness and candor any differences which might arise in the independent ratings. Both employee and supervisor have a responsibility to come to a mutual understanding on the final evaluation. If mutual understanding is not reached the second line supervisor may be asked by either the employee or the supervisor to help achieve mutual understanding on the Performance Evaluation Conference ratings. NOTE: In the space identified as "Employee Remarks" the employee is free to record any exceptions he/she takes to the ratings made by the supervisor on the Conference Report form.

4. Both the supervisor and employee should complete Section II, "Work Plan for the Future", on their Worksheets. Future performance plans are as important as the rating of past performance, therefore, Section II of the Conference Report must be completed in full by the supervisor with the employee's assistance. Either party can consult agency personnel or training officers for assistance in developing a Work Plan.

5. The supervisor is responsible to obtain signatures of the employee and the evaluating supervisor's supervisor and is also responsible for seeing to it that the employee receives a copy of the final evaluation and that a copy is placed in the employee's official personnel record. While the reviewer may serve as a mediator and can record comments on the Performance Evaluation Conference Report form, he/she is not permitted to alter the ratings recorded on the form. The

(Employee Performance Evaluation continues on page 214)

STATE OF WASHINGTON
EMPLOYEE PERFORMANCE EVALUATION (cont'd)

employee must sign the evaluation even though he/she may not fully agree with its content; any exceptions the employee takes to the content of the report can be recorded under "Employee Remarks".

6. The supervisor should monitor, at various intervals throughout the next evaluation cycle, how well the employee is doing relative to the Work Plan.

Evaluating employees is a difficult and demanding task; self-evaluation is likewise a very difficult but insightful enterprise. If both employee and supervisor work hard at using this basic tool of participative evaluation with confidence, honesty and mutual understanding, the relationship between them should be strengthened. A stronger supervisor-employee relationship based upon more effective communications should lead to an enhancement of the State's ability to provide effective and efficient public services.

DEFINITIONS: RATING CATEGORIES   **NOTE:** Use These Definitions of Rating Terms

---

Far Exceeds Normal Requirements—Truly exceptional performance generally attained by no more than an exceptionally small number of an organization's employees.

Exceeds Normal Requirements—Superior performance that surpasses what is generally expected of employees a majority of the time.

Meets Normal Requirements—Competent day-to-day performance is attained. Any shortcomings are generally balanced by some superior performance characteristics. This level of performance is generally attained by the majority of an organization's employees.

Meets Minimum Requirements—Day-to-day performance generally shows some limitations that are not balanced by any superior performance characteristics. This level of performance is generally demonstrated by only a small number of an organization's employees.

Fails to Meet Minimum Requirements—Day-to-day performance shows significant limitations and definite need for improvement is noted. This level of performance is generally demonstrated by no more than an exceptionally small number of an organization's employees.

NOTE: All of these definitions are prefaced by the term generally; conditions and people vary from agency to agency and the quality of performance similarly varies widely. These definitions are phrased in terms of the typical, generally encountered situation in State government. Make your ratings in terms of this understanding of the terms far exceeds normal requirements, meets normal requirements, etc. It is possible that in your agency there are more or fewer persons in each rating category than is typical of State government.

(Employee Performance Evaluation continues on page 215)

STATE OF WASHINGTON
EMPLOYEE PERFORMANCE EVALUATION (cont'd)

FORM **S.F. 9128** (9/78)	STATE OF WASHINGTON **EMPLOYEE PERFORMANCE EVALUATION**

NOTE: This is a triple-use form. Mark the appropriate box below.

☐ SUPERVISOR'S WORKSHEET
(To be prepared before the evaluation with the employee)

☐ EMPLOYEE'S WORKSHEET
(To be prepared before the evaluation with your supervisor)

☐ PERFORMANCE EVALUATION CONFERENCE REPORT

EVALUATION PERIOD
FROM _____ TO _____

PURPOSE OF APPRAISAL
☐ ANNUAL REVIEW   ☐ PROBATIONARY REVIEW
☐ TRIAL SERVICE REVIEW   ☐ OTHER _____

DOES THIS EMPLOYEE HAVE SUPERVISORY RESPONSIBILITY?
☐ YES   ☐ NO

JOB DESCRIPTION REVIEW
☐ THE CLASSIFICATION QUESTIONNAIRE HAS BEEN REVIEWED IN DETAIL

EMPLOYEE'S NAME (Last, First, Middle Initial)	JOB CLASSIFICATION TITLE		SOCIAL SECURITY NO.
AGENCY	DIVISION/SECTION	ANNIVERSARY DATE	SUPERVISOR'S NAME

SECTION I: PERFORMANCE FOR THE RATING PERIOD

ACCOMPLISHMENT OF JOB REQUIREMENTS: Performance Dimension A

ELEMENTS:

- QUANTITY OF WORK —
- COMPLETION OF WORK ON TIME —
- QUALITY AND ACCURACY OF WORK COMPLETED —
- INITIATIVE IN ACCEPTING RESPONSIBILITY —
- OTHER ELEMENTS (TO BE DEFINED BY EMPLOYEE AND/OR SUPERVISOR) —

COMMENTS

OVERALL RATING (Check Only One)
☐ FAR EXCEEDS NORMAL REQUIREMENTS
☐ EXCEEDS NORMAL REQUIREMENTS
☐ MEETS NORMAL REQUIREMENTS
☐ MEETS MINIMUM REQUIREMENTS
☐ FAILS TO MEET MINIMUM REQUIREMENTS

JOB KNOWLEDGE AND COMPETENCE: Performance Dimension B

ELEMENTS:

- KNOWLEDGE OF WORK UNIT PURPOSES, GOALS AND DUTIES —
- COMMAND OF SKILLS NEEDED FOR EMPLOYEE'S POSITION —
- COMMITMENT TO IMPROVING SERVICES TO THE PUBLIC —
- ADAPTABILITY TO NEW DEVELOPMENTS IN THE JOB —
- OTHER ELEMENTS (TO BE DEFINED BY EMPLOYEE AND/OR SUPERVISOR) —

COMMENTS

OVERALL RATING (Check Only One)
☐ FAR EXCEEDS NORMAL REQUIREMENTS
☐ EXCEEDS NORMAL REQUIREMENTS
☐ MEETS NORMAL REQUIREMENTS
☐ MEETS MINIMUM REQUIREMENTS
☐ FAILS TO MEET MINIMUM REQUIREMENTS

JOB RELIABILITY: Performance Dimension C

ELEMENTS:

- DEPENDABILITY AND RELIABILITY REGARDING WORK INSTRUCTIONS —
- PURSUIT OF EFFICIENCY AND ECONOMY IN THE USE OF STATE RESOURCES —
- DEGREE OF NEED FOR SUPERVISION —
- EFFICIENCY IN THE USE OF WORK TIME —
- OTHER ELEMENTS (TO BE DEFINED BY EMPLOYEE AND/OR SUPERVISOR) —

COMMENTS

OVERALL RATING (Check Only One)
☐ FAR EXCEEDS NORMAL REQUIREMENTS
☐ EXCEEDS NORMAL REQUIREMENTS
☐ MEETS NORMAL REQUIREMENTS
☐ MEETS MINIMUM REQUIREMENTS
☐ FAILS TO MEET MINIMUM REQUIREMENTS

STATE OF WASHINGTON
EMPLOYEE PERFORMANCE EVALUATION (cont'd)

PERSONAL RELATIONS: Performance Dimension D

ELEMENTS:	COMMENTS	OVERALL RATING (Check Only One)
• ABILITY TO GET ALONG WITH OTHERS IN THE WORK UNIT —		☐ FAR EXCEEDS NORMAL REQUIREMENTS
• CONTRIBUTES TO THE PROMOTION OF MORALE —		☐ EXCEEDS NORMAL REQUIREMENTS
• ACCEPTS APPROPRIATE DIRECTION FROM SUPERIORS —		☐ MEETS NORMAL REQUIREMENTS
• CONTRIBUTES TO THE PRODUCTIVITY OF THE WORK UNIT —		☐ MEETS MINIMUM REQUIREMENTS
• OTHER ELEMENTS (TO BE DEFINED BY EMPLOYEE AND/OR SUPERVISOR) —		☐ FAILS TO MEET MINIMUM REQUIREMENTS

COMMUNICATIONS SKILLS: Performance Dimension E

ELEMENTS:	COMMENTS	OVERALL RATING (Check Only One)
• COMPREHENSION OF ORAL AND WRITTEN DIRECTIONS —		☐ FAR EXCEEDS NORMAL REQUIREMENTS
• ABILITY TO COMMUNICATE ORALLY AND IN WRITING —		☐ EXCEEDS NORMAL REQUIREMENTS
• ABILITY TO LISTEN AND ABSORB NEW FORMS OF INFORMATION —		☐ MEETS NORMAL REQUIREMENTS
• KNOWLEDGE AND USE OF CORRECT MEANS AND CHANNELS FOR THE COMMUNICATION OF NOTICES, COMPLAINTS, ETC —		☐ MEETS MINIMUM REQUIREMENTS
• OTHER ELEMENTS (TO BE DEFINED BY EMPLOYEE AND/OR SUPERVISOR) —		☐ FAILS TO MEET MINIMUM REQUIREMENTS

PERFORMANCE AS SUPERVISOR: Performance Dimension F
(For Supervisor's Use Only)

ELEMENTS:	COMMENTS	OVERALL RATING (Check Only One)
• PLANS, ORGANIZES AND MONITORS WORK UNIT ACTIVITIES FOR EFFICIENT OPERATION —		☐ FAR EXCEEDS NORMAL REQUIREMENTS
• DIRECTS AND PROVIDES GUIDANCE TO SUBORDINATES —		☐ EXCEEDS NORMAL REQUIREMENTS
• CONDUCTS EFFECTIVE PERFORMANCE APPRAISALS AND PROMOTES EMPLOYEE DEVELOPMENT —		☐ MEETS NORMAL REQUIREMENTS
• SETS PERSONAL EXAMPLE OF HIGH PERFORMANCE FOR THE WORK UNIT —		☐ MEETS MINIMUM REQUIREMENTS
• OTHER ELEMENTS (TO BE DEFINED BY EMPLOYEE AND/OR SUPERVISOR) —		☐ FAILS TO MEET MINIMUM REQUIREMENTS

EMPLOYEE REMARKS: (For employee use only for Performance Evaluation Conference Report)

The employee is free to record additional comments or raise objections to the ratings made by the supervisor on the Performance Evaluation Conference Report; these comments become a permanent part of the employee's personnel file (attach additional sheets as needed).

STATE OF WASHINGTON

EMPLOYEE PERFORMANCE EVALUATION (cont'd)

SECTION II. WORK PLAN FOR THE FUTURE

NOTE: BOTH THE EMPLOYEE AND THE SUPERVISOR SHOULD FILL OUT SECTION II ON THEIR WORKSHEETS

WORK PLAN FOR PERFORMANCE AND PLANNING EMPLOYEE DEVELOPMENT OF _____

EMPLOYEE'S NAME

FOR PERFORMANCE ON THE PRESENT JOB, THIS EMPLOYEE SHOULD CONCENTRATE ON THE FOLLOWING PERFORMANCE ELEMENTS:

FOR LONG TERM DEVELOPMENT, THIS EMPLOYEE SHOULD CONSIDER THE FOLLOWING COURSE OF ACTION

SECTION III: REVIEW

REVIEWER'S COMMENTS

I have reviewed this report	DATE		
REVIEWER'S SIGNATURE			
This report is based on my best judgment of this employee's job performance	DATE	I have received a copy of this evaluation and it has been discussed with me	DATE
EVALUATING SUPERVISOR'S SIGNATURE		**EMPLOYEE'S SIGNATURE**	

FORM S.F. 9128 (9/78)

4

UNIVERSITY OF CALIFORNIA - LOS ANGELES

EMPLOYEE PERFORMANCE EVALUATION
(Instructions)

PURPOSE OF PERFORMANCE EVALUATIONS

Periodic written performance evaluations provide a supervisor and employee an opportunity to discuss the employee's job performance over a specific period of time. An important part of the evaluation process is agreement by both the supervisor and employee on what the job duties are. The supervisor should clearly express how well the employee is doing, and as appropriate, establish goals for improving performance. If the employee being evaluated is a supervisor who has direct responsibility for meeting established commitments to equal employment opportunity and affirmative action goals, a review of the individual's good faith efforts in this area must be included in the performance evaluation. In addition, written performance evaluations are included as an essential part of several personnel policies and many affect many actions such as completion of probationary period, layoff, merit increase, corrective action, dismissal, and transfer or promotion.

TIMING OF EVALUATIONS

While established personnel policies indicate the minimum frequency of evaluations, evaluations may be conducted anytime the supervisor or employee feels a review would be of value. Written performance evaluations become part of the employee's departmental personnel file.

1. **Probationary Employees.** Normally, probationary employees are evaluated at least twice during the probationary period, as provided by the Personnel Policy 250. These evaluations shall be made at the mid-point of the probationary period and again at least one month prior to the completion of the probationary period. More frequent written evaluations may be made whenever circumstances indicate an evaluation would be beneficial.

2. **Career Employees Who Have Attained Regular Status.** The performance of each continuing career employee shall be evaluated in writing at least once a year, preferably several months prior to his annual salary review date.

3. **Casual Employees.** Casual employees should be evaluated at any time the department head, supervisor, or the employee feels a written evaluation would be beneficial. Casual employees **must be** evaluated prior to receiving a casual increase.

4. **Employees Who Have Unsatisfactory Performance.** When an employee has been evaluated as having unsatisfactory performance, if retained, he should be evaluated again within three months of the date of the previous evaluation.

PERFORMANCE EVALUATION INTERVIEWS

1. **Pre-appraisal Interview.** In advance of the date an evaluation is due, the supervisor should clarify with the employee the standards and criteria upon which he will be evaluated. In addition, the supervisor should acquaint the employee with the evaluation form to be used. A date for the formal evaluation should be set at this time.

2. **Formal Evaluation Interview.** The supervisor should convey to the employee his evaluation of the employee's performance and they should plan for future job development. The supervisor should encourage the employee to ask questions, express his views concerning his job performance, and to discuss job problems. It is suggested that a draft of the written performance evaluation be prepared for the interview for as a result of the interview the supervisor may wish to add, delete or clarify the language.

COMPLETION OF THE PERFORMANCE EVALUATION FORM

GENERAL. The employee performance evaluation form consists of three (3) duplicated pages with a covering duplicated certification sheet. **BECAUSE OF CARBONIZED BACKINGS, THE FOUR DUPLICATED**

PAGES MUST BE SEPARATED PRIOR TO FILLING OUT. With exception of Section Two of the form (which is optional), the remainder of the form and certification should be filled out for each employee evaluation conducted.

EMPLOYEE PERFORMANCE EVALUATION CERTIFICATION. Note that only a copy of the certification is to be sent to the Staff Personnel Department. **DO NOT SEND THE COMPLETED EVALUATION FORM TO THE STAFF PERSONNEL DEPARTMENT.**

In the case of a Final Probationary Period Review, the Staff Personnel Department copy of the certification should be retained in the initiating department until the end of the employee's probationary period. At that time the bottom portion of the form (i.e. Report of Probationary Period - Final Evaluation) should be completed and the certification then submitted to the Staff Personnel Department.

SECTION ONE. Provides basic information on the nature of employee's work and personal achievements since the last performance evaluation.

Current Assignment. If present tasks being performed remain essentially unchanged from, either the description of such tasks on a previous performance evaluation form, or a description of such tasks on an established job description for the position, - it would be sufficient in this section to only make reference to the previous evaluation form on the job description.

Other Assignments During Year. (comments above are also applicable to this section) This section should reflect other assignments on employee's present position, or assignments on other positions employee may have held during the appraisal period.

SECTION TWO. Provides the supervisor with a simplified checklist evaluation of factor measurements generally inherent in all jobs. This section is optional, and is primarily included to facilitate review of substantial numbers of positions bearing the same classification or within the same classification series, or which are routinely similar in nature or duties performed.

Factor Measurements. A supervisor's understanding of what exemplifies performance at the various rating levels is of great importance to successful evaluation. It is recommended, for the sake of consistency, that supervisors in a unit get together periodically and compare standards and expectations they attach to each rating level. The following is a general guide - -

"**Satisfactory**" - employee's performance **meets** the standards for the job.

"**More than Satisfactory**" - employee's performance **frequently exceeds** the standards for the job.

"**Superior**" - employee's performance **most always far exceeds** the standards for the job.

"**Improvement Needed**" - employee's performance, while not unsatisfactory, **has not yet met** the standards expected by the supervisor.

"**Unsatisfactory**" - employee's performance has been **far below** the standards expected by the supervisor.

Factor Relationship to Job. Provides the supervisor an opportunity to weigh the relative importance to the job of each factor measurement.

SECTION THREE. In those instances in which Section Two is used, the supervisor should insure that the SUPERVISOR'S OVERALL EVALUATION is consistent with the outcome of the checklist ratings.

SECTION FOUR. Permits supervisor and employee to indicate specific steps to be taken toward performance improvement and personal development.

REMOVE THIS INSTRUCTION SHEET BEFORE PREPARING FORM

P21359 (R.5/78) 71465-130

UNIVERSITY OF CALIFORNIA — LOS ANGELES
EMPLOYEE PERFORMANCE EVALUATION (cont'd)

UNIVERSITY OF CALIFORNIA
EMPLOYEE PERFORMANCE EVALUATION

**EMPLOYEE PERFORMANCE EVALUATION CERTIFICATION
AND REPORT OF PROBATIONARY PERIOD**

Department _____

This is to certify that a performance evaluation of _____
(Name)

was conducted on _____ .
(Date)

A copy of the appraisal was given to the employee on _____ .
(Date)

Type of Review

☐ Annual

☐ Probationary

    ☐ Mid-Point

    ☐ Final: Retain certification until end of probationary period and complete the bottom section of the form before submitting
to the Personnel Department.

☐ Casual

☐ Supplemental

_____   _____
Supervisor   Date

_____   _____
Employee   Date

Report of Probationary Period — Final Evaluation

Date Probationary Period
Ends _____

Date Probationary Period Ends
If Extended _____

The above employee has:

☐ satisfactorily completed the probationary period and has been granted regular employee status.

☐ failed to satisfactorily complete the probationary period and has received notification of release.

_____   _____
(Date)   (Signature of Supervisor)

DETACH AND SUBMIT TO THE PERSONNEL DEPARTMENT

P21359 IR 5 78) RETENTION PERIOD: u 5 YRS. AFTER SEPARATION

UNIVERSITY OF CALIFORNIA — LOS ANGELES
EMPLOYEE PERFORMANCE EVALUATION (cont'd)

University of California — Los Angeles **EMPLOYEE PERFORMANCE EVALUATION**		Two copies of this form are to be made and distributed to: 1) Department 2) Employee	
NAME	DEPARTMENT	DIVISION	DATE PREPARED
PAYROLL TITLE	DATE HIRED	LENGTH OF TIME IN PRESENT POSITION	DATE OF LAST REVIEW
SUPERVISOR	SUPERVISOR'S PAYROLL TITLE		

SECTION ONE — Complete For All Staff Employees

CURRENT ASSIGNMENT (Describe Tasks Being Performed)

OTHER ASSIGNMENTS DURING YEAR (Indicate Major Assignments During Year Not Presently Being Performed)

NOTEWORTHY ACHIEVEMENTS DURING YEAR (Degrees, Certificates, Awards, Publications, Education, Training, etc.)

P21359 (R.5/78) RETENTION PERIOD: 0.5 YRS. AFTER SEPARATION

DEPARTMENT COPY

UNIVERSITY OF CALIFORNIA — LOS ANGELES
EMPLOYEE PERFORMANCE EVALUATION (cont'd)

SECTION TWO (optional)

CHECK (✓)	FACTOR MEASUREMENTS	CHECK (✓)	FACTOR RELATIONSHIP TO JOB
	I. Superior		1. Great importance
	II. More than satisfactory		2. Average importance
	III. Satisfactory		3. Little importance
	IV. Improvement needed		
	V. Unsatisfactory		

1. WORK QUALITY | I | II | III | IV | V | | 1 | 2 | 3
Accuracy, Neatness, Thoroughness

REMARKS

2. PRODUCTIVITY | I | II | III | IV | V | | 1 | 2 | 3
Extent to which the amount of work produced compares to quantity standards for the job.

REMARKS

3. JOB KNOWLEDGE | I | II | III | IV | V | | 1 | 2 | 3
Basic knowledge and skills, understanding of specific job duties and familiarity with other job functions.

REMARKS

4. RELATIONS WITH OTHERS | I | II | III | IV | V | | 1 | 2 | 3
Extent to which employee works effectively with fellow employees and with the public.

REMARKS

5. DEPENDABILITY | I | II | III | IV | V | | 1 | 2 | 3
Extent to which employee accepts and follows through on assignments.

REMARKS

6. WORK HABITS | I | II | III | IV | V | | 1 | 2 | 3
Care of equipment, observation of Department policy and procedures, attendance and punctuality.

REMARKS

7. _____ | I | II | III | IV | V | | 1 | 2 | 3
OTHER (SPECIFY)

REMARKS

DEPARTMENT COPY   P21359 (R.5/78)

UNIVERSITY OF CALIFORNIA – LOS ANGELES
EMPLOYEE PERFORMANCE EVALUATION (cont'd)

SECTION THREE – Complete For All Staff Employees

SUPERVISOR'S COMMENTS (Include Description of Employee's Major Strengths; Areas of Weakness; Affirmative Action Efforts, if Applicable; Potential for Future Growth; etc.)

SUPERVISOR'S OVERALL EVALUATION (Check One)

☐ SUPERIOR ☐ MORE THAN SATISFACTORY ☐ SATISFACTORY ☐ IMPROVEMENT NEEDED ☐ UNSATISFACTORY

SECTION FOUR – Complete For All Staff Employees

ACTION TO BE TAKEN BY SUPERVISOR TO ASSIST EMPLOYEE IN IMPROVING PERFORMANCE (Indicate Time Frame)

ACTION TO BE TAKEN BY EMPLOYEE TOWARDS IMPROVING OWN PERFORMANCE (Indicate Time Frame)

SECTION FIVE   Employee Comments

SECTION SIX – Signatures

This employee has been under my supervision for _____ months.

* Employee's Signature: _____

Supervisor's Signature: _____ Date: _____

Department Head Signature: _____ Date: _____

Date: _____

* Your signature indicates neither agreement nor disagreement with this evaluation, but it does indicate the evaluation has been reviewed by you.

RETENTION PERIOD: 0-5 YRS. AFTER SEPARATION

DEPARTMENT COPY

P21359 (R.5/78)

CITY OF HOUSTON

MUNICIPAL EMPLOYEE PERFORMANCE REVIEW
(For Professional, Technical, Supervisory or Staff Employees)
(Reprinted by permission from the Houston Public Libraries)

Name of Employee_____ Classification_ _____

Employee Number_____ How long in Above Classification_____

Dept./Div./Section_____ Date of Review_____

LEVEL OF PRESENT CLASSIFICATION: Supervisory_____ Technical_____
                                  Professional_____ Administrative/Staff_____

Reason for Review: Six Month_____ Annual_____
                    Unscheduled (Please Explain)_____

EXPLANATION OF APPRAISAL GUIDE:

Outstanding (O) - Performs this aspect of work in a manner that far exceeds minimun require-
                  ments; demonstrates unusual skills or abilities.
Good (G) _ Performs this aspect of work in a manner that meets or exceeds minimum requirements;
           demonstrates satisfactory skill or abilities in this area while leaving room for
           improvement.
Fair (F) - Performs this aspect of work in a manner that barely meets minimum requirements;
           demonstrates a need for improvement of skills or abilities in this area.
Unsatisfactory (U) - Performs this aspect of work in a manner that does not meet minimum
                     requirements; demonstrates a lack of skills or abilities in this area;
                     the need for definite improvement in this area is crucial.

INSTRUCTIONS: For each factor below, circle the applicable rating scale to the right. Only
               one should be circled for each factor.

I. EVALUATION OF PRIMARY DUTIES

    (Rating authority should list these prior to review meeting. They can be taken from
    the job description for this position.)

	U	F	G	O
A._____	X	X	X	X
B._____	X	X	X	X
C._____	X	X	X	X
D._____	X	X	X	X
E._____	X	X	X	X
F._____	X	X	X	X
G._____	X	X	X	X

(Municipal Employee Performance Review continues on page 224)

CITY OF HOUSTON

MUNICIPAL EMPLOYEE PERFORMANCE REVIEW (cont'd)

I. EVALUATION OF PRIMARY DUTIES (continued)

Comments:_____
_____
_____
_____

II. WORK-RELATED FACTORS DEMONSTRATED IN BEHAVIOR

		U	F	G	O

A. JOB RESULTS

		U	F	G	O
1.	Demonstrated ability to perform work of satisfactory quality	X	X	X	X
2.	Demonstrated ability to perform satisfactory quantity of work	X	X	X	X
3.	Demonstrated ability to work without close supervision	X	X	X	X
4.	Demonstrated ability to schedule activities so that work is completed on time	X	X	X	X
5.	Demonstrated ability to work on several assignments simultaneously.	X	X	X	X
6.	Demonstrated ability to deal with new problems, situations, or pressures related to job performance.	X	X	X	X
7.	Demonstrated ability to follow instructions with minimum delay	X	X	X	X
8.	Demonstrated willingness to keep superiors informed of significant developments in his/her area	X	X	X	X
9.	Demonstrated punctuality and regularity of attendance	X	X	X	X
10.	Demonstrated potential to supervise the work of others (to be rated only if present job is non-supervisory)	X	X	X	X

Comments:_____
_____
_____

B. WORKING RELATIONSHIPS

		U	F	G	O
1.	Demonstrated willingness to aid other employees both inside and outside his/her department	X	X	X	X
2.	Demonstrated ability to maintain good relations with other employees and/or the public	X	X	X	X
3.	Demonstrated ability to use proper amount of tact in issuing criticism to superiors, subordinates or peers	X	X	X	X
4.	Demonstrated ability to communicate effectively verbally and in writing	X	X	X	X

Comments:_____
_____
_____

C. MANAGEMENT SKILLS

		U	F	G	O
1.	Demonstrated ability to delegate authority in such a manner as to utilize all of subordinate's skills and abilities	X	X	X	X
2.	Demonstrated ability to obtain maximum quantity of acceptable work from subordinates	X	X	X	X
3.	Demonstrated ability to maintain control of section activities	X	X	X	X
4.	Demonstrated ability to properly train subordinates	X	X	X	X
5.	Demonstrated ability to assign effective work scheduled for subordinates	X	X	X	X
6.	Demonstrated ability to determine need for new manpower, equipment or methods	X	X	X	X

Comments:_____
_____
_____

CITY OF HOUSTON

MUNICIPAL EMPLOYEE PERFORMANCE REVIEW (cont'd)

III. OVERALL PERFORMANCE SINCE LAST APPRAISAL

Has shown improvement
Has maintained prior level
Has shown reduction
Has no previous evaluation

Comments: _____

IV. EXPLANATION OF APPRAISAL

This portion of the review is important because you list the basis for your evaluation of the employee. Discuss with the employee his or her behavioral strengths and/or weaknesses and list them below. Also list your suggestions for improving performance. Use additional paper if necessary.

Strengths and/or Weaknesses: _____

Suggestions for Improving Performance: _____

Other Comments: _____

EMPLOYEE ACKNOWLEDGEMENT:

I certify that this Performance Review has been discussed with me and I understand that I may appeal this evaluation to the head of my department within ten (10) days from the date of my signature.

Employee Signature: _____ Date: _____

Comments: _____

Rating Authority: _____ Date: _____
How long have you supervised employee? _____
Reviewing Authority (If applicable): _____ Date: _____
Head of Department: _____ Date: _____

Civil Service Director: _____ Date: _____

MINNEAPOLIS PUBLIC LIBRARY

STAFF PROGRESS REPORT
Unclassified Service
(Reproduced by permission from the Minneapolis Public Library
and Information Center)

Date of Report_____

Employee_____ Date of Present Assignment_____

Position_____ Date of Initial Appointment_____

Assignment_____

INSTRUCTIONS: Please read the instruction sheet for rating unclassified employees
before filling out this report. Items A-D are for supervisors to complete; item E
is for the employee to complete. Date and sign the report when it has been completed and discuss it with the employee who will also sign to indicate he has read
it. Send the report to the appropriate chief who will read, sign and send it to
the Personnel Office.

A. List duties and % of time   Comment on employee's performance of each duty
    spent on each duty

_____   _____

_____   _____

_____   _____

_____   _____

_____   _____

_____   _____

_____   _____

_____   _____

_____   _____

_____   _____

    List any special activities,   Comment on performance of special activities
    i.e. one-of-a-kind assignment,
    staff committee assignment

_____   _____

_____   _____

_____   _____

_____   _____

MINNEAPOLIS PUBLIC LIBRARY

Unclassified Service (cont'd)

B. The figures on the following scales indicate: 1-not satisfactory, 2-fair, 3-good, 4-very good, 5-outstanding.

Please check above the line at the proper degree of performance. Comment on any rating at either extreme and on any others where it would be helpful.

1. QUALITY OF WORK
   Accuracy, thoroughness, neatness; 1   2   3   4   5
   application of knowledge and skills.

2. QUANTITY OF WORK
   Amount of work completed; speed. 1   2   3   4   5

3. DEPENDABILITY
   Prompt accomplishment of duties; 1   2   3   4   5
   punctuality; adherence to schedule;
   follow-through; reliability.

4. INITIATIVE
   Ability to think creatively; 1   2   3   4   5
   imagination; resourcefulness;
   needs little supervision.

5. PERSONAL RELATIONSHIPS
   Courtesy, tact, friendliness, 1   2   3   4   5
   self-control; behavior toward staff
   and public; acceptance of criticism.

6. ATTITUDE TOWARD JOB
   Interested in job, eager to improve; 1   2   3   4   5
   strives to constructively support
   the MPL program.

7. SUBJECT KNOWLEDGE
   Reads widely and intelligently, 1   2   3   4   5
   knows literature of subject; has
   critical ability.

8. ORGANIZATION OF WORK
   Analyzes and organizes work well; 1   2   3   4   5
   budgets time appropriately.

9. PROFESSIONAL ATTITUDE
   Interest beyond particular job; keeps 1   2   3   4   5
   informed of and evaluates developments
   in the profession; sees library service
   in its entirety; is responsive to
   changing needs.

MINNEAPOLIS PUBLIC LIBRARY

Unclassified Service (cont'd)

Supervisory Qualities (check if appropriate)

10. MANAGEMENT OF AGENCY
    Has well-organized, well-maintained,
    agency or unit; is alert to labor-
    saving methods; delegates tasks wisely.

    1   2   3   4   5

11. STAFF RELATIONS
    Trains, directs and develops subordi-
    nates, maintains good morale and
    discipline, makes good judgments.

    1   2   3   4   5

12. PUBLIC RELATIONS
    Maintains good public relations;
    communicates effectively with persons
    and groups in the community.

    1   2   3   4   5

13. PROBLEM-SOLVING
    Has ability to analyze problems; uses
    imagination in solving problems; makes
    sound suggestions and good decisions.

    1   2   3   4   5

14. LEADERSHIP
    Has ability to carry through ideas and
    improvements; ability to inspire others;
    confidence, courage, respect of others.

    1   2   3   4   5

C.

1. Does employee's health adversely affect his job performance? Yes____ No____
   If yes, comment.

2. Are there any problems with employee's appearance (neatness, cleanliness,
   appropriateness of dress)?
   If yes, comment.   Yes____ No____

3. List any abilities or interests not being used in present position:

4. List any special steps taken to assist in improving employee's performance:

MINNEAPOLIS PUBLIC LIBRARY

Unclassified Service (cont'd)

D. Overall Judgment:_____

_____

Supervisor's signature_____ Date_____

I have read this report. I understand my signature does not necessarily mean that
I agree with the rating on all items.

Employee's signature_____ Date_____

_____

E. For the employee:

1. List any community activities in which you participated this year.

2. List courses taken or given during the past twelve months.

3. Note any significant travel during the past twelve months.

4. Note any abilities or interests not being used in present position.

5. List memberships, offices, committee assignments, etc., in professional
organizations in the past twelve months.

6. Comments on the report:

_____

Chief's signature_____ Date_____

Comments:

MINNEAPOLIS PUBLIC LIBRARY

STAFF PROGRESS REPORT
Classified Service
(Reproduced by permission from the Minneapolis Public Library
and Information Center)

Employee_____ Date of report_____

Classification_____ Date of Initial Assignment_____

Assignment_____ Date of Present Assignment_____

INSTRUCTIONS: Please read the instruction sheet for rating employees before filling
out this report. Fill out items A-E, date and sign the report and discuss it with the
employee. Ask the employee to fill out item F and sign the report as an indication he
has read it. When this has been done send the report to your supervisor.

A. Comment on performance of the attached list of duties:

    1.

    2.

    3.

    4.

    5.

B. Comment on relationships with:

    1. the public

    2. fellow employees

    3. supervisory personnel

MINNEAPOLIS PUBLIC LIBRARY
Classified Service (cont'd)

C. Comment on any problems with punctuality, attendance, physical fitness, appearance:

D. List steps taken to assist employee in improving his performance:

E. OVERALL JUDGMENT:

Supervisor's signature_____

I have read this report. I understand my signature does not necessarily mean that I agree with the rating on all items.

Signature of employee_____ Date_____

F. FOR THE EMPLOYEE:

1. List community activities in which you participated this year:

2. List courses taken or given during the past 12 months:

3. Note any significant travel during the past 12 months:

4. Note any abilities or interests not being used in present position:

5. Comments on the report:

Reviewed by_____ Reviewed by_____

PO 1972

MINNEAPOLIS PUBLIC LIBRARY

Classified Service (cont'd)

Staff Progress Report
Library Page I

Employee_____ Date of Report_____

Assignment_____ Appointment Date_____

INSTRUCTIONS: Comment briefly on the following items, date and sign the report. Discuss it with employee and have him sign. He may comment if he wishes. Send the completed report to your supervisor. A copy of a report on the first six months of a Library Page I, part time, will be forwarded to the Civil Service Commission.

1. Knowledge of duties:

2. Performance of duties (include accuracy, neatness, speed, willingness):

3. Ability to follow instructions, accept suggestions:

4. Relationship with others on the staff:

Comment on any problems with punctuality, attendance, physical fitness:

List steps taken to assist employee in improving his performance:

Overall judgment:

Supervisor's signature_____

I have read this report. I understand my signature does not necessarily mean that I agree with the rating on all items.

Signature of employee_____ Date_____

Comments:

| Signature | Title | Date |

Reviewed by:

PO 1973

1979

Labor Agreement

Between

The Library Board of the City of Minneapolis

and

AFSCME, Local 99

Minneapolis, Minn.

(General Unit)

(Used with the permission of the
Minneapolis Public Library and Information Center)

(Text of Agreement begins on page 234)

Labor Agreement (cont'd)

THIS AGREEMENT, made and entered into this _____ day of _____,
1979, by and between the Library Board of the City of Minneapolis, Minnesota,
(hereinafter referred to as the "Library"), and the American Federation of
State, County and Municipal Employees, Local No. 99, Minneapolis, Minnesota
(hereinafter referred to as the "Union"). The parties hereto agree as
follows:

ARTICLE I.   Purpose.
              It is the purpose and intent of this Agreement to achieve
and maintain sound, harmonious and mutually beneficial working and economic
relations between the parties hereto; to provide an orderly and peaceful
means of resolving differences or misunderstandings which may arise under
this Agreement; and to set forth herein the complete and full agreement
between the parties regarding terms and conditions of employment.

ARTICLE II.   Recognition.
              The Employer recognizes the American Federation of State,
County and Municipal Employees, Local No. 99, as the certified exclusive
representative for the unit, consisting of the employees in the classifications of:

Accounting Clerk I	Duplicating Machine Operator II
Accounting Clerk II	Library Aide II
Graphic Artist	Circulation Department Clerk
Bindery Worker I	Bibliographic Control Clerk
Bindery Worker II	Library Continuations Clerk
Bookbinder	Stock Clerk II
Library Page I	Keypunch Operator I
Clerk Typist I	Computer Operator I
Library Aide I	Computer Operator II
Library Page II	Acquisitions Clerk
Library Processing Aide	Attendant, Library
Clerk I	Telephone Operator I
Audio Visual Aide I	Delivery Worker
Offset Plate Preparation Clerk	Community Libraries Clerk
Book Preparation Aide	Library Technician - Homebound Volunteers
Clerk Typist II	

but excluding those part time employees whose service does not exceed 14 hours
per week or 35 per cent of the normal work week.

ARTICLE III.   Definitions.
              For the purpose of this Agreement, the words defined have
the meaning given them.
              "Employee" - Any person who holds a position in the unit
for which the Union is the certified exclusive representative.
              "Employer" - The Library Board of the City of Minneapolis,
Minnesota.

ARTICLE IV.   Non-Discrimination.
              The provisions of this Agreement shall be applied equally
by the Employer and the Union to all employees without discrimination as to sex,
race, color, creed, religion, ancestry, national origin, affectional preference,
disability, age, marital status, or status with regard to public assistance,
or membership in the Union.

-1-

ARTICLE V.   Strikes and Lockouts.
            A.   The Union, its officers or agents, or any of the
employees covered by this Agreement, shall not cause, instigate, encourage,
condone, engage in, or cooperate in any strike, work slowdown, mass resignation, mass absenteeism, the willful absence from one's position, the
stoppage of work, or the abstinence in whole or in part of the full, faithful
and proper performance of the duties of employment, regardless of the reason
for so doing.

            In the event the Employer notifies the Union that an
employee may be violating this Article, the Union shall immediately notify
such employee in writing of the Employer's assertion and the provisions of
this Article.

            Any employee who violates any provision of this Article
may be subject to disciplinary action or discharge, pursuant to the Minneapolis City Charter, Chapter 19. (Civil Service)

            B.   The Employer will not lock out any Employee during the
term of this Agreement as a result of a labor dispute with the Union.

ARTICLE VI.   Management Rights.
            The Union recognizes the right of the Employer to operate
and manage those affairs which are matters of inherent managerial policy,
which include but are not limited to, such areas of discretion or policy as
the functions and programs of the Employer, its overall budget, utilization
of technology, the organizational structure and selection and direction and
number of personnel.

ARTICLE VII.   Grievance Procedure.
            A.   This grievance procedure is established to resolve
any specific dispute between the employee and the Employer concerning, and
limited to, the interpretation or application of the provisions of this
Agreement.

            B.   An employee presenting a grievance may elect to be
represented by a Union representative of his choice at any step of the
procedure.

            C.   A grievance shall be resolved in the following manner:

Step 1.   Any employee claiming a specific disagreement concerning the
          interpretation or application of the provisions of this Agreement
          shall, within twenty (20) calendar days of its first occurrence or
          within ten (10) calendar days of the time the employee reasonably
          should have knowledge of the occurrence, whichever is later,
          discuss the complaint orally with the employee's immediate super-
          visor as designated by the Employer. The supervisor shall attempt
          to adjust the complaint at that time.

Step 2.   If a complaint is not resolved in Step 1 and the employee wishes to
          file a grievance, the employee shall, within seven (7) calendar

-2-

days of the oral discussion with the immediate supervisor, serve
a written copy of the grievance to the immediate supervisor and to
the Union. The written grievance shall set forth the nature of the
grievance, the facts on which it is based, the specific provision
or provisions of the Agreement allegedly violated, and the relief
requested. The supervisor shall respond in writing to the employee,
and to the Union, with a copy to the Associate Director, within
seven (7) calendar days after receipt of the grievance.

Step 3. If a grievance is not resolved in Step 2 and the Union wishes to
continue the grievance, the Union shall, within seven (7) calendar
days after receipt of the supervisor's answer, present the written
grievance and reply to the Chief concerned (Chief of central library,
Chief of community libraries, Chief of technical services, Superintendent of Buildings, or Associate Director). The Chief,
Superintendent or Associate Director shall give the Union and the
employee his written answer, with a copy to the Associate Director,
within seven (7) calendar days after receipt of the grievance.

Step 4. If the grievance is not resolved in Step 3 and the Union wishes
to continue the grievance, the Union shall, within seven (7)
calendar days after receipt of the Chief's answer, present the
written grievance and reply to the Director or his designee.
The Director or his designee shall give the Union and the employee
the Employer's written answer, with a copy to the Associate Director,
within seven (7) calendar days after receipt of the grievance.

Step 5. If a grievance is not resolved in Step 4 and the Union wishes to
continue the grievance, the Union may, within ten (10) calendar
days after receipt of the answer of the Director or his designee,
refer the written grievance and replies to arbitration. The
parties shall attempt to agree upon an arbitrator within seven (7)
calendar days after receipt of notice of referral; and in the event
the parties are unable to agree upon an arbitrator within said seven
(7) calendar day period, either party may request the Public Employment Relations Board of Minnesota to submit a panel of five (5)
arbitrators. Both the Employer and the Union shall have the right
to alternately strike two (2) names from the panel. In the event
the parties cannot agree on the party striking the first name, the
decision will be decided by a flip of a coin. The remaining person
shall be the arbitrator. The arbitrator shall be notified of his
selection by a joint letter from the Employer and the Union requesting
that he set a time and a place, subject to the availability of the
Employer and Union representatives.

-3-

The arbitrator shall have no right to amend, modify, nullify, ignore, add to or subtract from the provisions of this Agreement. He shall be limited to only the specific written grievance submitted to him by the Employer and the Union, and shall have no authority to make a decision on any other issue not so submitted to him. The arbitrator shall submit in writing his decision within ten (10) days following the close of the hearing or the submission of briefs by the parties, whichever is later, unless the parties agree to an extension thereof. The decision shall be based solely upon his interpretation of the meaning or application of the express terms of this Agreement as applied to the facts of the grievance presented. The decision of the arbitrator shall be final and binding.

The fee and expenses of the arbitrator shall be divided equally between the Employer and the Union provided, however, that each party shall be responsible for compensating its own representatives and witnesses.

      D. The Employer and the Union mutually agree that the grievance and arbitration procedures contained in this Agreement are the sole and exclusive means of resolving all grievances arising under this Agreement.

      E. The time limits established in this Article may be extended by mutual written consent of the Employer, the employee and the Union.

      F. If the finding or resolution of a grievance at any step of the procedure is not continued within the prescribed time limits, said grievance shall be considered resolved on the basis of the last answer provided, and there shall be no further appeal or review. Should the Employer not respond within the prescribed time limits, the grievance will proceed to the next step.

      G. When an employee has elected to pursue a remedy by State Statute or Minneapolis City Charter, for alleged conduct which may also be a violation of this Agreement, the employee shall not have simultaneous nor subsequent resort to this grievance procedure and the grievance then or thereafter processed shall be forever waived. The filing of a grievance based on the same issue or subject matter shall act as a bar for any action based on the same grievance brought in any court or administrative body pursuant to Federal or State law, or Minneapolis City Charter provision.

ARTICLE VIII.   Payroll Deduction for Dues.
      The Employer shall, upon request of an employee in the unit, deduct such sum as the Union may specify for the purpose of dues to the Union. The Employer shall remit monthly such deductions to the appropriate designated officer of the Union.

      The Union will indemnify, defend and hold the Employer harmless against any claims made and against any suits instituted against the Employer, its officer or employees, by reason of payroll deductions for dues.

      In accordance with M.S.A. 179-65, Subd. 2, the Library agrees that upon notification by the Union the Library shall deduct a fair share fee from all certified employees who are not members of the exclusive representative.

ARTICLE IX.   Salaries.
Salaries for full time employees shall be computed and
paid on a bi-weekly basis. The regular amount of pay for full time employees
shall be the bi-weekly rate regardless of the number of hours on duty for
that period provided that the employee is on duty as scheduled or is on
authorized paid leave.

Salaries for part time employees shall be computed and
paid on an hourly basis for the number of hours worked in a bi-weekly pay
period.

Appendix A, attached hereto and incorporated herein, shall
be the schedule of bi-weekly and hourly salaries for employees.

ARTICLE X.   Hours, Overtime.
A. Hours: This Article is intended to define the normal
hours of work and to provide the basis for the calculation of overtime pay.
Nothing herein shall be construed as a guarantee of hours of work per day or
per week.

The normal work day shall be seven and one half (7.5) hours
of work and the normal work week, regardless of shift arrangements, shall be
an average of thirty seven and one half (37.5) hours,

except that with respect to the position of Delivery Worker
the normal work day shall be eight (8) hours of work and the normal work week,
regardless of shift arrangements, shall be an average of forty (40) hours of
work.

Should it be necessary for the Library temporarily to
establish work schedules departing from the normal work schedule, notice of
such change shall be given to the Union as soon as is reasonably practicable.

B. Overtime: Overtime for Library employees shall be
paid according to Library Board policy adopted June 1969 (Personnel Manual
440.1, .2, .4). Compensation shall not be paid more than once for the same
hours under any provision of this Agreement.

ARTICLE XI.   Severance Pay.
Employees who retire from positions in the qualified
service and who meet the requirements set forth in this Article shall be
paid a severance pay allowance in the manner and amount set forth herein.

Payment of severance pay shall be made only to employees
and officers who at the time of retirement have accrued sick leave credit
of no less than sixty days, and who have no less than twenty years of
qualified service as computed for retirement or who have reached 60 years
of age or who are required to retire earlier because of either disability
or having reached mandatory retirement age.

When an employee having no less than sixty days accrued
sick leave dies prior to retirement, he shall be deemed to have retired
because of disability at the time of death and severance pay benefits shall

-5-

be paid to the beneficiary designated on his Minneapolis group life insurance policy or to the employee's estate if no beneficiary is listed, or in the case of an eligible part time employee to the beneficiary named on his application for the Municipal Employees Retirement Fund.

The severance pay for each employee qualified hereunder, shall be one-half the daily rate of pay for the position held by the employee on the day of retirement, notwithstanding subsequent retroactive pay increases, for each day of accrued sick leave subject to a minimum of sixty days and a maximum of 200 days.

Such severance pay shall be distributed at the monthly rate equal to the total amount of severance obligation divided by sixty (60) or $50.00, whichever is greater, to be paid on the last pay day for the City employees of each month, provided that the first of such payments shall begin in the calendar month next following termination of employment, but not less than thirty (30) days after the date of the employee's termination.

If a severance pay recipient dies prior to receiving the full amount of such benefit, the remaining payments shall be made in a lump sum to the beneficiary designated at the time of retirement or to the employee's estate if no beneficiary is listed.

ARTICLE XII.   Insurance Benefits.
Library employees receive the benefits of the City plan for hospitalization and life insurance.

A. Hospitalization: The Library agrees to contribute one hundred per cent (100%) of the cost of hospitalization insurance for each employee who has completed six (6) months of permanent actual full-time employment in any period of twelve (12) consecutive months. This amount shall be paid to the City's Group Health and Hospitalization Plan. Commencing in January of 1980, for each employee who selects dependent coverage, the City will contribute up to $47.55 per month toward the cost of dependent coverage. Commencing in January of 1981, for each employee who selects dependent coverage, the City will contribute up to $52.76 per month toward the cost of dependent coverage.

Health Maintenance Organization plans shall be available at the employee's annual option. The Library will pay one hundred per cent (100%) of single coverage for each employee who has completed six (6) months of permanent actual full-time employment in any period of twelve (12) consecutive months so long as this Health Maintenance Organization rate does not exceed that of the indemnity plan by more than $2.50 per month. The employee's contribution for dependent coverage shall be the same as in Article XII, Section A, unless the employee selects a more costly plan.

B. Life Insurance: Effective July 1, 1979 the Library agrees to provide paid life insurance coverage in the amount of $6,000 for each employee who has completed six (6) months of permanent full-time employment in any period of twelve consecutive months. The Library shall continue to provide arrangements for employees to purchase additional amounts of life insurance.

-6-

ARTICLE XIII.   Bulletin Boards.
          The Employer provides a bulletin board at the Central
Library for use by the Union in posting notices of Union business and
activities; said bulletin board space shall not be used by the Union for
political purposes other than Union elections.

ARTICLE XIV.   Examination Time.
          When an employee is schedule to take a Minneapolis Civil
Service promotional examination in his or her promotional line during his
or her regular scheduled hours of duty, the Employer shall grant time off
to take the examination when reasonably possible.

ARTICLE XV.   Rules and Regulations.
          It is understood that the Employer has the right to
establish reasonable rules and regulations. The Employer agrees to enter
into discussion with the Union on additions or changes of the existing rules
and regulations prior to their implementation.

ARTICLE XVI.   Civil Service Rules.
          The Employer and the Union agree that they will abide by,
for the term of this Agreement, the existing Civil Service rules relating
to leaves of absence, discharges and appeals, lay-off and re-employment,
and suspensions and demotions.

ARTICLE XVII.   Discipline Clause.
          The Library will discipline employees who have completed
the required probationary period only for just cause. Just cause shall be
defined in accordance with the Rules and Charter Provisions of the Minneapolis
Civil Service Commission. A written reprimand, suspension, demotion or discharge of an employee who has completed the required probationary period may
be appealed through the grievance procedure as contained in Article VII of
this Agreement. In the alternative, where applicable, an employee may seek
redress through a procedure such as Civil Service, Veteran's Preference, or
Fair Employment. Once a written grievance or appeal has been properly filed
or submitted by the employee or on the employee's behalf through the grievance
procedure of this Agreement or another available procedure the employee's
right to pursue redress in an alternative forum or manner is terminated.
The aggrieved employee shall indicate in writing which procedure is to be
utilised, and shall sign a statement to the effect that the choice of any
other hearing procedure precludes the aggrieved employee from making a
subsequent appeal through the grievance procedure of this Agreement.

ARTICLE XVIII.   Savings Clause.
          The parties agree to abide by all Federal laws, the laws
of the State of Minnesota, and the rules and regulations of the Minneapolis
Civil Service Commission.

          Any provisions of this Agreement held to be contrary to
law by a court of competent jurisdiction from whose final judgment or decree
no appeal has been taken within the time provided shall be void. All other
provisions shall continue in full force and effect.

ARTICLE XIX.   Duration and Effective Date.
          This Agreement shall be effective as of the first day
of July 1979 and shall remain in full force and effect to and including
the thirtieth day of June 1981, subject to the right on the part of the
Employer or the Union to open this Agreement by written notice to the other
party no later than February 1, 1981. Failure to give such notice shall
cause this Agreement to be renewed automatically for a period of twelve
(12) months from year to year.

          In the event such written notice is given and a new
Agreement is not signed before the expiration date of the old Agreement,
then said Agreement is to continue in force until a new Agreement is signed.
It is mutually agreed that the first meeting will be held no later than
seven (7) calendar days after the Employer or Union receives such notification. At this meeting each side shall set forth the sections to be
revised and the proposed provisions therein, and/or any addition thereto.
It is mutually agreed by both parties hereto that in the event of such
notice each Article of this Agreement not referred to in such notice shall
remain in full force and effect throughout the subsequent Agreement year(s).

Recommended for approval on this _____ day of _____

FOR THE LIBRARY BOARD   FOR THE UNION

_____   _____
Joseph Kimbrough   Stanley Stabno
Director   Business Representative
Minneapolis Public Library

_____   _____
Library Board   Anita B. Berglund
                                         President

                                         Approved as to Legality:

                                         _____
                                         Assistant City Attorney

                    City of Minneapolis

_____
Jerome Jallo
Assistant City Attorney

                                         Countersigned :

                                         _____
                                         City Comptroller-Treasurer

APPENDIX A

MINNEAPOLIS PUBLIC LIBRARY
Salary Schedules for the General Unit
Effective July 1, 1979

Title (C.S.grade)	Step	Bi-wk	Title (C.S.grade)	Step	Bi-wk
Accounting Clerk I	1	366	Library Page I	1	253
(III)	2	393	(I)	2	270
	3	441		3	288
	4	461		4	306
	5	480		5	318
	6	501		6	332
	7	521		7	346
				8	360
Accounting Clerk II	1	449			
(V)	2	483			
	3	538	Clerk Typist I	1	305
	4	562	Library Aide I	2	328
	5	587	Library Page II	3	367
	6	611	Library Processing	4	382
	7	638	Aide	5	398
			Clerk I	6	416
Graphic Artist	1	498	(II)	7	434
(V)	2	531			
	3	564			
	4	598	Keypunch Operator I	1	330
	5	624	(III)	2	355
	6	651		3	394
	7	679		4	411
				5	427
Bindery Worker I	1	347		6	446
(III)	2	373		7	465
	3	416			
	4	434			
	5	451	Audio Visual Aide I	1	347
	6	470	Offset Plate Prepara-	2	373
	7	491	tion Clerk	3	416
			(III)	4	434
Bindery Worker II	1	366		5	451
(IV)	2	393		6	470
	3	441		7	491
	4	461			
	5	480			
	6	501	Book Preparation Aide	1	366
	7	521	Clerk Typist II	2	393
			Duplicating Machine	3	441
Bookbinder	1	449	Operator II	4	461
(IV)	2	483	Library Aide II	5	480
	3	538	Computer Operator I	6	501
	4	562	(IV)	7	521
	5	587			
	6	611			
	7	638			

APPENDIX A

Salary Schedules for the General Unit - 2

Title (C.S.grade)	Step	Bi-wk	Title (C.S.grade)	Step	Bi-wk
Stock Clerk II	1	385	Acquisitions Clerk	1	503
(V)	2	414	Bibliographic Control	2	541
	3	464	Clerk	3	604
	4	484	(VI)	4	630
	5	505		5	656
	6	526		6	685
	7	549		7	714
			Telephone Operator I	1	347
Library Continuations	1	417	(III)	2	373
Clerk	2	448		3	416
(V)	3	497		4	434
	4	519		5	451
	5	541		6	470
	6	565		7	491
	7	591			
			Attendant, Library	1	305
			(II)	2	328
Circulation Department	1	449		3	367
Clerk	2	483		4	382
Computer Operator II	3	538		5	398
Community Libraries	4	562		6	416
Clerk	5	587			
Library Technician –	6	611			
Homebound Volunteers	7	638	Delivery Worker	See page 3	
(V)					

Provided that employees in the first pay step of a classification into which they were hired prior to July 1, 1979, shall be advanced to the 3rd pay step when granted an incremental increase on their anniversary date (when they have worked one full year), with the exception of Library Page I, where they will be advanced to the 4th pay step. Employees in the first pay step hired after July 1, 1979, will advance to the 2nd step when granted an incremental increase on their anniversary date (when they have worked one year).

Provided also that employees in other than the 1st pay step of a classification shall be advanced one pay step effective July 1, 1979 with the exception of Library Page I and Graphic Artist who will advance two pay steps effective July 1, 1979.

Provided that employees in this section shall receive 5 cents per hour additional at the beginning of the 15th year of service; and shall receive 10 cents per hour additional at the beginning of the 20th year of service; and shall receive 15 cents per hour additional at the beginning of the 25th year of service. These payments shall be based on a maximum of 80 hours biweekly.

Effective July 1, 1980

Effective July 1, 1980, the rates will be increased by the greater of 5.5% of the base pay rates or 90% of the percentage increase in the Minneapolis/St.Paul Consumer Price Index for Urban Wage Earners and Clerical Workers published by the Bureau of Labor Statistics, United States Department of Labor (1967=100) for the period of April, 1979, to April, 1980. Any calculation involving the above cost of living formula resulting in other than a whole percent shall be computed to the next whole percent. In no event shall the July 1, 1980, base pay rates exceed a maximum increase of 7.5%.

Salary Schedules for the General Unit - 3

Delivery Worker
(III)

Hourly

1	6.325
2	6.795
3	7.255
4	7.705
5	8.165
6	8.615

Provided that an employee in the third step of the classification, Delivery Worker, into which he was hired prior to July 1, 1979, shall be advanced to the sixth step effective July 1, 1979.

Provided that employees in this section shall receive 5 cents per hour additional at the beginning of the 15th year of service; and shall receive 10 cents per hour additional at the beginning of the 20th year of service; and shall receive 15 cents per hour additional at the beginning of the 25th year of service. These payments shall be based on a maximum of 80 hours biweekly.

Effective July 1, 1980

Effective July 1, 1980, the rates will be increased by the greater of 5.5% of the base pay rates or 90% of the percentage increase in the Minneapolis/St.Paul Consumer Price Index for Urban Wage Earners and Clerical Workers published by the Bureau of Labor Statistics, United States Department of Labor (1967=100) for the period of April, 1979, to April, 1980. Any calculation involving the above cost of living formula resulting in other than a whole percent shall be computed to the next whole percent. In no event shall the July 1, 1980, base pay rates exceed a maximum increase of 7.5%.

TOWN OF WATERTOWN, MUNICIPAL EMPLOYER MASSACHUSETTS MUNICIPAL LIBRARY EMPLOYEES COUNCIL #93, AMERICAN FEDERATION OF STATE, COUNTY AND MUNICIPAL EMPLOYEES, AFL-CIO, LOCAL #2436 MUNICIPAL EMPLOYEES UNION

AGREEMENT

This Agreement is made and entered into this day of July 1, 1980 by and between the Town of Watertown, as represented by its Board of Selectmen and its Board of Library Trustees, (hereinafter referred to as the EMPLOYER) and the Massachusetts Municipal Library Employees, Watertown Chapter, Local #2436 Massachusetts State Council No. 93, American Federation of State, County and Municipal Employees, AFL-CIO, (hereinafter referred to as the UNION). The Massachusetts Municipal Library Employees, Watertown Chapter, is the successor to the Watertown Public Library Staff Association.

ARTICLE I

RECOGNITION

Section A

The EMPLOYER recognizes the UNION for purposes of collective bargaining as the sole and exclusive representative of a Unit as certified by the Labor Relations Commission of the Commonwealth of Massachusetts Case No. MCR-441 described as follows:

All permanent employees of the Watertown Free Public Library in the professional position of Librarian, Pre-professional Librarians, and all permanent non-professional employees in the classification of Senior or Junior Library Assistants and/or clerical employees, including all regular part-time employees.

Excluded from the Unit are the Director of the Library, all custodial and maintenance employees, all pages, all casual and/or emergency employees and all other employees of the Municipal Employer (including specifically temporary employees and the Confidential Secretary to the Director).

As used in this section the phrases:

"Permanent Employee", shall mean an employee retained in continuous employment of a full-time basis or on a regular part-time basis of not less than twenty (20) hours per week as may be averaged over the previous eight (8) week cycle, including an employee in probationary status pending appointment to permanent status.

(Used with permission of the Board of Trustees of the Watertown, Massachusetts Public Library)

Agreement (cont'd)

"Continuous Employment", shall mean uninterrupted employment except for required military service and authorized legal holidays, vacation leaves, sick leaves, maternity leaves, and other authorized leaves of absence.

"Temporary Employee", shall mean an employee retained to fill a temporary position or to fill a full-time or regular part-time position for a period of less than fifty-two (52) calendar weeks in continuous employment.

"Temporary Position", shall mean a position in the Library Service which exists for a period of less than fifty-two (52) calendar weeks in continuous employment.

Section B

1.   The EMPLOYER retains all the powers conferred upon it by law (except insofar as said powers may be expressly restricted by the terms of this Agreement), including but not limited to the right to establish and administer policies and procedures relating to operations, services and functions of the EMPLOYER; to reprimand, suspend, discharge or otherwise discipline employees for just cause; to hire, promote and transfer employees; to determine the number of employees and the duties to be performed by them; to maintain the efficiency of employees; to establish, expand, reduce, alter, combine, consolidate, or abolish any department, operation or service; to make reasonable changes in job classifications; to determine staffing patterns and areas worked; to control and regulate the use of facilities, supplies, equipment and other property; to determine the number, location and operation of divisions and departments of the EMPLOYER, the assignment of duties, the qualifications required and the size and composition of the Library Staff; to make or change rules, regulations, policies and practices not inconsistent with the terms of this Agreement and otherwise generally to manage and direct the Library Staff, provided that such rights shall not be exercised so as to violate any of the provisions of this Agreement.

2.   The parties are agreed that no restrictions are intended on the rights and powers of the EMPLOYER except those specifically and directly set forth in expressed language in specific provisions of this Agreement.

3.   The parties recognize that the Director of the Library, as the chief executive officer of the Board of Library Trustees, shall continue to act as the administrator of Board policies and powers. Nothing herein contained shall be interpreted to limit or restrict the discretion and authority inherent in the office of the Director of the Library, (except insofar as said powers may be expressly restricted by the terms of this Agreement).

2

ARTICLE II
GRIEVANCE PROCEDURE

Section A - Definitions

1.   A "grievance" shall mean that there has been a complaint by an employee of a violation, misinterpretation or inequitable application of any of the provisions of this Agreement. As used in this article, the term "employee" shall also include a group of employees having the same grievance.

2.   A "party in interest" is the person or persons making the complaint and any person who might be required to take action or against whom action might be taken in order to resolve the complaint.

3.   An "aggrieved person" is the person or persons making the claim

Section B - Purpose

1.   The purpose of this procedure is to secure, at the lowest possible administrative level, equitable solutions to the problems which may from time to time arise affecting the welfare or working conditions of the employees. Both parties agree that these proceedings will be kept as informal and confidential as may be appropriate at any level of the procedure.

2.   Nothing herein contained will be construed as limiting the right of any employee having a grievance to discuss the matter informally with any appropriate superior, and having the grievance adjusted without intervention of the UNION, provided the adjustment is not inconsistent with the terms of this Agreement and that the UNION has been given the opportunity to be present at such adjustment and to state its views.

Section C - Procedure

Since it is important that grievances be processed as rapidly as possible, the number of days indicated at each level should be considered as maximum, and every effort should be made to expedite the process. The limits specified may, however, be extended by mutual agreement.

1.   Level One   An employee with a grievance will first discuss it with his immediate supervisor either directly or through a representative of the UNION, with the objective of resolving the matter informally.

2.   Level Two   (a). If the aggrieved person is not satisfied with the disposition of his grievance at Level One, or if no decision has been rendered within ten (10) work days after presentation of the grievance, he may file the grievance in writing with the Director of the Library. (Director) The written grievance shall be filed with the Director within five (5) work days after the decision at Level One or within fifteen (15) work days after the grievance was first presented at that Level, whichever is sooner.

3

(b). The Director will represent the EMPLOYER at this
level of the grievance procedure. Within ten (10)
work days after the written grievance has been so
filed, the Director will meet with the aggrieved
Person in an effort to resolve it.

(c). If an employee does not file a grievance in writing
with the Director within thirty (30) days after the
employee knew or should have known of the act or
condition on which the grievance is based, then the
grievance will be considered as waived. A dispute
as to whether a grievance has been waived under this
paragraph will commence at Level Three of this procedure.

3. **Level Three** If the aggrieved person is not satisfied
with the disposition of his grievance at Level Two, or
if no decision has been rendered within ten (10) work
days after he has first met with the Director, he may
file the grievance in writing with the Board of Library
Trustees. (Board) The written grievance shall be filed
with the Board within five (5) work days after the
decision by the Director or fifteen (15) work days after
he has first met with the Director, whichever is sooner.
Within ten (10) work days after the written grievance has
been so filed, a majority of the Board of Library Trustees
or a sub-committee of the Board (Sub-Committee) will meet
with the aggrieved person for the purpose of resolving the
grievance. The ultimate decision on the grievance at Level
Three will, however, be rendered by a majority of the Board
of Library Trustees.

4. **Level Four** (a). If the aggrieved person is not satisfied
with the disposition of his grievance at Level Three, or
if no decision has been rendered within ten (10) work days
after he has first met with the full Board or the Sub-
Committee, he may within five (5) work days after a decision
by the Borad or within fifteen (15) work days after he has
first met with the full Board or the Sub-Committee, whichever
is sooner, request in writing that the UNION submit his
grievance to arbitration. If the UNION determines that the
grievance is meritorious, it may submit the grievance to
binding arbitration within fifteen (15) work days after receipt
of the request for arbitration made by the aggrieved person.

(b). Within ten (10) work days after such written notice of
submission to arbitration, the full Board or the Sub-Committee
and the UNION will agree upon a mutually acceptable arbitrator
and will obtain a commitment from said arbitrator to serve. If
the parties are unable to agree upon an arbitrator or to obtain
such a commitment within the specified period, a request for a
list of arbitrators may be made to the American Arbitration
Association by either party.

(c). The parties will be bound by the rules and procedures of
the American Arbitration Association.

4

(d). The arbitrator so selected will confer with the representatives of the EMPLOYER and the UNION and hold hearings promptly and will be requested to issue his decision not later than twenty (20) work days from the date of the close of the hearings, or, if oral hearings have been waived, then from the date the final statements are submitted to him. The arbitrator's decision will be in writing and will set forth his findings of fact, reasoning and conclusion on issues submitted. The arbitrator will be without power or authority to make any decision which requires the commission of an act prohibited by law or which is violative of the terms of this Agreement. The decision of the arbitrator will be submitted to the EMPLOYER and the UNION and will be final and binding.

(e). The costs for the services of the arbitrator, including per diem expense, will be borne equally by the EMPLOYER and the UNION.

Section D – Rights of Employees to Representation

1. No reprisals of any kind will be taken by the EMPLOYER or by any of its agents or representatives against any party in interest, any representative of the UNION or any other participant in the grievance procedure by reason of such participation.

2. Any party in interest may be represented at all stages of the grievance procedure by a person of his own choosing. When an employee is not represented by the UNION, the UNION shall have the right to be present and to state its views at all stages of the grievance procedure.

3. Decisions rendered at Levels One, Two and Three of the grievance procedure will be in writing setting forth the decision and the reasons therefor and will be transmitted promptly to all parties in interest. Decisions rendered at Level Four will be in accordance with the procedures set forth in Section C, Paragraph 4(c).

4. While both parties may maintain files of grievances and the dispositions thereof, the EMPLOYER shall not make any entry or file any paper in the personnel file of any employee involved in a grievance except as may be required to implement the disposition thereof.

5. Forms for filing grievances, serving notices, taking appeals, making reports and recommendations, and other necessary documents, will be jointly prepared by the Library Director and the UNION and given appropriate distribution so as to facilitate operation of the grievance procedure.

6. Notwithstanding anything to the contrary, no dispute or controversy shall be a subject for arbitration unless it involves a grievance as defined in this Article, Section A, No. 1 of this Agreement; the arbitrator shall have no power to add to, subtract from, or modify any of the terms of this Agreement. The arbitrator shall arrive at his decision solely upon the facts,

evidence and contentions as presented by the parties during the arbitration proceedings.

7.   Grievances involving disciplinary action which will or might result in monetary loss to the employee shall commence at Level Two of the Grievance Procedure.

ARTICLE III
PROBATIONARY PERIODS

Section A

All original appointments to permanent full-time positions or regular part-time positions in the Library Service shall be subject to the following probationary periods:

Professional Positions, One (1) year;

Pre-Professional Positions, Six (6) months: and

Non-Professional Positions, Six (6) months.

Section B

1.   All promotions of employees of the Library in permanent status from one grade to a higher grade in the same class of positions or from one class of positions to a higher class of positions shall be subject to the following probationary periods:

Professional Positions, Three (3) months;

Pre-Professional Positions, One (1) month; and

Non-Professional Positions, One (1) month.

2.   In the case of an employee who is appointed to a permanent position in which he is then serving on a temporary basis (excluding vacation fill-in time), the probationary period shall commence as of the date he first assumes the duties of the position.

Section C

The probationary periods stated in this Article shall mean periods of full-time service or their equivalent in regular part-time service.

ARTICLE IV
TEMPORARY SERVICE IN A HIGHER POSITION

Section A

Whenever a vacancy exists in any position in the Library Service and an employee in a lower grade and salary is assigned by the Board of Library Trustees to cover the vacancy on a temporary basis, the employee so assigned shall receive the compensation of the higher graded position beginning with

6

the thirtieth (30th) work day following the assignment retroactive to the first (1st) work day and continuing while performing satisfactorily in the higher grade until such temporary service is terminated.

Section B

Section A, of this Article, shall not apply to the assignment of a person to cover a higher position when the holder of the higher graded position is absent on vacation leave but shall apply when the holder of such higher graded position has resigned or is absent on sick leave or other authorized leave of absence.

Section C

In the event the employee so serving in the higher graded position is appointed to that position, the probationary period shall commence as of the date he first assumed the duties of the higher graded position, as provided in Article III, Section B(2).

ARTICLE V

NON-DISCRIMINATION

Section A

The UNION agrees that as the sole and exclusive bargaining agent for all employees in the Unit described above, and as so recognized by the EMPLOYER, it will continue to act, negotiate and bargain collectively for all employees in the Unit, and shall be responsible for representing the interests of all such employees without discrimination, and without regard to Union membership or participation in Union activities. The UNION further agrees to continue its policy of recognizing that membership in the UNION is voluntary and is open to all employees in the Unit without discrimination and without regard to race, color, creed, national origin, age, sex or marital status.

Section B

In its employment practices the EMPLOYER agrees to continue its policy of dealing with all persons without discrimination and without regard to race, color, creed, national origin, sex, age or marital status, and without regard to Union membership, participation in Union activities or to the assertion by any employee of any rights under this Agreement.

ARTICLE VI

EMPLOYEE EVALUATION

Section A

A performance evaluation of all employees of the Library shall be made

7

at least annually by their supervisors. Employees will be given a written
copy of their evaluation reports and will have the right to discuss such
reports with their supervisors, including the Director of the Library. The
evaluation reports shall then be entered in the employees' personnel files.

Section B

Employees shall have the right upon request and at reasonable times to
review the contents of their personnel files except for materials of a confidential nature received at the time of their original appointments. An
employee shall have the right to have a representative of the UNION present
during such review.

Section C

No material derogatory to an employee's conduct, service, character or
personality will be placed in his personnel file unless the employee has had
an opportunity to review the material. The employee will acknowledge that
he has had the opportunity to review such material by affixing his signature
to the copy to be filed, with the express understanding that such signature
in no way indicates agreement with the contents thereof. The employee will
also have the right to submit a written answer to such material and his
answer shall be reviewed by the Director and attached to the file copy.

ARTICLE VII

USUAL LEAVE OF ABSENCE

Section A - Vacation Leave

1. Vacation leave earned during any calendar year shall be credited on the
last day of that year and shall be available during the following calendar
year, except that during the first year of employment any vacation leave
earned prior to June 1st shall be available in the same calendar year and any
vacation leave earned after June 1st shall be available in the following
calendar year. Vacation leave credit not used in the calendar year in which it
becomes available except where an employee is required to perform services
during his vacation period, may not be accumulated and used in a subsequent year.

2. All permanent part-time employees whose hours of work follow a regular
weekly schedule of an average of twenty (20) hours or more shall be entitled
to receive vacation periods, without loss of pay, in such proportion as their
part-time service bears to full-time service in the Library.

3. All permanent, full-time employees shall be entitled to receive vacation
periods, without loss of pay, as follows:

8

(a)Less than six (6) months of continuous service, no vacation; (b) At least six months of continuous service, two (2) weeks; (c) Each month after six (6) months of continuous service, one and one-half (1 1/2) days; and (d) Annually, after one (1) year of continuous service, four (4) weeks.

4.   Employees who have available to them more than two (2) weeks of vacation leave credit shall be entitled to receive a two (2) week summer vacation between June 15th and September 15th and the remainder of their vacation leave credit as a whole or in fractional amounts of not less than one-half (1/2) working day at any time during the year of availability. In lieu of a summer vacation, an employee, with the approval of the Director of the Library, may be granted a two (2) week vacation period at some other time during the year of availability.

5.   The Director of the Library shall grant vacation leave as prescribed above at such times during the vacation year as will best serve the public interest and convenience. Employees may indicate their preference for a summer vacation period by submitting a request in writing to the Director before May 15th; requests for other periods of vacation of one week or more should be submitted at least thirty (30) days prior to the proposed commencment of such vacation period. Preference shall be given to employees on the basis of their years of service in the Library.

Section B - Sick Leave

1.   All permanent, full-time employees shall be entitled to receive sick leave with pay at the rate of one and one-fourth (1 1/4) working days for each month of service, not to exceed fifteen (15) working days for each year of service. Sick leave not used in any year may be accumulated from year to year, such accumulation not to exceed two hundred and forty (240) working days during the entire period of employment.

2.   All permanent, part-time employees whose hours of work follow a regular weekly schedule of an average of twenty (20) hours or more which average shall be computed over the previous eight week cycle, shall be entitled to receive sick leave with pay in such proportion as their part-time employment bears to full-time employment in the Library Service.

3.   Requests for additional sick leave shall be referred by the Director to the Board of Library Trustees and the Board may extend the employee's paid sick leave if, in their discretion, such extension is justified on the basis of extreme and extenuating circumstances.

9

4. An employee who is laid off or resigns from his position under conditions that are not discreditable to him, if reemployed within one (1) year, shall have available any unused sick leave credit existing at the time of said layoff or resignation. When an employee is transferred to another department of the Town, any unused sick leave which may have accumulated to his credit shall continue to be available for his use as necessary.

5. "Sick Leave" shall mean that period of time for which an employee is entitled to receive compensation while a) unable to perform his duties because of illness or injury; or b) caring for a sick or injured child or spouse living in the same residence as the employee; or c) caring for a sick or injured parent, whether living in the same house or not at some location within the state of Massachusetts. Sick leave allowance shall be limited to five (5) days for each occurrence under (b) or (c) above.

6. When an employee finds it necessary to be absent from his duties because of illness or injury, he or his representative shall at once notify the Director of the Library and no sick leave benefits shall accrue to an employee who fails to give such notice.

7. The Director of the Library may require the presentation of a doctor's certificate or report in connection with any claim for sick leave. If absent from duty for more than three (3) consecutive working days due to illness or injury, the employee shall present to the Director a doctor's certificate or report in writing and under oath regarding his condition. the EMPLOYER specifically reserves the right to obtain independent medical certificates and reports and otherwise to obtain independent verification of the employee's claim for sick leave due to illness or injury.

8. Sick leave under this Article shall not apply in cases where injuries are sustained in the line of duty.

9. If an employee has received sick leave contrary to the provisions of this Article or through any misrepresentations made by him or by others in his behalf he shall reimburse the Town in an amount equal to the sick leave pay so received.

10. The Director of the Library shall cause to be kept a uniform attendance record on such forms as shall be approved and audited by the Town Auditor, showing the amounts of sick leave accrued and granted. Upon request, the Director shall transmit such records to any member of the Board of Library Trustees, the Town Treasurer or the Town Auditor.

10

Section C - Paid Holidays

1.   All employees covered by this Agreement shall be excused from all duty on the following legal holidays: New Year's Day, Martin Luther King Day, Washington's Birthday, Patriot's Day, Memorial Day, Independence Day, Labor Day, Columbus Day, Veteran's Day, Thanksgiving Day, and Christmas Day. All permanent, full-time employees shall be entitled to these designated holidays without loss in pay. All permanent, part-time employees whose hours of work follow a regular weekly schedule of an average of twenty (20) hours or more, which average may be computed over the previous eight week cycle, shall be paid in such proportion as their part-time service bears to full time service in the library.

2.   If a holiday falls on the employee's regular day off duty, the employee, in lieu of such paid holiday, shall receive some other day off consistent with the public interest and convenience, without loss in pay. If a holiday falls on one of the employee's vacation days, the employee shall receive an additional day of vacation or some other day off as aforesaid, without loss in pay.

ARTICLE VIII
OTHER LEAVES OF ABSENCE

Section A - Bereavement Leave

1.   In case of the death of a parent, step-parent, husband, wife, child, step-child, brother, sister, father-in-law, mother-in-law, son-in-law, or daughter-in-law of any employee, said employee will be granted a leave of absence from his duties, without loss of pay and without having any part of said employee's sick leave benefit charged against his accumulated sick leave time, from the day of death up to, but not beyond, the first working day following the funeral of the deceased; but in no case will said employee receive pay for absence of more than three (3) working days, except with the expressed approval of the Board of Library Trustees, and then only in cases of extreme emergency.

2.   In case of the death of a grand-child, grand-parent, brother-in-law, sister-in-law, nephew, niece, uncle or aunt of any employee, he shall be granted a leave of absence of one (1) working day on the day of the funeral without loss of pay and without having any part of the employee's sick leave benefit charged against his accumulated sick leave time; but in no case shall the employee receive pay for absence of more than one (1) working day day except with the express approval of the Board of Library Trustees and then only in case of extreme emergency.

3.   In the event a death occurs while an employee is on vacation leave, the

11

employee shall immediately notify the department head, who, at the request of the employee, shall change said employee's status from vacation to bereavement leave. This provision will not operate to extend the employees original period of absence. In the event an employee substitutes bereavement leave for vacation leave under these circumstances, said vacation leave shall be taken at a later date with the approval of the department head.

Section B - Court Leave

Employees who are called for jury duty or summoned on behalf of the Town as witnesses shall be granted court leave, without loss of pay. If the fees for jury duty or witness fees amount to less than the employee's regular rate of compensation, he shall be paid an amount equal to the difference between them. Notice of service shall be filed with the Director of the Library upon receipt of summons. When an employee has been granted court leave and is excused by proper court authority, he shall report back to his regular place of duty whenever the interruption in said court related service will permit four or more consecutive hours of employment during the hours of his tour of duty.

Section C - Maternity Leave

Permanent female employees shall be granted a maternity leave period not exceeding twenty four (24) weeks, without pay. An employee who is on maternity leave shall notify the Director in writing, at the end of eight weeks as to her intent to return to work at the termination of her leave.

Section D - Unpaid Sick Leave

The Board of Library Trustees, in their discretion, may grant periods of unpaid sick leave in cases where employees, due to longterm illness, have used all their available sick leave credit and have also used all their available vacation leave credit.

Section E - Unpaid Sick Leave and Maternity Leave

Group Insurance costs shall be paid by the employer up to sixteen (16) weeks. After sixteen (16) weeks the employee shall pay back to the employer within six (6) months one-half (1/2) of the cost of group insurance expended during the unpaid sick leave and/or maternity leave.

Section F - Paternity Leave

Permanent male employees shall be granted a paternity leave period not exceeding four (4) weeks, without pay.

ARTICLE IX

GROUP INSURANCE

The present Group Insurance Plan shall remain in full force and effect for the duration of this Agreement: the EMPLOYER agrees to pay the same share

12

of the cost as at present. In the event that the EMPLOYER is empowered by law to increase the employer share of group insurance benefit costs, and in the event that the EMPLOYER does so provide for any other employee group, all employees under this Agreement shall receive the benefit of the same employer share of said costs.

ARTICLE X
LONGEVITY PAY

All permanent part-time employees who work 20 hours or more per week shall receive longevity pay in the same proportion that their work week bears to the work week of a permanent full-time employee. All full-time employees shall receive longevity pay in accordance with the following schedule:

Effective July 1, 1979

10 years	$500
15 years	$550
20 years	$650
25 years and over	$800

ARTICLE XI
DUES DEDUCTION AND AGENCY SERVICE FEE

Section A - Authorization for Dues Deductions

Upon receipt by the EMPLOYER of a signed voluntary authorization by an employee, the EMPLOYER agrees to deduct the initiation fee (if any) and monthly UNION membership dues which may be duly levied by the UNION from the pay of said employee and remit the aggregate amount to the Treasurer of the UNION together with a list of employees from whose pay said dues have been deducted. Such remittance shall be made by the 10th day of the next succeeding month. An authorization may be revoked by the employee by sending a signed written notice thereof to the Town Auditor, such revocation to take effect sixty (60) days after receipt thereof. The EMPLOYER shall send a copy of the revocation to the UNION.

The following form of authorization for dues deduction shall be used:

AUTHORIZATION FOR PAYROLL DEDUCTION

By_____
    Last Name   First Name   Middle Name

To_____
    Employer   Department

Effective_____
                 Date

    I hereby request and authorize you to deduct from my earnings the UNION membership initiation fee, and, once each month, an amount duly established by the UNION as dues. The amount deducted shall be paid to the Treasurer of the UNION.

13

The authorization shall continue for a period of one (1) year from the date or until the termination of this Agreement (whichever occurs first) and shall be automatically renewed for successive periods of one (1) year unless written notice of revocation is given by me to you in writing, upon the receipt whereof this authorization shall expire sixty (60) days thereafter.

SIGNED_____

Section B - Indemnification

The UNION shall indemnify and save the EMPLOYER harmless against any claim, demand, suit or other form of liability that may arise out of or by reason of action taken by the EMPLOYER for the purpose of complying with this Article.

Section C - Agency Service Fee

An Agency Service Fee in accordance with the provisions of Massachusetts General Laws, Chapter 150E, shall be in effect for all bargaining unit employees as of 1/1/80, except that present employees will be Granfathered.

Pursuant to the provisions of Chapter 150E, all employees in the Bargaining Unit shall, as a condition of employment, pay to the UNION, the exclusive Bargaining Agent and Representative, an amount of money equal to that paid by other employees in the Bargaining Unit who are members of the UNION, which shall be limited to an amount of money equal to the Union's regular and usual membership dues as provided for by the Union Constitution. For existing employees such payment shall commence thirty-one (31) days following the date of their employment.

ARTICLE XII
ADVANCE STUDY PROGRAM

Section A

In the discretion of the Board of Library Trustees, any employee may be granted time off from his regular duties to take or continue to take courses of study in library science, or other library related courses of study, for the purpose of acquiring or of increasing his professional ability. The proposed courses of study must be reviewed and approved in advance by the Director of the Library. The Board may also, in their discretion, grant not more than four (4) hours of leave with pay during each week such employee is actually taking said courses of study. Travel time to and from the schools where such courses of study are taken shall be included in the said four (4) hours of leave with pay.

14

Section B

     An employee who has been granted leave with pay from his regular duties as aforesaid shall file with the Director a declaration of his intention to remain in the employ of the Library for a period of six (6) months following completion of said courses of study.

Section C

     An employee who has satisfactorily completed eight (8) to twelve (12) semester hours of study which have been previously approved by the Director may, in the discretion of the Board of Library Trustees, be placed on the next higher step of the salary schedule for the class and grade of the employee's position, except that an employee at maximum in the class and grade of a Pre-Professional I (L-4) may be placed on an appropriate step in the class and grade of a Pre-Professional II (L-5), without loss to the employee of his eligibility to receive his next annual step rate increment. In exercising their discretion hereunder, the Trustees shall consider whether the employee has actually increased his professional ability as a result of taking such courses of study.

ARTICLE XIII
BULLETIN BOARDS

     The EMPLOYER agrees to make space available to the UNION on bulletin boards located in non-public areas in the Main Library and in each of the Branch Libraries for the purposes of posting routine UNION notice, circulars and other materials relating to UNION business. The UNION agrees not to post any material containing derogatory language or criticisms of the EMPLOYER. All material must be approved for posting by an officer of the UNION and a copy thereof should be furnished to the Director of the Library.

ARTICLE XIV
PROFESSIONAL MEETINGS

     When an employee attends a professional meeting with the prior approval of the Director of the Library, such attendance shall be compensated as for time worked, as follows: if the professional meeting is held during the employee's regular working hours, the employee may attend without loss in pay; if held outside the employee's regular working hours, the employee shall be entitled to receive compensatory time off. An employee's request to attend a professional meeting must be made in writing to the Director at least one (1) week before the date thereof, and the Director's approval must likewise be in writing.

15

ARTICLE XV

HOURS OF WORK AND OVERTIME

Section A - Work Week

The regular work week for full-time employees shall be thirty-seven (37) hours scheduled in five (5) working days during any seven (7) day payroll period. The regular work week shall include Saturday but not Sunday. A full-time employee's working day shall provide for a duty free lunch period; and a fifteen (15) minute rest period during each one-half (1/2) shift. To the extent practicable, the rest period should be scheduled in the middle of said one-half (1/2) work shift. If a full-time employee is required to work in excess of thirty-seven (37) hours in a regular work week he may, in the discretion of the Director of the Library, be granted compensatory time off consistent with the public interest and convenience.

Section B - Overtime

If a full-time employee, after completing his regularly scheduled thirty-seven (37) hour work week, is required to work on the following Sunday, the employee shall be compensated at the rate of one and one-half (1 1/2) times his regular rate for such Sunday employment. A permanent part-time employee is not entitled to receive overtime compensation for work performed on a Sunday. To the extent practicable, Sunday assignments shall be made on a voluntary basis.

ARTICLE XVI

SALARIES

Salary agreements are set forth in Appendix "A" which is attached hereto and made a part hereof. Effective July 1, 1980 and continuing to and including June 30, 1981, the salary schedule for the employees covered by this Agreement shall be as follows:

	Min.	II	III	IV	Max.
	Appendix A - Salary Schedule 1980				
L-1	7,652.14	8,041.03	8,394.02	8,747.00	9,094.02
L-2	9,094.02	9,536.75	9,973.51	10,416.25	10,852.99
L-3	9,794.02	10,242.73	10,679.49	11,122.23	11,558.97
L-4	10,505.98	11,116.24	11,732.48	12,354.70	12,964.96
L-5	11,205.99	11,822.22	12,438.46	13,054.70	13,670.94
L-6	11,732.48	12,438.46	13,138.45	13,850.43	14,550.43
L-7	12,438.46	13,138.45	13,850.43	14,550.43	15,256.41
L-8	13,138.45	13,850.43	14,550.43	15,256.41	15,956.42
L-9	16,482.91	17,344.44	18,199.99	19,061.54	19,923.08

ARTICLE XVII

PERSONNEL BY-LAWS

Section A

    Except as provided in Section B of this Article, all existing provisions of the Town By-Laws relating to the hours, wages and conditions of employment of the employees covered by this Agreement, whether or not such provisions are referred to in any Article hereof, are to remain in full force and effect during the term of this Agreement.

Section B

    In the event that any of the aforesaid Town By-Laws are amended so as to provide more favorable hours, wages, or conditions of employment for such employees, then it is agreed and understood that this Agreement is to be reopened for the limited purpose of incorporating such new provisions in the Agreement.

ARTICLE XVIII

GENERAL

Section A

    The parties acknowledge that this Agreement is entered into in order to promote harmonious relations between the EMPLOYER and the UNION, to establish equitable and peaceful procedures for the prompt resolution of differences, to establish suitable salaries, hours of work, and other Library Service and retain the services of qualified and industrious employees of the Library.

Section B

    There will be no reprisals of any kind taken by the EMPLOYER, their officers, agents or representatives against any employee of the Library by reason of his membership in the UNION or participation in its activities, or his assertion of any right hereunder.

Section C

    The UNION may have three (3) members of its Negotiating Committee attend contract negotiation meetings with the EMPLOYER's representatives during working hours without loss of pay.

Section D

    In the event that any part or provision of this Agreement is in conflict with any law, ordinance or by-law, such law, ordinance or by-law shall prevail so long as such conflict remains, but all other parts and provisions of this Agreement will remain in full force and effect.

17

Section E

The UNION agrees that for the duration of this Agreement it will not engage in, induce, or encourage any strike, work stoppage, slowdown, or with-holding of services by the employees represented by it. Any employee who engages in such activity will be subject to disciplinary action, including discharge.

Section F

The EMPLOYER and the UNION agree that each has had a right to bargain for any provision that they wished in this Agreement. Except as provided the contract for any further demands or proposals, and that the present Agreement constitutes a complete contract on all matters, and that if other proposals have been made, the same have been withdrawn in consideration of this Agreement.

Section G

If funds are necessary to implement this Agreement, a request for the necessary appropriation shall be submitted to the Town Meeting by the EMPLOYER. If such request is rejected, the matter will be returned to the parties for further bargaining. (See G.L. Chapter 149, Section 1781).

Section H

On December 24, all employees of the Library will be excused from all duty at 12:00 noon, without loss of pay.

ARTICLE XIX

SICK LEAVE BUY-BACK

Upon his retirement or death, an employee covered by this Agreement shall be paid an amount equal to the value of twenty-five percent (25%) of his accumu-lated, unused sick days, not to exceed sixty (60) days. Any employee hired on or after July 1, 1980, shall upon retirement receive twenty-five percent (25%) of his accumulated sick leave not to exceed fifteen hundred dollars ($1,500.00).

ARTICLE XX

TRANSPORTATION EXPENSE

Employees traveling on Library business authorized by the Director shall be reimbursed in accordance with the following schedule:

    A. Public transportation reimbursed in full.
    B. Private auto at 0.14 cents per mile.

A voucher shall be signed by the employee and submitted to the Library Director for payment authorization. Transportation expenses to and from conferences and meetings are excluded from this Article.

18

ARTICLE XXI
JOB POSTINGS AND PROVISIONS FOR APPLICATION

When a position becomes vacant, notification shall be posted on staff bulletin boards in all agencies, inviting applications from qualified candidates. The Library is an equal opportunity employer, and does not discriminate for reasons of sex, age, religion, race or national origin. Notice of vacancies will be posted for a minimum of three weeks before the deadline for applications. Job descriptions and specifications for posted positions shall be made available to all interested applicants in the Director's Office. Applications will be accepted from both within and without the library system.

ARTICLE XXII
DURATION

This Agreement shall continue in force and effect from July 1, 1980 up to and including June 30, 1981 at which time it will terminate. The parties agree to enter into negotiation for a new contract not later than January 15, 1981. In order to expedite such negotiations, each party agrees that not later than December 28, 1980 it will notify the other party hereunto of the alterations, modifications and amendments it desires to discuss with respect to the subject matter of any or all of the Articles of this Agreement and of its proposals with respect to each new matter, and the negotiations shall be limited to the terms specified in such notice.

_____

In Witness whereof, the parties hereunto set their hands and seals this _____day of _____, 1980.

FOR THE TOWN OF WATERTOWN   FOR THE BOARD OF LIBRARY TRUSTEES

_____   _____
Chairman   Chairman

_____   _____
Clerk   Trustee

_____   _____
Member   Trustee

FOR THE UNION   Trustee
                                     _____
_____
Executive Director, Council #93   Trustee
                                     _____
_____
Business Representative   Trustee

_____
_____
_____

19

(End of reprint)

A. Washington State Library

B. Houston Public Library

C. New York State Library

D. University of California,
   Los Angeles Library

A. WASHINGTON STATE LIBRARY

Examples of:

1) Instruction for Budgetary Process
2) Objective Setting Form
3) Statistic Worksheet
4) Calendar for Budget Planning
5) Decision Package Form

(Used with the permission of the Washington State Library
and the Viability Group)

(Examples begin on page 267)

Washington
State Library

Memorandum

TO: WSL Management   DATE: January 16, 1980

FROM: Roderick G. Swartz, State Librarian

RE: 1981-1983 Biennial Budget

It is time to begin the planning process for the 1981-1983 biennial budget. As soon as further instructions are received from OFM, we will relay this information to you. This is expected around mid-March.

Several new or different areas of emphasis will be made this time:

1) First, we are working very closely with the two new Commission committees — Long Range Planning and Budget. Included is a memo of 12-27-79 (revised 1-5-80) which outlines some of the thinking of the Long Range Planning Committee. Both committees will continue to exercise oversight as we continue through the year. (See Appendix A)

2) Concentration on quantifiable objectives — The goals we projected for 1979-81 are still fairly valid. With minor changes and an updated mission statement (Appendix B), I am including these for you to review and return by 1-31-80. Major concentration between now and the March Commission meeting will be on the development of quantifiable objectives. To aid you in this task, we are outlining the following:

CREATION OF QUANTIFIABLE OBJECTIVES   DUE: 2-29-80

Review and edit your decision packages. This may mean discarding some, adding others, or doing some editing on others. These decision packages should reflect your area's efforts at implementing the agency's goals.

Outline your objectives for each decision package at the outside; there should probably be no more than five objectives for each decision package. For each objective we will want the following:

1) An objective which is quantifiable

2) A realistic time line for each objective

3) A statistic or measurement process outlined to assess success

To help formulate these three items, we are including two worksheets: one on objective setting and another on statistics or measurement. (Appendix C & D)

Keep in mind you will probably be focusing on three different types of objectives:

1) Normal work outputs — i.e., you will basically be quantifying the day to day work of the library.

2) Normal work output improvements — These objectives would focus on significant innovations, breakthroughs or new developments.

3) Organizational capability improvements — These objectives may not relate directly to normal work output, but should result in increased efficiency and effectiveness, ability to take on new and different assignments, improved working environment, or greater versatility.

WASHINGTON STATE LIBRARY (cont'd)

WSL Management
January 16, 1980
Page Two

The following 14 steps in "objective" writing might be of some help to you: *

1) It starts with the word "to," followed by an action verb.

2) It specifies a single key result to be accomplished.

3) It specifies a target date for its accomplishment.

4) It specifies maximum cost factors.

5) It is as specific and quantitative (and hence measurable and verifiable) as possible.

6) It specifies only the "what" and "when"; it avoids venturing into the "why" and "how."

7) It relates directly to the accountable manager's roles and missions and to higher-level roles, missions, and objectives.

8) It is readily understandable by those who will be contributing to its attainment.

9) It is realistic and attainable, but still represents a significant challenge.

10) It provides maximum payoff on the required investment in time and resources, as compared with other objectives being considered.

11) It is consistent with the resources available or anticipated.

12) It avoids or minimizes dual accountability for achievement when joint effort is required.

13) It is consistent with basic library policies and practices.

14) It is willingly agreed to by both superior and subordinate, without undue pressure or coercion.

(* Taken from *Setting Objectives*, page 62.)

You can see from the time line (Appendix E) we have built in time for review and additional effort. Complete work packets, including 1979-81 decision packets will follow.

This effort is important! Involve your team and give it your best shot!

RGS:rw
cc: WSL Commission

WASHINGTON STATE LIBRARY (cont'd)

Objective Setting Worksheet

A. Brief Statement of What You Want to Achieve:

B. By When (within one year):

C. Specific Amounts (How much, what quality, %, etc.):

D. Brief Statement of What Your Boss Wants You to Achieve:

E. Rewrite Your Objective Exactly Including A, B, C & D:

F. Time line within Biennium to Reach Objective

WASHINGTON STATE LIBRARY (cont'd)

Objective Evaluation Form

If any answer to the questions below are not definitely "yes", go back to the "Objective Setting Worksheet" and rework your objective:

	Yes	Maybe	No
1. Is the objective statement constructed properly? To (action verb) (single key result) by (target date) at (cost).	___	___	___
2. Is it measurable and verifiable?	___	___	___
3. Does it relate directly to the manager's roles and missions and to higher-level roles, missions, and objectives?	___	___	___
4. Can it be readily understood by those who must implement it?	___	___	___
5. Is the objective a realistic and attainable one that still represents a significant challenge to the manager and his organization?	___	___	___
6. Will the result, when achieved, justify the expenditure of time and resources required to achieve it?	___	___	___
7. Is the objective consistent with basic company and organizational policies and practices?	___	___	___
8. Can the accountability for final results be clearly established?	___	___	___

1/16/80   Copyright 1979 The Viability Group

WASHINGTON STATE LIBRARY (cont'd)

1 of 2   (3)

STATISTIC WORKSHEET

OBJECTIVE

WAYS TO MEASURE

WHICH SHOW BOTH QUALITY AND QUANTITY

WHICH ARE EASILY AND ACCURATELY MEASURABLE

CHOICE OF STATISTIC

WASHINGTON STATE LIBRARY (cont'd)

CHOOSING PRODUCTION STATISTICS

To be relevant and useful in motivation and evaluation of staff, your choice of a production statistic ("Stat") must pass all of the following tests:

	Yes	No
1. Does the stat reflect valued action, real accomplishment and degree of service?	___	___
2. Does the statistic directly or indirectly reflect the quantity of work done or its value in money?	___	___
3. Does the stat reflect quantity of desired product actually completed?	___	___
4. Does the stat clearly show the quality of those products?	___	___
5. Can the stat be simply and quickly calculated daily or weekly by the workers themselves?	___	___
6. Is the stat accurately measurable?	___	___
7. Can the stat be reported immediately after the tabulation period (day, week, fortnight, etc.) is over?	___	___
8. Can the worker control the rise and fall of the statistic?	___	___
9. Can the stat's accuracy be verified easily by management?	___	___
10. Will watching and discussing the statistic make the worker more responsible and productive?	___	___

1/16/80

WASHINGTON STATE LIBRARY (cont'd)

WSL BUDGET & PLANNING PROCESS

TASK

1. Review of 79-81 Goals & Objectives

2. 81-83 Goals: Review down through Division Chief level

3. Creation of Objectives: Involvement to Section Head level

   A. Quantifiable objectives
   B. Time line for each objective
   C. Measurements needed to assess success

4. Review by State Librarian of the following:

   A. Original work by section heads
   B. Review of work by division chiefs
   C. Final Review by Deputy State Librarian

5. Interim Review by WSL Commission Long Range Planning Committee

6. Retreat or meetings to refine objectives as completely as possible

7. Dollar decisions to implement goals & objectives

8. Review by State Librarian in manner similar to Item #4

9. Interim Review by WSL Commission Finance & Long Range Planning Committees

10. Finalization of Package for 1981-1983 Biennial Budget

11. Final review by appropriate WSL Commission Committees and the Commission itself

TIME LINE

1. and 2. January 31, 1980

3. February 29, 1980

4. March 7, 1980

5. March 12 or 13, 1980

6. late March or early April, 1980

7. May 30, 1980

8. June 13, 1980

9. June 18 or 19, 1980

10. July/August, 1980

11. July/August, 1980

WSL 1/2/80

WASHINGTON STATE LIBRARY (cont'd)

PLANNING AND BUDGETING DECISION PACKAGE

Activity Name:	Division	Prepared	Rank
Level of	Section	Approved	

Purpose of Activity	Resources Required	1979-81	1981-83
	Personnel		
	Salaries $		
	Services $		
	Travel $		
	Equipment $		
	Benefits $		
Description of Activity	Other $		
	$		
	Total $		

Alternative Ways of Performing Work or Program more efficiently/cost effective

Advantages of Retaining activity/expected benefit

Consequences if Activity is Eliminated

WSL 3/78

B. HOUSTON PUBLIC LIBRARY

Activity Description for Budgetary Purposes

(Used with the permission of the
Houston Public Library)

HOUSTON PUBLIC LIBRARY (cont'd)

ANNUAL BUDGET

| | | | Page No. | 1 |
| | | | Fund Activity No. | 2 |

BUDGET ACTIVITY OPERATIONS DESCRIPTION

| Fiscal Year | 1980 | Department | Library | Budget Activity | Branch Services |

DESCRIPTION OF OPERATIONS

Branch Services provides library service to the citizens of Houston through 26 branches and four reading & study centers located throughout the city and through three bookmobiles. A wide variety of fiction and nonfiction books, periodicals, pamphlets, records, tapes and other A-V materials are stocked for children and adults. Professional librarians assist patrons in locating materials, provide guidance in the selection of materials, answer reference questions on a wide variety of subjects, plan a variety of programs for children and adults of an educational and recreational nature, cooperate with other agencies and institutions in assisting the adult basic learner and the independent learner, and plan public relations and programs for outreach to the public. Specialized programs include Books By Mail and service to the County Jail and institutions that care for the elderly and handicapped. Children in disadvantaged areas are served by the Children's Carousel.

SERVICE DEMAND INDICATORS

Users of Branch Libraries	3,449,160	3,568,396	3,711,132
Registration of Library users	120,037	128,286	134,700
Plans and programs developed for new Branch Libraries	2	1	4
Sites purchased for additional libraries	1	1	2

OBJECTIVES

1. To answer 775,087 reference questions.
2. To circulate 5,209,426 books and materials.
3. To handle 30,000 questions requiring information and referral.
4. To develop programs and plans for four new library branches.
5. To expand existing Early Childhood/Parenting Centers and establish centers at two additional branches.
6. To locate and purchase sites for two additional branches.
7. To initiate a special program for teenagers at 1 branch.
8. To continue cooperative efforts with HCC in offering Adult Basic tutoring and ESL classes.

PERFORMANCE INDICATORS

Reference questions answered	557,878	692,942	775,000
Books and Materials circulated	4,538,297	4,961,358	5,200,000
Information and referral questions handled	29,215	29,500	30,000
Users attending library activities	491,387	628,672	660,106

COMMENTARY AND ANALYSIS

Branch Services will open the newly enlarged and renovated Heights Branch in early 1980. The final plans for the Southeast Branch and the Canal/Milby Branch will be prepared in 1980 and furniture and equipment ordered for them. The demolishing of the Carnegie Branch and the beginning of the construction will take place in 1980 as well as the setting up of service for this branch in leased quarters. Branches will serve a minimum of 142,736 additional users in 1980, answer 83,000 more reference questions, circulate approximately 250,000 more books and AV materials, and have 32,000 more people in attendance at library programs than in 1979. Early childhood education and parenting centers will be developed at two additional sites. The most pressing problem facing Branch Services is adequate staffing for Heights Branch and the increasingly busy Kendall and Stanaker Branches.

CITY OF HOUSTON

HOUSTON PUBLIC LIBRARY (cont'd)

Fiscal Year	Department	Budget Activity	Page No. 2
1980	Library (Con't)	Branch Services	Fund Activity No. 2

ANNUAL BUDGET—
EXPLANATION

COMMENTARY AND ANALYSIS

Branch Services' total budget request for 1980 is $5,612,042.00. This includes a continuation request of $5,358,853.00 and a supplemental request of $253,189.00. Major increases in the continuation budget are:

1101 Salaries and Wages—increased by $320,532.00 (10.3% over the 1979 estimate) resulting from the annualization of all budgeted positions for the full year.

3100 Operation Services—increased by $88,273.00 (27.2% over the 1979 estimate) resulting from increased telephone cost mainly for on-line terminals and increased utilities costs.

4500 Capital Outlay—increased by $123,896.00 (up 12.2% over the 1979 estimate) resulting primarily from increased inflationary cost of books of 10% (from $834,156.00 to 917,572.00), AV materials of 25% ($61,150.00 to 76,438.00), and periodicals of 18% ($95,744.00 to 112,978.00).

The Priorities for supplemental request are:

1) To adequately staff Heights Branch and provide some funds for collection development in preparation for move back to the enlarged and renovated facility.

2) To bring our busiest branch, Kendall, up to the staffing and hours of service to Stanaker Branch (Magnolia) commensurate with the staffing of other branches doing the level of reference and circulation at their level.

3) A checkpoint materials security system for Jungman Branch, a special computerized self-instruction program at Walter Branch, and contracts with commercial firms for the care of bookmobiles and 12 typewriters in our busiest branches are very important to protecting materials from theft, providing innovation in programming, and the obtaining of quick and reliable maintenance for large vehicles and typewriters.

CITY OF HOUSTON

C. NEW YORK STATE LIBRARY

Summary Sheet for Supplemental Funds
for a "Program Request" for
Collection Management/Network Services

(Used with the permission of the
New York State Library)

NEW YORK STATE LIBRARY (cont'd)

STATE OF NEW YORK   AGENCY State Education Department

MAINTENANCE AND OPERATION DIV./INST. _____

    Explanation Sheet   PROGRAM_____

    Fiscal Year 1980-1981   FUND State Purposes

Class.
Code
No.

040
004

Policy Advice on Request
COLLECTION MANAGEMENT/NETWORK SERVICES
Summary of Request

New Positions	Temporary Service	Supplies & Materials	Travel	Contractual Service	Equipment
$55,420	$88,895	$54,000	$1,170	$362,300	$71,200

OBJECTIVES/ACTIVITIES:

1) Improve the response rate of the New York State Inter-Library Loan (NYSILL) System so that 50% of the requests are processed in two days or less ($35,500/15 existing, 2 new staff).

2) Provide tailored information to users ($64,300/1 existing, 3 new staff).

3) Consolidate automated catalog and add six terminals and four printers for increased public access to the automated catalog ($154,700/1 staff).

4) Provide 1.2 million photo reproductions of Library materials in response to user requests ($83,000/5 staff).

5) Continue collection preservation program through microfilming and binding ($155,000/6 staff).

6) Maintain materials in proper shelf order by checking shelving ($40,500/16 staff).

7) Control materials at the circulation desk, including bar coding ($5,639/3 staff).

8) Continue inventory of the collection ($38,056/1 staff).

9) Provide film services to users (2 positions).

10) Administer and provide supervision, training and evaluation for staff and programs ($800/3 staff).

BUDGET REQUEST:

New positions requested include a Senior Librarian (G-18) and Clerk (G-3) to improve NYSILL performance by reducing response time of requests, and a Senior Librarian (G-18), Assistant Librarian (G-14) and Senior Clerk (G-7) to provide data base services and computerized literature searches for state agencies and other users.

Temporary service funds ($88,895) are requested to maintain materials in proper shelf order and to provide photo reproductions of library materials in response to user requests.

Supplies and materials funds ($54,000) are needed for sensitive book labels and photocopy supplies.

Travel funds ($1,170) are necessary to attend workshops and conferences at both state and national levels.

Contractual services ($362,300) are needed for the further development of the automated catalog, microfilming and binding for preservation, and providing tailored information for patrons.

Equipment funds ($71,200) are requested for additional computer terminals and printers to increase access to automated files and to purchase three photocopiers to reduce rental costs.

SUPPLEMENTAL INFORMATION AVAILABLE UPON REQUEST

D. UNIVERSITY OF CALIFORNIA, LOS ANGELES

1) Budget request with schedule of deadlines
2) Unit request form for books

(Used with the permission of the
University of California, Los Angeles
University Library)

April 18, 1979

TO: Unit Heads

FROM: Judith M. Corin, Assistant University Librarian for Planning

RE: Attached Budget Request Package

The attached Unit Budget Request package includes forms and instructions for requesting S & E, E & F, Travel, Library Materials (Book Funds) and Library Publications support. Again, you are requested to present your programmatic needs in the 1978/79 Annual Report which you will be submitting to us in September. The Annual Report will assist us in preparing for our Executive Budget Review with Chancellor Young and in developing our next Budget Request. We will be sending you further instructions about the format and content of the Annual Report in the near future.

Also enclosed in this package is a listing of the E & F items being ordered for your unit from 1978-79 funds. You should already have received a xerox copy of your supplies request with order numbers and dates. If you have not received this listing or have any questions please call Janie Gillette on 51201.

JMC:sl

Attachments

(Budget request with schedule is on page 281)

UNIVERSITY OF CALIFORNIA, LOS ANGELES (cont'd)

2 of 2

April 18, 1979

1979-80 Budget Schedule

April 18	Forms sent to units summarizing purchases of 1978-79 requests. New request forms sent to units for the following: S & E, E & F, Travel, Library Materials, Publications
May 7	Requests due in Administrative Office
June 1	GA proposed allocations to be reviewed by Executive Committee
June 18	GA allocations, E & F order status, Library materials allocations
July 16	Copies of S & E order sheets sent to units
August	External Annual Reports prepared (ARL, Unified Annual, HEGIS)
September (dates to be set)	Library Annual Reports due
October	Unit visits by Executive Committee Begin preparation for Executive Budget Review (Chancellor)
January	Begin preparation for Target Budget

UNIVERSITY OF CALIFORNIA, LOS ANGELES (cont'd)

The information requested here may be used in the allocation of 1979-80 book funds, depending on the amount of the book budget we receive from the state, and we may also need it to request supplemental funding from the Chancellor's urgent need funds.

We are therefore asking that you present your 1979-80 book budget needs in the same terms as you did last year:

> If your 1978-79 book budget allocation has not been sufficient to provide adequate service to your users, based on your present estimate of what you will be able to purchase this year, indicate on the attached form the specific ways in which it will fall short. For each subject area in your collection which you have not been able to support adequately, indicate on the attached form the number and dollar amount of *additional* purchases you should make in 1979-80; indicate for each subject area in which you anticipate decreased needs the number and dollar amount of this decrease. Estimate costs at 1978-79 prices. *Do not include price increase figures in this projection.* We will add in the appropriate price increase figures, based on the subjects you are collecting and the Bowker figures. If, however, you wish to indicate your estimate of the overall price increase percentage for 1979-80 for your materials, please do so at the bottom of the form.

> The 1979-80 state book budget for U.C. libraries will again contain a sum for shared purchases, so we will need from you specific items recommended for purchase with shared purchase funds, with a justification for each item. Use the attached U.C. Libraries Consideration form. If you need additional copies, they are available from Sherry Lyons. You will be given another opportunity to submit shared purchase recommendations later.

UNIVERSITY OF CALIFORNIA, LOS ANGELES (cont'd)

Library Unit Budget Request

Name of Unit or Fund _____

LIBRARY MATERIAL REQUIREMENTS

INCREASED NEEDS (ADDITIONAL ONLY)

SUBJECT	CURRENT MONOGRAPHS		SERIAL SUBSCRIPTIONS		RETROSPECTIVE MONOGRAPHS & SERIALS		OTHER (SPECIFY)		TOTAL DOLLARS
	Number of Volumes	Dollars	Number	Dollars	Number of Volumes	Dollars	Form	Dollars	
TOTAL INCREASES									

DECREASED NEEDS (EXPRESS AS MINUS FIGURES)

TOTAL DECREASES									
NET TOTALS									

Indicate specific ways, if any, in which your unit serves as a regional resource.

UNIVERSITY OF CALIFORNIA, LOS ANGELES (cont'd)

Library Unit Budget Request

Book Funds

Name of Unit or Fund

NARRATIVE STATEMENT (optional):

Indicate any special circumstances which could have a direct bearing on your need for book funds:

Estimated percentage of price increase for library materials in 1977/78 over 1976/77:

UNIVERSITY OF CALIFORNIA, LOS ANGELES (cont'd)

FORM A

U.C. LIBRARIES CONSIDERATION FORM

Date: _____

Bibliographic Description:

Justification for Purchase & Location:

Signature of CDO & Recommending Campus

Price	Suggested Location(s)	Ref. Access Only OK	Order Deadline (for Rushes Only)

RESPONSE

COMMENTS

Recommendation

Holdings	Purchase (Yes or No)	Statewide Only (1 cop.) (Yes or No)	Location	Ref. Access Only OK
		Regional (2 cop.) (Yes or No)	If yes, vote N or S	
			N. at _____	

Signature of CDO & Responding Campus